LEARNING
AND TEACHING
TOGETHER

Michele T.D. Tanaka

LEARNING AND TEACHING TOGETHER

Weaving Indigenous Ways of Knowing into Education

UBCPress · Vancouver · Toronto

25 24 23 22 21 20 19 18 17 16   5 4 3 2 1

Printed in Canada on FSC-certified ancient-forest-free paper
(100% post-consumer recycled) that is processed chlorine- and acid-free.

Library and Archives Canada Cataloguing in Publication

Tanaka, Michele T. D., author
Learning and teaching together : weaving indigenous ways of knowing into education /
Michele T.D. Tanaka.

Includes bibliographical references and index.
Issued in print and electronic formats.
ISBN 978-0-7748-2951-9 (hardback). – ISBN 978-0-7748-3086-7 (mobi). –
ISBN 978-0-7748-2953-3 (pdf). – ISBN 978-0-7748-2954-0 (epub).

1. Native peoples – Education – Canada. 2. Multicultural education –
Canada. 3. Critical pedagogy – Canada. 4. Teaching – Canada. I. Title.

E96.2.T35 2016   370.89'97071   C2016-905414-4
                                                                          C2016-905415-2

Canadä

UBC Press gratefully acknowledges the financial support for our publishing program of the Government of Canada (through the Canada Book Fund), the Canada Council for the Arts, and the British Columbia Arts Council.

Printed and bound in Canada by Friesens
Set in Myriad SemiCondensed and Minion by Artegraphica Design Co. Ltd.
Copy editor: Jillian Shoichet
Indexer: Judy Dunlop
Cover designer: Alexa Love

UBC Press
The University of British Columbia
2029 West Mall
Vancouver, BC V6T 1Z2
www.ubcpress.ca

May any merit arising from my efforts

benefit all sentient beings

without exception.

\0/

Contents

Figures

Foreword

GREG CAJETE

One of the most important elements of Indigenous teaching and learning revolves around "learning how to learn." The cultivation of the human capacities for listening, observation, experiencing with all one's senses, development of intuitive understanding, and respect for time-tested traditions of learning naturally formed the basis for skills used in every process of Indigenous learning and teaching. Michele Tanaka's study illustrates these processes in vivid detail, using the creation of a multi-textile mural in a teacher education course at the University of Victoria (on the traditional lands of the Lkwungen, Esquimalt, and W̱SÁNEĆ peoples) as an opportunity to study Indigenous learning and teaching traditions as they unfold in an Indigenous context.

Over several thousand years, Native people in both North and South America developed a diverse variety of approaches to teaching and learning. These approaches ranged from the loosely organized informal contexts for learning and teaching in hunter-gatherer tribes to the formally organized "academies" of the Aztecs, Maya, Inca, and other groups of Mexico and Central and South America. Whatever the approach, there was a continuum of education in tribal American societies that involved an array of ritual/initiatory practices that closely followed the human phases of maturation and development. At each point on this continuum, an important aspect of learning how to learn was internalized. Within tribal societies, learning how to learn may be seen to unfold around four basic areas of orientation.

First, attention is focused on the real and practical needs of the tribal society, which systematically addresses learning related to the physical, social, psychological, and spiritual needs of tribal members – most importantly, learning how to survive in the natural environment and be a productive member of the tribal society. Second, individuals are taught in individual ways when they show the readiness or express the willingness to learn. Emphasis is on allowing for the uniqueness of individual learning styles and encouraging the development of self-reliance and self-determination. Third, the application of special intellectual, ritual, psychological, and spiritual "teaching tools" facilitates deep levels of learning and understanding. Throughout, Indigenous teaching is predicated on three basic criteria: flexibility, viability, and effectiveness. Fourth, the honouring and facilitation of the psychological and transformational process of students' "flowering," or opening up to a self-knowledge and natural capacities for learning, is usually accomplished in the context of tribal societies by helping individuals overcome their own self-generated impediments to learning and other obstacles to understanding. These four areas of orientation are all present in the earth fibres course experience described in this book, although the language and organization differs somewhat from what I use here.

The following axioms of Indigenous teaching serve as a context for the reader's exploration. These axioms represent a small portion of the storehouse of wisdom and creative approaches to teaching applied by tribal teachers throughout history in creating an educational process that reflected and continues to reflect a sophisticated "ecology of education." Indigenous education allows for a diversity of sophisticated teaching "tools" that few modern Western educational approaches are able to duplicate in breadth and creativity. These interpretations of Indigenous teaching axioms are derived from my own readings, including this book, and observations related to Indigenous education. I offer them in a simplified descriptive form in the hope that teachers will apply their own creative interpretations and implementations to the development of their own lessons and curricula. As processes, the axioms are applicable to the holistic presentation of any kind of content and adaptable to every age level.

Tribal teachers begin teaching by building on the commonplace. We all have experiences, understandings, and traits in common with one another. These can be used to pose a problem in terms, forms, or descriptions of experiences that are familiar to students. Learning is a natural instinct, and success in learning something new is tied to human feelings of self-worth. When we create a learning environment that flows with this natural current of humanness, we are taking an essential step in cultivating motivation and enhancing self-confidence in learning.

Observing how things happen in the natural world is the basis of some of the most ancient and spiritually profound teachings of Indigenous cultures.

Basic understanding begins with exploring how things happen. Nature is the first teacher and model of process. Learning how to see Nature enhances our capacity to see other things. When teaching is focused on such perennial phenomena as, for example, solar and lunar cycles, we stimulate our "learning how to learn" instincts at a deep level and encourage the development of self-knowledge.

Real situations provide the basic setting for most Indigenous learning and teaching. Overt intellectualization is kept to a minimum in favour of direct experience and learning by doing. Teaching within a real situation expands the realm of learning beyond speculation and allows the student to judge the truth of a teaching for him- or herself. Indigenous teaching also revolves around some form of work. Indigenous teachers recognize that work invites concentration and facilitates a quietness of the mind, which in turn leads to illuminating insights about what is being taught.

Indigenous teaching focuses as much on "learning with the heart" as it does on "learning with the mind." It also facilitates learning to see who one really is rather than the image of self manufactured by one's ego or by the ego of another. This real perception of self helps the student realize that he or she is essentially responsible for any barriers to his or her own learning.

Indigenous practices such as creative dreaming, art, ritual, and ceremony help the student externalize inner thoughts and qualities for examination. Such practices help students to establish a connection with their "real" selves and learn how to bring inner resources to bear in their lives. Helping students gain access to the real self is part of the "transformative" education that is an inherent part of Indigenous teaching.

Learning about the nature of self-deception is a key aspect of Indigenous preparation for learning. A first step to understanding the nature of true learning is to reach a level of clarity regarding *why* one is learning. Students must become aware of how ambition, self-gratification, power, and control as purposes for learning are forms of self-deception that must be avoided because they lead eventually to the misuse of knowledge and the further perpetuation of self-deception. Striving for real knowledge requires a cultivated sense of humility. The human tendencies toward pride, arrogance, and ego-inflation must be recognized and avoided in the search to find one's true "face," "heart," and "vocation."

Readiness to learn is a basic determinant for the ultimate success or failure of a teaching. Indigenous teachers recognize that readiness for learning important things must be conditioned through repetition and the relative "attunement" of the student to the teaching. They watch for "moments of teach-ability" and repeat the teaching of key principles in numerous ways and at various times. A regular practice of Indigenous teachers is to place students in situations where they must re-examine assumptions and confront preconceived notions. In the position of having to constantly reconsider what they think they know, students remain open to new dimensions of learning and prepared for higher levels of thinking and creative synthesis.

Indigenous teaching is always associated with "organic development." Indigenous teaching is planted like a seed and then nurtured and cultivated through the relationship of teacher and student until it bears fruit. The nature and quality of the relationship and its perseverance over time will determine the ultimate outcome of a teaching process. Apprenticeship and learning through ritual stages of learning-readiness are predicated on the planting of these seeds and the nurturing of the growing seedlings through time. In this way, teaching and learning can also be viewed as a matter of serving and being served. Service is the basis of the relationship between student and teacher. This foundation is exemplified most completely in the apprentice-teacher relationships found in all expressions of Indigenous education.

Indigenous teaching is understood to be a communicative art, based on the nature and quality of communicating at all levels of being. Indigenous teachers practise the art of communicating through language, relationship to social and natural environments, art, play, and ritual. Tribal teachers also understand that all teaching is relative and that each path to knowledge has its own require-ments, which need to be addressed. Flexibility and learning how to adjust to the demands of the moment are key skills cultivated throughout Indigenous education.

Indigenous teaching involves making students think "comprehensively," facilitating their awareness of the higher levels of the content they are learning and its relationship to other areas of knowledge. Such comprehensive think-ing forms a firm foundation for the creative processes of teaching and learning. That is, comprehensive preparation and immersion in a learning process invites new understandings and perceptions of dimensions of knowledge – dimensions that are there all the time but that need to be worked before they reveal themselves.

Mirroring the consequences of a teaching back to students in order to expand their perspective and deepen their learning is a technique often used in Indigenous education. Tribal teachers facilitate learning through direct, and at times provoked, perception – by setting up a situation that forces students to see the limitations of what they think they know. In this way, students are en-couraged to reach deeper within and to realize the deeper levels of meaning represented by a teaching. This practice helps students cultivate a degree of humility necessary for maintaining openness to new learning and the creative possibilities of a teaching.

The cultivation of humility prepares a foundation for students to learn the nature of "attention." Attention may be considered a foundation of Indigenous learning in that almost every context, from learning basic hunting and fishing skills to memorizing the details of ritual, from listening to a story to mastering a traditional art form, rely on the practised application of attention. Attention, within an Indigenous understanding, has to do with the focus of all the senses. Seeing, listening, feeling, smelling, hearing, and intuiting are the senses that are developed and applied in the Indigenous context of attention.

Learning the nature of appropriate activity is a natural consideration of Indigenous teaching. Activity in Indigenous life always has a purpose. "Busy work" is not a concept that tribal teachers are interested in perpetuating, since helping students learn how to engage in effective activity appropriate to the situation at hand is a required skill for more advanced Indigenous teaching.

Knowledge and action are considered parts of the same whole. Properly contextualized and developed knowledge leads to the same balance in terms of action. Therefore, in order to assure the integrity and relative "rightness" of an action, a great amount of time must be spent on reflection and seeking broad levels of information and understanding – before one forms an opinion or takes action. Prayer, deep reflection, patience, and "waiting for the second thought" are regularly practised in Indigenous decision making.

The concept of "each person's work," akin to the Hindu concept of karma, is honoured in the processes of Indigenous education. Indigenous teachers view each student as unique, each with a unique path of learning to travel during his or her lifetime. Learning the nature of that path was often (and is) the focus of Indigenous rites of initiation and vision questing. The trials, tribulations, and "work" that become a part of each individual's learning path constitute the basis for some of the most important contexts of Indigenous teaching and learning.

From an Indigenous perspective, true learning and the gain of significant knowledge do not come without sacrifice – even, at times, deep wounds. Indigenous teachers realize that sometimes only by experiencing extreme hardship and trauma do some individuals reach their maximum level of learning development. The ritual incorporation of this reality into such ceremonies as the Sun Dance transforms this "woundedness" into a context for learning and reflection. In this way, the wound or traumatic life event serves as a constant reminder of an important teaching. As long as the wound or the repercussions of an event are used to symbolize something deeply important to know and understand, they provide a powerful source for renewal, insight, and the expansion of individual and community consciousness.

Michele Tanaka's in-depth and personal study of the earth fibres course illustrates how both teachers and learners expressed each of these axioms in various ways within the course. The axioms are alive still in this book, as Tanaka offers them to the reader.

One of the primary foundations of Indigenous education is that each person is, fundamentally, his or her own teacher and that learning is connected to the individual's life process. Meaning is to be looked for in everything, especially in the workings of the natural world. All aspects of Nature are teachers of mankind; what is required of the learner is a cultivated and practised openness to the lessons the world has to teach. Within Indigenous contexts, ritual, mythology, and the art of storytelling, combined with the cultivation of relationship to one's inner self, family, community, and natural environment, were utilized to help individuals realize their potential for learning and a complete life. Participants were enabled to reach "completeness" by being encouraged to learn how to trust their natural instincts, to listen, to look, to create, to reflect and see things deeply, to understand and apply their intuitive intelligence, and to recognize and honour the teacher of spirit within themselves and the natural world.

This is the educational legacy of Indigenous peoples. In *Learning and Teaching Together*, Michele Tanaka brings forward the legacy of the Indigenous wisdom keepers of the earth fibres course. It is encouraging to see how learning to learn differently has so profoundly affected the pre-service teachers' understanding of learning and, hence, their teaching practice. It is imperative that such messages and ways of educating be revitalized "for Life's sake" at this time of ecological crisis. Tanaka's work has opened the door to an increased understanding of how this can be done.

Acknowledgments

I lift my hands in acknowledgment and say HÍSW̱ḴE SIÁM~thank you \0/, honoured ones, to the Coast Salish peoples on whose land this work was created. I give heartfelt thanks to Wanosts'a7, Lorna Williams, for her willingness, generosity, and trust as she welcomed me as a researcher into the earth fibres experience. She has modelled a gentle, determined way forward that continues to inspire me. I am also especially appreciative of kQwa'ste'not, Charlene George, a creative, wise, and courageous woman who shared her time and teachings with patience, kindness, and clarity.

I thank the wisdom keepers, May Sam, Gay Williams, Gina Robertson, Lynne and James Hemry, Carolyn Memnook, Fran Memnook, Janet Rogers, and Della (Rice) Sylvester for taking the time to tell me their stories of learning and teaching. The offerings of these remarkable Earth-conscious elders extend beyond the course to touch so many lives in a good way. I am also ever appreciative of the twelve pre-service teachers whose flexibility amidst unfamiliar ways, willingness to be watched, and energetic embracing of indigenous pedagogy inspires me to improve my own teaching. I wish them all the best in the next stages of their learning and teaching.

This book would not have happened without the help of my friend and editorial assistant Moira Cairns – her careful attention, unwavering persistence, constructive feedback, and loving support kept me going when I couldn't see the way. I extend further appreciation to Darcy Cullen and the editorial team at UBC Press, who recognized the importance of my work despite its rough edges; they patiently and expertly worked with me through the editorial process.

I also thank the anonymous reviewers whose honest appraisals and expressions of support spurred me to dig deeper and make significant revisions so that my work has become more accessible, focused, and relevant.

To my parents Marie and Dick, thank you for bringing me into this world and for encouraging me to be a lifelong learner – your faith in my abilities, intellectual nourishment, and unending support lifted me up to do this work. I still use a version of Dad's system of yellow pads and index cards to organize my thoughts! To my husband Jim, your steadfast love and patience have supported my career in countless ways – more importantly, your love continues to open my heart to all that is possible. To Emma and Jeff, I give my unending love and gratitude; through watching your gifts unfold, I see the evolution of peace and integrity. Special thanks to Lynne and James, who continue to feed my spirit through love and compassion. And to all my spirit relations, both on TENEW~Earth and beyond, your guidance and love mean everything.

The support of the Social Sciences and Humanities Research Council of Canada has been key to the completion of this work and is greatly appreciated. My gratitude also goes to the members of the University of Victoria community who championed and participated in the earth fibres course. Despite adversity, I can see the earth fibres teachings ripple out into crosscultural endeavours across campus. Special thanks goes to the Curriculum Library staff, current caretakers of XAXE SIÁM SILA. Thank you to kQwa'ste'not~Charlene George, for the images of the moons and the title page watermark design of HÍSW̱ḴE hands; X̱EMȾOLTW̱, Nick Claxton, for help with the SENĆOŦEN; and Emma Tanaka for her photography and graphic design work.

The stories of the earth fibres course are fluid and alive. The static realm of the written word is an unnatural place for being-knowing-doing based in oral traditions. I wish to acknowledge to all the participants of the experience that, through this writing, I am consciously bringing these stories forward to the best of my abilities at this particular point in time. Trusting in your kind-heartedness, I take full responsibility for any errors, omissions, and/or misinterpretations that may have occurred through the telling.

HÍSW̱ḴE SIÁM \0/

SENĆOŦEN
Pronunciation and Glossary

Pronunciation

A   SHORT "A" sound

Á   "AE" sound with abrupt stop

Ӿ   long "A" sound

B   sharp "B," popping sound

C   hard "C" sound

Ć   "CH" sound

₵   hard "CW" sound

D   sharp "D" sound between a "T" and a "D"

E   short "U" sound

F·   "F" sound, as in English

H·   "H" sound, as in English

I·   long "E" sound

Í·   long "I" sound

J·   sharp "J" sound

K·   sharp "K" sound

Ҝ·   sharp "KW" sound

Ḵ·   soft "K" sound

Ḱ·   soft "KW" sound with rounded mouth

L·	"L" sound, as in English
Ł·	a real SENĆOŦEN sound made by a slight blowing under the tongue
M·	"M" sound, as in English
N·	"N" sound, as in English
N̲	"ng" sound
O·	short "O" sound
P·	"P" sound, as in English
Q·	hollow "QW" sound
S·	"S" sound, as in English
Ś·	"SH" sound
T·	"T" sound, as in English
T̵·	"TS" sound
Ŧ	"TH" sound
T̲	"TL" sound
U·	"OO" sound
W·	"W" sound, as in English
W̲·	wind sound or sharp "WH" sound
X·	a real SENĆOŦEN sound made by placing the tongue close to the roof of the mouth and exhaling
X̲·	"XW" sound
Y·	"Y" sound, as in English
Z·	"Z" sound, as in English

Glossary

The tilde (~) denotes an approximate translation.

ĆELÁN̲EN SW̲IKE	~Ancestor or Old Man; ĆELÁN̲EN means "teaching of the ancestors" or "to be a true history"; SW̲IKE means "male person"
HÍSW̲K̲E	~thank you
IY, ŚK̲ÁLEȻEN	~our very best presence, good mind, good heart

I would like to acknowledge Dave Elliott for developing the alphabet and the pronunciation guide and Nick Claxton for sharing it with me.

ḴENI	~seagulls
KEXMIN	~seeds of the Indian consumption plant also known as Indian celery
kQwa̓ste̓not	Charlene George
NUTSA MAHT ŚW̱ḴÁLEȻEN	~with one heart, one mind of our being, we work together
s (little "s")	he/she/its; action
SLEHÁL	~bone games
SENĆOŦEN	language of the W̱SÁNEĆ peoples
SI,ĆENEN̲	~stepping into or becoming W̱SÁNEĆ
SMÍEŦ	~deer
T̲,SOS	~poor of spirit/judgment
SQIX̱I	~small sea urchin
SX̱ÁNEⱢ	~bullheads (as well as Orion's Belt stars)
ŦEḴI	~Sockeye salmon
TEN̲EW	~Earth (literally "a wish for the people")
theé lellum	~an honoured home to welcome all our guests
T'SOU-KE	indigenous nation of the west side of Vancouver Island in British Columbia
TUT'SUP	~fronts of cedar headbands
Wanosts'a7	Dr. Lorna Williams
W̱EM	~tears
WEXES	~frog, croaking, March moon
W̱SÁNEĆ	indigenous nations of the north coast of the Gulf and San Juan islands, southern Vancouver Island, and the southern edge of the Lower Mainland in British Columbia
XAXE SIÁM SILE	~Honoured Grandmother of Many Generations: Wise, Learned, and Respected as Mother Earth
XEMŦOLTW̱	Nick Claxton

LEARNING
AND TEACHING
TOGETHER

Introduction: A Welcoming

In the fall of 2005, a remarkable course was offered within a teacher education program on the traditional Coast Salish territory of the Lkwungen, Esquimalt, and W̱SÁNEĆ peoples. This place, SI,ĆENEṈ~becoming W̱SÁNEĆ, is also known as the University of Victoria, in British Columbia, Canada.

The course, titled "Earth Fibres, Weaving Stories: Learning and Teaching in an Indigenous World," was the second in a continuing series designed and implemented by Lorna Williams, Wanosts'a7, Lil'wat scholar and professor emerita, University of Victoria. Taught in partnership with local elders, or wisdom keepers, from several First Nations, the course provided direct and humble access to indigenous knowledge and holistically addressed issues of crosscultural awareness and pedagogy. The calendar description states:

> In this course students will be engaged in an experiential educational practice. They will learn firsthand how teaching and learning occur in an Indigenous world. Undergraduate and graduate students will work alongside artists-in-residence and wisdom keepers/mentors to witness, experience, learn, and work with a variety of traditional Indigenous fabric and textile arts. The learning community will engage in hearing the traditional stories and songs associated with each of the textile pieces. The course will integrate hands-on practical activities with theoretical and academic goals. Students will experience the principles of traditional Indigenous ways of teaching and learning such as: mentorship and apprenticeship learning; learning by doing;

learning by deeply observing; learning through listening and telling stories and singing songs; and learning as a member of a team; learning by sharing and providing service to the community. (Williams, 2006)

Through the innovative experience, Lorna demonstrated that it is possible to give space and time for significant crosscultural awareness and dispositional change within the context of teacher education. Her vision created a place where learning and teaching emerged from indigenous ways rather than from the status quo, so that educators could gain a deeper sense of indigenous worldviews (for more information on Lorna's vision, see Tanaka, 2009; Tanaka, Williams, Benoit, Duggan, Moir, and Scarrow, 2007; Williams and Tanaka, 2007; Williams, Tanaka, Leik, and Riecken, 2014; Sanford, Williams, Hopper, and McGregor, 2012).

This book highlights the experience of twelve pre-service teachers who were enrolled in the course: Leanne, Courtney, Garrett, Jayne, Sara, April, Nicole, Kevin, Danielle, Chelsea, Heather, and Jade (all pseudonyms). These soon-to-be teachers worked alongside other course participants in a collaborative team environment of six smaller groups, each led by wisdom keepers who engaged them in working with one of the following traditional materials: sheep's wool (May Sam, Tsartlip), buckskin (Gay Williams, Lil'wat), button blankets (Gina Robertson, Laichwiltach/Kwakuitl), woven sashes (Lynne Hemry, Métis), cedar bark (Carolyn and Fran Memnook, Hesqiaht Saddle Lake/Cree), and print buckskin (Janet Rogers, Mohawk/Tuscarora). In addition, Della (Rice) Sylvester (Cowichan) led the group on a poignant nature walk.

In the course, the participants created a variety of items, including a cedar bark shawl, knitted wool garments, a ceremonial button blanket, beaded medicine bags, woven sashes, beaded moccasins, and a printed buckskin blanket. These handcrafted creations were placed on a large multi-textile mural (see page 26) designed by T'SOU-KE artist and lead instructor Charlene George (kQwa'ste'not). Named XAXE SIÁM SILA~Honoured Grandmother of Many Generations: Wise, Learned, and Respected as Mother Earth, the mural created what Charlene called a "theé lellum, an honoured home to welcome all our guests." The stories of the thirteen moons depicted on this mural are shared in depth on pages 30–37.

In designing and implementing the course, Lorna and Charlene made a concerted effort to ensure that the experience was rooted in place, and so it is in SI,ĆENEN, the land upon which the course took place, that my stories begin. Honouring the traditions of this land, I introduce myself as I begin. My name is Michele Therese Duke Tanaka, and my ancestry is rooted in many cultures, including Scottish, Irish, German, English, Creole French, and 'Cajun (Acadian). I was born and raised in the United States and began my immigration to Canada in 2003. Since that time, I have been an appreciative visitor on this land as my family and I have been nourished – body, mind, and soul – by the richness and gifts of SI,ĆENEN̄. With gratitude, I acknowledge and respect the ancestral knowledge of this inspirited place.

This theé lellum welcoming now extends to you; I invite you to leave your familiar beliefs around education and to imagine a different setting embedded with ancestral teachings extending beyond time. Here, gentle, capable hands intuit their way as they weave, sew, knit, and create. Strewn about the busy classroom are various fabrics, velvety hides, strips of cedar, and supple, spun wool. Colourful beads, threads, paints, and shell buttons pass through deft fingers. Sounds of laughter, tears, and wondering intermingle with the telling of stories, both joyful and sad. The taste of fresh salmon and berries is infused with the smoke of a fire and the rich, clean scent of cedar as the course participants enter into an indigenous world.

As we shall see, Lorna and Charlene wove the theé lellum moon stories throughout the course. These offerings suggest the importance of learning to live in a good relationship with the natural and sustaining rhythms and cycles of life. What does Charlene's indigenous perspective offer to educators? What can we learn by listening and embracing indigenous ways? In the increasingly diverse context of North American schools, most teachers are white, middle-class women (Ladson-Billings, 2001; Sleeter, 2008). To inform their teaching practice, these educators draw primarily on experience from their own familiar upbringing and sometimes struggle with how to understand and teach students who are from backgrounds that differ culturally from their own. In addition, non-Aboriginal pre-service teachers are often so immersed in their own cultural beliefs that they are unaware their beliefs are culturally biased; some even see themselves as somehow being without a culture (Schmidt, 1999). Charlene's stories and the earth fibres course experience offered other pedagogical possibilities.

Teachers hold positions of power and bear the responsibility of developing deep crosscultural awareness, given an increasingly culturally diversified student body. Too often, habits of the dominant culture are privileged to the exclusion or detriment of other cultural ways of knowing brought into the classroom by students. In Canada, in the case of Aboriginal learners, this presents a particularly poignant case: as one of the fastest growing student populations, Aboriginal learners continue to face significant struggles in school disproportionate to those faced by the larger student body (Cowley and Easton, 2006; Statistics Canada, 2005a, 2005b).

All educators across Canada, whether they are in classrooms or community settings, whether they are teacher educators or policy makers, are tasked with attending to the resurgence of indigenous ways of knowing and the emergence of indigenous perspectives in educational contexts. In particular, teacher educators should give special attention to helping pre-service (student) teachers become more familiar with ways of learning and teaching that embody indigenous ways of knowing. We have arrived on the shore of a new paradigm. Now, we have to stand on the ground in which we believe and make our way forward in a good way.

Indigenous approaches can be useful not only for youth of Aboriginal heritage but also for all learners, especially those who are steeped in the traditions of the dominant Western paradigm (Tanaka, 2011). Making indigeneity an educational priority is challenging and requires bringing experiential and holistic emphasis to formal education settings that have typically privileged intellectual knowledge to the exclusion of other ways of knowing. Crosscultural understanding requires a shift in *teacher disposition* – the beliefs, attitudes, and values held by teachers (Kanu, 2006). While shifting pre-service teachers' dispositions can be difficult (Richardson, 1996), educational scholars are beginning to identify and define important factors that support deep and lasting change towards cultural inclusion (Gay, 2000; Kumashiro, 2008; Sleeter, 2008).

The challenging work of shifting dispositions requires stepping outside of, and sometimes resisting, deeply embedded social, cultural, and institutional structures as well as personal ways of being-knowing-doing. This text shares a rich example of such an effort in the context of teacher education, where pre-service teachers engaged in a course that deepened their knowledge, insight, and receptivity to indigenous epistemologies and worldviews, resulting in notable dispositional shifts.

Immersed in an indigenous learning environment, the pre-service teachers set aside their Western habits of being-knowing-doing and suspended their judgment to engage differently in the creation of the various earth fibre textile pieces. They carefully observed both their own processes as learners and the ways in which the wisdom keepers acted in their role as teachers. The insight gained through this immersive experience unsettled the pre-service teachers' deep-seated Eurocentric perspectives around the twinned processes of learning and teaching. They reported changed attitudes towards incorporating indigenous approaches within their teaching practice. This book describes the experiences of these emerging teachers and how the course became for them a formative *touchstone* (Strong-Wilson, 2008), an anchor from which to consider what might be true of learning and teaching.

As a researcher, I was fortunate to be able to walk alongside the participants in this course – the pre-service teachers, the wisdom keepers, and the earth fibres. I wish to acknowledge my gratitude to both Lorna and Charlene for welcoming me into the experience to do this research. Over a six-month period in the fall and winter of 2006 and 2007, I was able to listen to many poignant and interwoven stories of learning and teaching. I was also a participant in the creation of XAXE SIÁM SILA, and together we wove, sewed, painted, and knit with cedar bark, wool, buckskin, cloth, shells, buttons, and beads. We listened to stories of the ancestors and of the earth fibres themselves. We laughed and cried together over what was, what is, and what might be possible for learning and teaching in our schools.

Something significant happened during the creation of the Honoured Grandmother mural and, as an educator, I believe the stories of the course are worth sharing as part of the larger conversation about indigenizing curricula and crosscultural understanding. Through the vibrant, though relatively brief, encounter with the wisdom keepers and the earth fibres, the non-indigenous participants (including me) were changed. Many of us were willing to let the epistemological and ontological ground on which we thought we stood shift and be re-formed. We became different teachers, more open to indigenous students and more understanding of other cosmologies and possible ways of being.

This book describes how the pre-service teachers, as they engaged deeply in indigenous ways of learning and teaching, altered their assumptions and beliefs about pedagogy. While walking alongside the wisdom keepers, the pre-service teachers listened deeply across cultures (Schultz, 2003), engaged in emotional reflexivity (Dressman, 1998), and became comfortable in the discomfort of knowing while not knowing (Kumashiro, 2008). The increased sensitivity and insight gained through the experience of walking alongside the wisdom keepers helped these young teachers both to increase their cultural knowledge of particular indigenous people and to develop their conceptual understanding of learning and teaching. They then adopted teaching dispositions – beliefs, values, and attitudes – that were more inclusive of indigenous ways of being-knowing-doing. They brought forward this pedagogy into their practica in ways that were supportive and encouraging of all students within the classroom, regardless of their particular cultural worldview.

As an educator, I care a great deal about the usefulness of actions and about how to do things in a "good" way. My aspiration echoes the teachings of the wisdom keepers; useful and good actions help us to be our very best, both in the classroom and in other areas of our lives. Such actions require having an openness to getting along with each other, without causing harm, and to live in good relation with TEṈEW~Earth that sustains us. Useful and good actions nourish our souls. Charlene speaks of using good hands, "to be a tool for all that needs to happen and have an openness to do the things that need to be done" (field notes). Using good hands means proceeding "humbly, with skills it takes a lifetime to learn properly and an openness to the spirits of the place and the wonder of the unpredictable moment when the connection is made" (Chamberlin, 2003, p. 236). As an educator, I often discuss the importance of using good hands. I believe that promoting useful and good action is our primary purpose as teachers.

A Note about Terms

There is no simple or precise definition of *indigenous*. It can be used as a political or racialized term that indicates one's birth in a particular place (Battiste and Henderson, 2000). It can be a term of self-identification, often indicated by capitalization (i.e., *Indigenous*). I use the term in lower-case (i.e., *indigenous*) to describe people and ways of being that are *of the Earth*. Thus, "being indigenous" implies a place-based, relational understanding of TEṈEW~Earth that acknowledges and draws from the interrelated realms of mind, body, emotion, and spirit. The term *Aboriginal* refers specifically to the first inhabitants of Canada and includes First Nations, Inuit, and Métis peoples. The term *participants* refers to the broad group of people who took part in the earth fibres course, including the wisdom keepers (Aboriginal instructors, or elders) and the pre-service teachers. The first time a name is used in each chapter, the reader will be reminded as to whether the name refers to a wisdom keeper (WK) or a pre-service teacher (PST).

While English is my learned familial language, I use some indigenous language where appropriate, primarily SENĆOŦEN, as this is the language of the Aboriginal people upon whose traditional land the course took place. Some of the indigenous terms used are derived from the diverse languages of the wisdom keepers, and I have tried to be true to the way these terms were shared with me. Much of what I write here comes from oral teachings. There are variant alphabetical representations for oral languages; for the SENĆOŦEN words, I follow the W̱SÁNEĆ orthography, which uses capital letters, except for the lower-case *s*. Spellings for Aboriginal words were determined in consultation with Lorna Williams, Charlene George, and Nick Claxton. I thank them for their guidance through this complex terrain.

I use the term *education* to include experiences of learning and teaching and particularly formalized structures of schools and schooling. The term *teacher education* refers to the formal processes of educating teachers within higher education contexts. Of course, what is useful and true in education more generally is often useful and true within teacher education as well. Therefore, I also use the term *(teacher) education* and *(teacher) educator* to remind the reader that education broadly and teacher education more specifically are intimately intertwined through common history, lived experience, and hopes for the future. Finally, I use a hyphen to indicate fluidity between terms; static notions of either/or are outdated. We are not *either* a learner *or* a teacher but always hold the potential of being both simultaneously; we are *learner-teachers*. It is not possible to *be* without *knowing* and *doing*; rather, we hold the immediate plasticity of *being-knowing-doing*.

Mindful Reflexivity: My Attitude of Gathering

As a teacher, I bring to the classroom my own past experiences that have shaped my disposition towards learning and teaching (Britzman, 1990/2003). As educator Parker Palmer (1998) says, we teach who we are. Our beliefs, values, and attitudes shape the learning in our classrooms, the larger community, and beyond. I recognize that what I do as a teacher educator affects the pre-service teachers with whom I spend time. My actions ripple outwards, however subtly, through these young people as *they* go out to teach many more students over the years. Because of this environment of accountability, I engage in a type of *mindful* inquiry (Bentz and Shapiro, 1998).

My personal teaching actions are motivated by concerns for humanity, ecology, and spirituality. Around the world, peoples, plants, animals, and ways of life are rapidly disappearing and our "elbow room" in the world is shrinking. Indigenous knowledge matters now, more than ever before (Davis, 2009; Hawken, 2007). At the same time, I have become more conscious of how my privileged position as an educator entails a certain responsibility of awareness. I feel the need to clarify my bearings, my guiding disposition, my values, and my attitudes and beliefs through a recursive practice of *reflexivity*. I consciously pay attention to my own practice, which is embedded in complex relationships with my learner-teachers, my professional community, my home community, and the larger world. If we teach who we are, I need to know who I am and where I stand. From there, I set my bearings for how to proceed in a good way, with good hands.

Reflexivity requires me, and all educators, to extend skills of reflection (Dewey, 1933; Schön, 1983). While *reflection* involves looking carefully at teaching practice and how that practice affects students' learning, *reflexivity* entails a deeper, more nuanced process that includes attention to one's ontological and epistemological positioning. As an educator, I need to know what my beliefs are about the nature of existence and the nature of knowledge. What ground am I standing on? From where do my actions flow? What feeds my soul? What shapes my worldview? It is immensely practical for me to name and understand where I stand, as that in turn affects my beliefs, values, attitudes, and, ultimately, my actions.

Teacher identity is deeply embedded in educational practice. Drawing on personal narratives helps the teacher to make sense of personal practical knowledge gained through teaching experience (Clandinin and Connelly, 2000). One reflexive technique is to bring memories forward by paying attention to *touchstone* experiences, particularly in crosscultural settings (Strong-Wilson, 2008). The term *touchstone* refers to "that which serves to test or try the genuineness or value of anything" (*Oxford English Dictionary*). Salient memories, such as favourite books from childhood, can shape teaching practice (Strong-Wilson, 2008). The stories we remember, read, tell, and hear can become significant points of reference, touchstones by which teachers can "judge the worth of other stories and experiences" (Strong-Wilson, 2008, p. 95). Through a process of remembering, teachers become more fully situated in their "landscape of learning" (Greene, 1978, p. 2). The earth fibres course became for many participants a significant touchstone for indigenous ways of learning and teaching (Tanaka, 2011).

In using the term *reflexivity,* I wish to accentuate a process in which "the subject/researcher sees simultaneously the object of her or his gaze and the means by which the object (which may include oneself as subject) is being constituted" (Davies et al., 2004, p. 360). Here, the learner-teacher becomes learner-teacher-researcher. As Dressman (1998) suggests, reflexivity is a process that goes beyond reflecting on the more mechanical aspects of practice to include deep attention to individual positioning within social and, I would argue, ecological and spiritual contexts. Effective crosscultural pedagogy requires both reflection and reflexivity on the part of (teacher) educators.

Reflexive scholarly work requires attention to and acceptance of emotional engagement. As a learner-teacher-researcher, I am motivated by a heartfelt sadness and concern about the palpable disrespect that people too often show for each other, other living creatures, and TENEW~Earth. I believe that in the context of my work, this emotional connection should be acknowledged rather than ignored under the guise of so-called scholarly objectivity. Despite the tendency on the part of many educators to separate their emotions from their academic work, passion is an integral and important part of scholarly investigation (Neumann, 2006). The inclusion of my personal emotions in my academic writing is intentional, and I am unapologetic. The role of emotion in learning has become increasingly clear (Artz, 1994; F.L. Brown, 2004) and is particularly important to acknowledge in teacher education (Bullough and Young, 2002; Hayes, 2003). If there is one thing that I have learned from indigenous elders, it is that we must try to bring together the intellectual (objective) knowing of the mind and the emotional (situated) knowing of the heart, in order to bring increased balance and wellness both to ourselves and to the world. Bentz and Shapiro (1998, p. 108) suggest that this be done through heightened mindfulness as "the closer you are to the source of the text, the more valid your interpretation is likely to be."

An Indigenist Worldview

So: Who am I? As an educator, who am I being-becoming – that is, both being and coming to be, at the same time? On what ontological and epistemological ground do I currently stand? What is my personal cosmology? How do I understand, relate to, and locate myself in the universe? These are important questions for me to pose, as they are the homeland of this scholarly work. After much consideration and reflexive exploration of my own touchstone stories (Tanaka, 2015; Tanaka, Nicholson, and Farish, 2012), I find myself humbly rooted in what Shawn Wilson (2007) calls an "indigenist" worldview. In the same way that a man can be a feminist, a non-indigenous person such as I can be an indigenist. While this terminology feels awkward, it is the best way I have found to describe my location.

This setting of my moral and ethical compass was reinforced for me during an educational research conference I attended in San Diego a number of years ago. I had to choose whether to go hear indigenous scholar Gregory Cajete speak or stay in my hotel room to meet an imminent writing deadline. Luckily, I followed my heart: Cajete's words now shape much of the work I do today.

He began by mentioning environmental educator David Orr (1994/2004), who believes it is imperative for educators to think carefully about what education is *for*. What is the purpose of having all those kids with us in those places we call schools? What learning or teaching do we want to have happen? In response to Orr's challenge, Cajete (2009) suggested three simple questions that every teacher should ask: How are we going to deal with the environmental crisis as it is today? How are we going to live with each other? And how do we take care of our own souls? For me these questions have both stayed with me and evolved, becoming luminous guides, useful in all educational contexts. Note that throughout the book, my articulation of these questions changes slightly. While I am consciously trying to keep the spirit of Cajete's original voicing, I am at the same time letting the questions breathe and expand within the new context of this work and in relation to my own thinking. I hope Cajete will be pleased to see that the questions take on a life of their own once put into practice.

Like many Aboriginal and Native American scholars of education (e.g., see Cajete, 1994; Fixico, 2003; S. Wilson, 2008), I believe that the notion of who we are is defined by our relationships (with ourselves, with each other, and with the Earth) and cannot be defined outside of them. Identifying my location serves to help the reader identify his or her own location. Once we have identified our locations, we can all act in relationship to transform our educational practice. My reflexive practice has brought me to believe deeply in the importance of relationships and relational accountability that demonstrate respect, reciprocity, and responsibility (S. Wilson, 2008). Many non-Aboriginal scholars do work that is highly complementary to, or shares fundamental similarities with, indigenous perspectives, particularly in the area of environmental and ecological studies (e.g., see Capra, 1996; Hawken, 2007; Orr, 1994/2004; Saul, 2008).

The Gathering of Stories

At first glance, readers may wonder if I, a non-Aboriginal woman of mixed European descent, am inappropriately telling the stories of others – those of the indigenous wisdom keepers, the pre-service teachers, and the earth fibres. But as I was a participant-observer in the course (Spradley, 1980), these stories were shared with me, and my personal story has become intertwined with them. As a researcher, I listened from a phenomenological perspective, with an openness to the experience at hand (Thomas and Pollio, 2002; van Manen,

1990/1997); our entwined stories have touched my heart. Through this intimacy of understanding, I have come to believe that I am *obliged* to tell these stories. I don't own this knowledge; I am a caretaker of it. And now, as Charlene's teachings advise, it is my responsibility to bring this knowledge forward in a good way. Thomas King (2003), a Canadian American novelist of Greek and Cherokee descent, reminds us that once we've heard the stories, it's up to us what we do with them. And so I choose the uncertain path of storyteller, with the intent and willingness to share what I hold, to help good change to happen through this writing. Once you have heard these stories, it will also be up to you what you do with them.

Across Canada, teachers struggle to create inclusive environments in their multicultural classrooms and, in particular, to welcome indigenous students. The purpose of this book is to respond to this struggle by shedding light on the process of dispositional change within the non-indigenous pre-service teachers who were enrolled in the earth fibres course. The book offers a focused glimpse into the immersion of pre-service teachers in indigenous pedagogy and a sense of how that experience changes teaching practice.

My enthusiasm for this work is embedded in what I have come to know, and what I realize I don't know, through my practice as a teacher. My intent is twofold: first, to better inform myself in my journey towards becoming a useful and good teacher; and second, to share this new understanding with the practising community of teachers, teacher educators, and policy makers in the hope that this will improve the capacity of educational programs to meet the diverse needs of children in multicultural classrooms across North America and beyond.

The Significance of Stories

Stories and storytelling are integral parts of indigenous knowledge creation and research (Archibald, 2008; Smith, 1999). In his Massey lecture series, Thomas King (2003, p. 2) repeatedly tells a creation story about the world resting on the back of a turtle. What's under the turtle? Another turtle. And what's under that one? "It's turtles all the way down." King suggests that our beliefs are built on story upon story upon story: "The truth about stories is that that's all we are." Life is narrative – a sequence of events, an account of who and what we are. We express ourselves through stories, and we listen to the stories of others to find out who *they* are. We reflexively examine our life stories to better know ourselves, to figure out how the world works, and to find our place within a complex web of relationships. We give voice to where we are located, and where we are going, through the telling of our stories.

In the study, my approach to narrative inquiry was based on an assumption that the personal, practical knowledge of teachers can serve to inform theory (Clandinin and Connelly, 2000), and I embraced both descriptive and explanatory narratives (Polkinghorne, 1988). Using descriptive narrative, I tried to create accurate portrayals of the personal accounts shared with me in the interviews as well as what I saw during my role as a participant in the course. In using explanatory narrative, I focused on interpreting and understanding the causal relationships between the earth fibres experience and the dispositional changes within the pre-service teachers. Except where noted, all quotes used in the telling of these stories are from one-on-one interviews with the participants.

Nigerian storyteller Ben Okri (1997, p. 46) writes: "In a fractured age, when cynicism is god, here is a possible heresy: we live by stories, we also live in them. One way or another we are living the stories planted in us early or along the way, or we are also living the stories we planted – knowingly or unknowingly – in ourselves." The course was a serendipitous opportunity for the participants to pay close attention to the stories that had been planted within their landscapes of learning. The pre-service teachers were at a developmentally critical point in their teaching career, moving from an emphasis on their role as learner to an emphasis on their role as teacher. They came from a past that was steeped in strong stories of Euro-Western influence. The narrative expressions of these young people at this particular time and in this particular context were rich and informative as they struggled to make sense of their new role as teachers. The wisdom keepers lived other stories, stories planted generations ago by ancestors with significantly different worldviews. Within the interweaving of these stories exists a good and useful way forward for (teacher) educators.

The stories of the earth fibres study described here have been, and continue to be, disseminated in conversational rather than prescriptive ways. This approach intends to support educators to inform their practice intelligently and intuitively, particularly around ontological, epistemological, and pedagogical issues in multicultural classrooms. It is my hope that this book helps educators to think about what might be possible in their particular location and that it becomes a touchstone encouraging dominant-culture teachers to listen and converse more deeply across cultures.

Buckskin print, resonating complexity

Weaving Stories, Walking the Wheel

Before moving into the heart of the stories, it is important to understand the overarching structure of this work. The earth fibres course was rooted in a deeply complex pedagogy. Honouring that complexity required careful attention to framing the findings of the study in a way that reflected their web-like nature. The course served as a vessel for various experiential stories. There are many ways to narrate the events, and as many ways to present what might be considered significant in the data. I hope to put these stories into words in a way that honours the relational and living complexity of the course, that the experiences do not become too dissected or linear in the telling. Tafoya's (1995) principle of uncertainty suggests that the closer one gets to a definition or explanation of an idea, the more it loses its context. For this reason, I describe two particular framework images that I found useful in bringing the stories forward in a good way: those of a woven braid and of a Métis medicine wheel.

Charlene and learner tying braided strands of reed

The stories of the earth fibres course can be likened to the image of braided strands of cedar woven together into designs that are both interesting to look at and functional. In the context of this writing, I have chosen to highlight four specific storylines, or strands in the braid: those of the wisdom keepers, the pre-service teachers, and the earth fibres themselves, as well as my own personal account. Each of these strands (except for my own) embodies multiple stories representing multiple voices. The four strands weave around and through each other, revealing the reciprocal nature of the overall experience. To reflect the completeness of the course experience, I have chosen not to tell any individual's story on its own. Instead, I present the stories as they came to me, all parts of one complicated whole. This has become a tapestry of story, a story of stories, with each person's account rising to the surface at various times during the telling to add colour and texture to the overall piece.

The first strand in the story is that of the wisdom keepers, who held the intention of bringing their cultural teachings forward through sharing with us their traditional skills with various natural Earth fibres. Theirs is a storyline rooted in the lives of people who have lived for countless generations in a particular physical location, a story that extends back far before colonial impact. The wisdom keepers drew upon their profound connection to nature and introduced stories to the participants that were deep, rich, and true to their own personal cultural knowledge embedded in place. They brought cultural teachings forward with the conscious intent of showing us some of the different worldviews that co-exist in the contemporary context of Vancouver Island.

The second storyline is that of the non-indigenous pre-service teachers enrolled in the course. Their ancestors, of primarily European descent, came to the area of SI,ĆENEN relatively recently. For the most part, the pre-service teachers took the course because they felt unprepared to teach indigenous students. In addition, many expressed an intense longing for, as Courtney (PST) said, "a really genuine experience of learning at the university level." Throughout the course, the pre-service teachers carefully observed themselves as both learners and emerging teachers, while being acutely aware of finding their way through what Sara (PST) termed "a jumble of teaching beliefs."

The third storyline is that of the Earth fibres themselves – the cattails, cedar bark, wool, buckskin, shell, and other natural materials that were constantly held and felt by participants throughout the course. These fibres hold stories of physical place, of that which has endured in a particular location over time. Witnessing the wisdom keepers' present-day interactions with the fibres shed light on the relationships that people had with similar fibres in the past, and how those teachings are being brought forward today. The stories of the Earth fibres are embedded and revealed in the photos, the narratives of the participants, and the finished textile pieces in numerous and powerful ways.

The final story strand is my own. As both a participant in the course and an observer, I engaged in the process of working with the Earth fibres and watched myself as a learner-teacher-researcher. My experience in the course (and with the other storylines) was useful in considering the nature of the participants' experience. Together, the four storylines create a metaphorical braid of lived experience that emerges in stark contrast to the positivist-oriented backdrop of the university, a context that the course instructors so boldly tried to disrupt. As these storylines intertwined through our shared activity, the unusual learning experience disturbed the pre-service teachers' ways of being in the classroom and unsettled narratives that had been privileged in their prior school experience.

Alongside the image of the braid, the main themes in the data (those of place, spirituality, learner and teacher relationships, good hands, and integration)

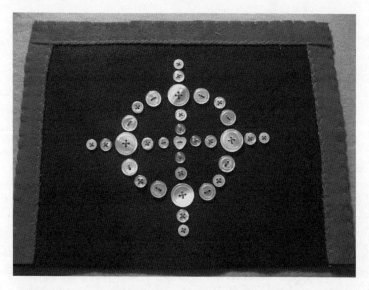

Button blanket medicine wheel made in the earth fibres course

emerged as being deeply congruent with a framework suggestive of the spiralling sensibilities found in the Métis medicine wheel. The teachings about the
wheel were first described to me in an interview with wisdom keeper Lynne,
midway through the course. In a later meeting, Lynne explained that the wheel
was a good image for my findings because she saw me as "teaching about circles
and not about squares." Further, the holistic and flowing nature of the wheel is
suggestive of the intricacies of the Earth fibres experience.

Lynne has generously shared with me her teachings of the wheel in order
that I may use them in the context of this writing; I thank her for her generosity of spirit. I want to be clear that it is my intention for this work to support
understanding between all peoples, including the Métis from whose tradition
this version of the wheel extends. I hope my indigenist interpretation will resonate with the teachings of the ancestors. My purpose is to use the wheel not as a
static model but, rather, as a resting place of sorts, a fluid framework that can
hold the data of the Earth fibres course experience in a gentle way, as it lives
and breathes in my hands. I see the wheel as a place where the experience can
rest for a time, as I tease out and convey some of the stories before they move
on, as stories do, to become whatever else they are meant to be.

After the course, as I moved through the various stages of data analysis, I
often struggled to find a suitable way to organize the stories. I wanted to honour

not only the complexity of the weave but my feeling that the stories were somehow still in motion. My frames were always too hierarchical or linear in nature. I consciously tried to let go of my own Euro-Western–oriented mindset, but I couldn't find a structure that felt right. This was due in part to the complexity and size of the data set (roughly thirty-four transcribed interviews and focus group sessions, totalling more than forty hours of audio data; numerous field notes; and dozens of field photographs) but also to the fact that I did not yet feel comfortable embracing an indigenist stance.

At one point in the process, when I felt particularly "stuck," I decided to pay another visit to Lynne, as she was one of the participants who had offered to meet with me beyond the initial interviews. My hope was that by sharing my ideas with someone who had an indigenous perspective, I might be able to realize a more organic way of presenting my findings. At this time, I had organized the data into approximately eighteen loose groupings, which I had been rearranging in different ways in my attempts to find a resonant structure. I showed my categories to Lynne and sketched a diagram of how I thought the data were unfolding. The diagram was visually similar to the structure of a DNA molecule, with the stories of the pre-service teachers and the wisdom keepers interweaving and spiralling upwards. Lynne quickly recognized its congruence with her own medicine wheel teachings. Working together, we placed my subthemes into the framework of the wheel. I then developed the five primary themes that are explored in Chapters 1 through 5.

As I understand it through Lynne's teachings, the medicine wheel is a simple, reflective tool that helps a person situate him- or herself amidst relationships in a given time and place. Lane, Bopp, Bopp, Brown, and elders (1984, p. 9) describe the medicine wheel as follows:

An ancient symbol used by almost all the Native people of North and South
America. There are many different ways that this basic concept is expressed:
the four grandfathers, the four winds, the four cardinal directions, and many
other relationships that can be expressed by four. Just like a mirror can be
used to see things not normally visible (e.g., behind us or around a corner),
the medicine wheel can be used to help us see or understand things we can't
quite see or understand because they are ideas and not physical objects.

In a similar way, wisdom keeper Charlene had spoken briefly about local Coast Salish teachings that draw on the image of four house poles holding up a lodge. Although the earth fibres course was offered on Coast Salish territory, I chose to use the Métis wheel as a framework, with Lynne's guidance, because the wheel was shared and talked about in the course and brought up by the participants themselves during the interviews. I believe that the image of the medicine wheel suggests a strong relational accountability to the participants in the course.

Lynne also shared with me that "the true power in the wheel is in the centre, in the hub, and the outer rim follows." The middle of the wheel is a place of strength and connection to spirit, reminiscent of a place where it is possible to connect to knowledge that endures (Aluli Meyer, 2008). Lynne told me:

> With your four directions, you have the four teachings: North, South, East, and West. North is strength; the East is the ancestors and illumination and wisdom; the South is purity and innocence and the child within and joy; and the West is the look within place, the place of here and now, paying your bills, looking after life, being responsible.

Lynne then described the process of "walking the wheel," a process used when one is trying to choose a good path to take in a given situation. For me, her description evoked a sense of spiralling movement: the walker of the wheel continuously comes back to the centre after visiting the four directions for clarification. This was a more suitable model for my analysis than my previous models had been.

After our conversation, I decided to experiment with walking the wheel in my personal life on various topics. Each time I did so, after "returning" to the centre, I noticed a shift in my understanding, a shift that also slightly adjusted my sense of self. In this way I experienced the wheel as a reflexive practice that helped me recognize and clarify my personal beliefs. When I placed the stories of the course into the frame of the wheel, this, too, became a reflexive process that furthered my analysis in a way that is congruent with the indigenous worldview articulated by the wisdom keepers. As discussed below, the chapters of this book take on a similar cyclical pattern.

This version of the story, then, is my interpretation, emerging through my own personal sensing and writing process. These stories would be different if someone else were to tell them. I ask the reader, as you consider the stories of the course, to keep in mind the images of the braid and the medicine wheel, as temporary vessels that help to hold the earth fibres course experience in time and place for the purpose of this writing. The stories are complex and interdependent. The path laid out in this writing is one of many possible ways through the lived experience in the course – a temporary snapshot. I invite and welcome you into my interpretation of the indigenous world of the Earth fibres course.

Overview of the Chapters

The book provides a small piece of a complicated, multi-dimensional, and animate puzzle that has different implications for all teachers, teacher educators, and teacher education programs, whether they are indigenous or not. It is written in the spirit of dialogue within the realm of education generally, and teacher education specifically, and describes how indigenous teachings were woven into the curriculum practice of these pre-service teachers.

Chapters 1 through 5 tell the entwined stories of the course participants, including the wisdom keepers, the pre-service teachers, the earth fibres, and me. Chapter 1 describes the importance of orienting to place in the context of the course, with an emphasis on interacting with the surrounding physical place,

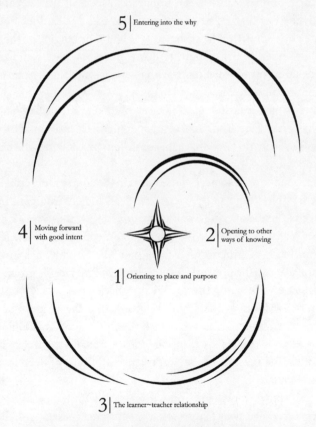

5 | Entering into the why

4 | Moving forward with good intent

2 | Opening to other ways of knowing

1 | Orienting to place and purpose

3 | The learner~teacher relationship

Walking the wheel of Chapters 1 through 5
(Graphic: Emma Tanaka)

understanding personal beliefs about learning and teaching, and engaging in a mutually derived sense of common purpose. The pedagogical beliefs of the wisdom keepers and the pre-service teachers are presented in detail in order to highlight pedagogical orientations and each individual's sense of direction.

Overall, the intent of the wisdom keepers in the course was to bring the teachings of their ancestral cultural knowledge forward to the members of the learning community. For the pre-service teachers, two primary intents were to learn more about indigenous culture and to have a genuine learning experience at university. The course was designed to create a space where these two groups could walk alongside each other and interact with a shared common goal. Here, a re-storied learning community emerged – one that was atypical of those generally found in university settings. This learning community thus highlighted a different sense of educational place.

Chapter 2 portrays spirit as an important aspect of the learning process. *Spirit* is defined as that mystery which makes us alive. It does not imply or necessitate any connection to a particular religion or religious belief. The participants describe the act of putting down their notebooks and of opening themselves up to other ways of knowing – ways that differ from the mental engagement commonly encouraged in university and school settings. Listening differently is a particular focus, as is a heightened awareness of language and its underlying meaning. The ritual of an opening circle is discussed as a way for participants to suspend knowing, gain comfort in unknowing, and access other ways of knowing.

The indigenous pedagogical stance taken in the course is described in Chapter 3. The wisdom keepers approached the learning environment by making, in their words, "gentle offerings" of information in ways that were akin to "laying a table" or "planting seeds" for the learner to do with as he or she saw fit. The endogenous learning process of each learner was carefully acknowledged by the wisdom keepers; the pre-service teachers were given fertile ground in which to access their own learning spirits. The pre-service teachers not only felt supported by the wisdom keepers but also knew that the wisdom keepers had faith in them as learners who could find their own way and fulfill their own learning needs. This pedagogy respected the learner and led many participants to feel that during the course they experienced the sort of deep learning that guides one's soul.

Chapter 4 shows how hands-on engagement with the earth fibres helped the participants move away from a solely mental engagement with the material towards other ways of knowing, interacting, and being in the learning environment. Notions of reciprocity, "Giveaway" (a phrase that is described in more detail on page 94–99), and using "good hands" by having a clear mind and healthy intent are deepened through a focus on physicality and doing. The unveiling ceremony for the final mural created in the course is discussed as a time of completion and connection.

Chapter 5 considers how the participants moved into a deepened awareness that helped them, as one participant said, understand "into the why" of another culture. The pre-service teachers' shifting perspectives and dispositions around notions of learning and teaching, as well as issues around the integration of indigenous teachings in classroom practice, are described and discussed.

Chapters 6 through 8 reflect on the stories of the course, framed through the lens of Cajete's (2009) questions for educators, presented now in reverse order: How do we deal with our own souls? How are we going to live with each other? How are we going to deal with the environmental crisis as it is today? These chapters include text boxes that highlight critical questions for practice. Many of these questions emerged in the margins as I first wrote about the course; all have stayed with me as an educator trying to improve and indigenize my practice. These questions are overlapping and interrelated and require extended conversations among educators about what it means to learn and to teach (Pinar, 2004). Chapters 6 through 8 reflect this complexity as key themes from Chapters 1 through 5 are woven more tightly together and brought to the fore.

Resting on the assumption that educators tend to focus on learning rather than teaching (Britzman, Dippo, Searle, and Pitt, 1997), Chapter 6 explores how the course teaches us to care for our souls, both our own and those of the learners we work with. It is about *re-membering* the wholeness of who we are because we teach who we are (Palmer, 1998). It is also about creating our sense of what wholeness means. Learning is the "membering" of the emotional, physical, and spiritual with the intellectual. Learning is circular, cross-disciplinary, and cross-cultural. Learning is complex and requires a kind of trust in the learner that is unfamiliar in Eurocentric educational thought. To take care of our souls, we do well to embrace what Freire calls the "death of the professor" (in Vella, 2002, p. 20) and let the learner find his or her own way. Learning requires us to be vulnerable, to engage our emotions, to follow our intuitive knowing.

Chapter 7 focuses on how we learn to get along with each other. Often this is about resisting the familiar and putting aside what we have come to know. A large part of this is *re-fusing* the status quo. This means "refuse" as in decline to participate, but also "re-fuse," as in to combine and coalesce. We need to re-wire and come together in a different way. (Teacher) education is founded on an industrial model where schools are like factories producing educated workers.

We must not only recognize that this idea is rooted deeply within us but also consciously move towards another paradigm. This is difficult work, and in the course this often meant moving into vulnerable spaces where our ontological beliefs were brought into question. This chapter looks at the importance of being honest and taking risks in liminal, but safe enough, spaces.

The environmental crisis and how we care for the planet are addressed in Chapter 8. One of the most alarming findings of the study is the degree to which the pre-service teachers felt disconnected from TENEW~Earth. At the beginning of the course, they were unaware of the origins of cedar bark, for example – that it comes from one of the *inner* layers of the tree. They were also unfamiliar with the relational positioning of cedar in the larger indigenous-knowledge context of the stories, spirit, and generational memory. The course experience expanded awareness of important issues of sustainability, asking us to consider how our activities might be useful for the seven generations to come.

Chapters 9 through 11 take a third cycle through the earth fibres experience, focusing on the larger context of resistance and the practical implications of implementation. How do we bring the teachings of the ancestors forward into the world of today? How do we listen to our grandparents and to our children at the same time? Crosscultural education asks teachers to shift their dispositions away from the habits of the dominant culture. This requires time and the right kind of space. Chapter 9 discusses how the Earth fibres course provided such time and space, and the opportunity to manifest resistance to Eurocentric ways of knowing on many levels, from the personal to the institutional. Resistance can take many forms, but what occurred in the course was a certain type of opposition that I call a *tender resistance,* a decolonizing act of social justice that is simultaneously caring, vulnerable, mindful, and dialogic. It is steeped in the act of a careful, open-minded, and generous listening.

Chapter 10 highlights the tensions the pre-service teachers found as they brought the teachings of the course into their practicum placements. Here we learn much from the fresh eyes of pre-service teachers, who became quite inventive as they brought the teachings forward into their unique practicum settings. Given the pervasiveness of what I call "positivism soup," the pre-service teachers had to address various challenges, including their feelings of disconnection, ideas of ownership, external motivation, assessment, efficiency, group work, and the lack of support for reflection.

Chapter 11 completes this third cycle by discussing how many of the problems in education are really better described as problems *of* education (Orr, 1994/2004). Educators are at a crossroads, where locating a sense of educational

Learning and Teaching Together

purpose is paramount. What is our intent? What do we want our classrooms, our world, to be? We have anxiety over these fundamental and often hidden issues in education. Suggestions are made as to how these issues might be addressed, including finding a sense of collaborative purpose, developing relational accountability, walking alongside each other, enacting a pedagogy of spirit, being-becoming mindful inquirers, and walking our talk. Chapter 12 completes the larger circle by returning us to a renewed sense of place within the earth fibres experience.

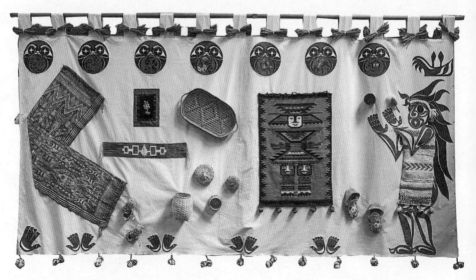

XAXE SIÁM SILA, Sides A and B. Photo by University of Victoria Photo Services

The Moons of XAXE SIÁM SILA

After the completion of the course and the raising ceremony for XAXE SIÁM SILA, Charlene wanted to be sure that the stories of the moons were remembered in a good way. One rainy afternoon, we met in a crowded coffee shop, and I turned on my audio recorder as Charlene spoke from her heart. Later, I transcribed her moon stories and then visited with her again to ensure the accuracy of my transcripts. A third such visit was made during the editorial process of this book to maintain cultural integrity.

On the following pages, kQwa'ste'not Charlene speaks, taking us deep into her cultural stories, illuminating the spirit that birthed the earth fibres course. Before you read on, I suggest you take a moment to pause – notice your breath – and imagine yourself in a cozy storytelling atmosphere. It's evening, family and friends gather by a fire, shadows flicker across time. Charlene's melodic voice begins.

This mural was created to honour our sisters, mothers, daughters, grandmothers, and aunties. It is meant to bring forward and recognize the women's gifts that are often behind the scenes. The canvas represents the sails brought by Western visitors and is the base of the piece. It honours WEXES~frog, who represents this incredible time of change. At the top are thirteen TUT'SUP~ fronts of cedar headbands that give honour to all the grandmothers who came before us. Below are thirteen wool pom-poms to balance the regalia for each moon. The two honoured Grandmothers on each side welcome us as our mothers would, lifting up their hands to say HÍSW̱ḴE \0/~thank you for all the gifts that we share. The large HÍSW̱ḴE hands in the corner are there so that we will know how to turn to the other side of the mural with no harm to our visitors. The small HÍSW̱ḴE hands are thankfully holding up the work. These images belong to the wisdom keepers and are on loan to the university to help with teaching.

Flowing from the first Grandmother's hair is the home that keeps us rooted in where we came from. The wolf is nearby to remind us of family and transformation. The wolf is at the head of the canoe that continues on the backside of the mural. This is one cycle of a never-ending journey. The pieces on the first side of the mural are beginners' pieces, humbly made by students in the course. On the other side, pieces have been gathered from across Turtle Island and from our relatives further south (from geographic areas known as South America and the island of Borneo). The pieces might look simple but have been put together with incredible skill transferred through the generations. The stories, history, and culture are in each knot, stitch, and twist of wool and cedar.

As we continue the traditions and the teaching from the past to be able to nurture and enhance what we have today, we honour the next generation by reminding them of our Grandmothers. This process gives a concrete translation tool to new teachers so that they can carry indigenous women's wisdom into their teaching. XAXE SIÁM SILA hangs from a spindle whorl that represents new turning, new twists that we are stepping into. One spindle whorl is Hummingbird, who flies between North and South. She is a female warrior: even though she is small, she has incredible strength and spends her time being self-sustaining, fighting and nurturing. The other whorl shows the old, old face of the Grandmother who cried the first WEM~tears, deep prayers to the Creator.

Overall, the mural provides balance to the male aspect of ĆELÁṈEN SW̱IKE, the welcoming house pole, which is also housed in the MacLaurin Building where the teacher education program resides [Author's note: ĆELÁṈEN has the double translation of "teaching of the ancestors" and "to be a true history"; SW̱IKE means "male person." ĆELÁṈEN SW̱IKE is often referred to affectionately as the Old Man]. The second half of the canoe allows us to continue our journey with good hands full of intention from our IY ŚW̱ḰÁLEȻEN~our very best presence: NUTSA MAHT ŚW̱ḰÁLEȻEEN~ with one heart, one mind of our being, we work together.

The thirteen moons tell the story of our year and bring awareness of life cycles. I am humbly thankful for the many teachings brought forward in the SENĆOŦEN language calendar [Claxton and Elliott, 1993]. My perspective of the moons is a Grandma's perspective from the T'SOU-KE [west] side of this island (W̱SÁNEĆ is on the east side). Each of the moons shows activities that *should* be occurring within a year cycle. This does not necessarily mean these activities happen today; many things have changed and gone off-kilter since the first Visitors came, the great change.

In each of the moon faces, I expanded the mouth area to show the incredible importance of what each moon is speaking to you about: the tradition of Coast Salish people. The work is done in a circle to show that this way of hearing, understanding, and giving information comes from the Creator. In my teachings, when you have a mouth with a circle, it represents things that come from the Creator. They are in a counter-clockwise direction, the direction that we dance. When we visit our relatives East from here, they go the other direction! The moon is shining on and telling about these things, but it is on TEṈEW~Earth that these things actually, physically happen.

When I sit to draw, these are the things that come out. I am honoured to be the holder of the pencil and don't question why what I draw needs to be there. What I've drawn might be different from what some other artists have depicted because this is from a feminine perspective more than the masculine. Of course, the moons don't always follow our current calendar system that the modern world has adopted to help with timekeeping in a linear fashion. Dominant-society calendars try to recreate their own rhythm, rather than having a natural cycle that is not neat or orderly in a linear way. Our calendar is overlapping circles within circles.

What I've shown follows the cycles of the moon seasons. They honour and highlight the activity, the gathering, and the social parts of our culture that were (and still are) practised for so many generations. I can't even begin to tell you how many! It's important to recognize what's still here, and also what is missing, such as many kinds of fish, sea life, and camas. My belief is that these relations are still here, but they have morphed and changed into what currently supports us. Sadly, some don't acknowledge, appreciate, or take care of these Gifts.

The Season of New–Spring

Spiritual Birth Moon – The New Baby

We always start the calendar with the new. This represents many things, and while I wouldn't publicly share some of the things that the new season represents, this moon is a time of renewing through our ceremonies in the long house. Drawing a baby inside this first moon's mouth represents a time when we all go within and are new again. There are many other kinds of activities that are happening at this time, but that's the one I wanted to promote most when I was looking at the first moon of the year.

WEXES~Frog Moon

The second moon shows the mouth being a WEXES~frog. To me, it's very much about transformation. We are making a big change in season. At the end of this moon, the frogs are singing, and we are transforming into the next part of our season. In this moon, WEXES is telling us that wintertime is coming to an end and we will make changes. WEXES calls to us in the spring and in the fall time. WEXES holds the first part of the year and, if I were drawing a bigger calendar, WEXES would hold up the second part of the year as well. This shows how we've gone from light to dark and dark to light.

Blossom Moon

As we move into our third moon, we start to have our blossoms. What I've drawn is the Creator's hand, or the Grandma's hand, which ends up being the TENEW~Earth. It's out of the palm of the hand that the blossoms grow. The circle in the middle of the palm represents TENEW~Earth. The back part of the hand has no beginning and has no end. It's represented by a dark design because that is where things come from spirit. I've shown the V-shaped blossoms; that one has the first ones that come up, the first pollens that come out. The hand design with crescents and double-S shapes shows that this is not just a hand; it has great significance. The double-S represents the song of how things go together for me. Somewhere between WEXES and the hand of the Creator bringing the blossoms is what we now call the Equinox, the change when we are starting towards our time of light.

Beginning Gathering Moon

In our fourth moon I drew SX̱ÁNEL~bullheads, the little brother to salmon. Everything has its season when it returns, and this moon is about many things that are returning. There's only a certain window of opportunity when you can gather some things for the whole year. Sometimes this gathering can only happen over cycles of a few years. Although we were very wealthy with our beaches and our food supplies, this would be one moon where some of our fish are just coming back. It's part of the cycle. I wanted to recognize that there are some climate differences from W̱SÁNEĆ to T'SOU-KE, so later on I put smelts in a different moon because those are the ones that return to our side of the island.

This moon is the beginning of when we would peel cedar bark if the weather cooperated. So in this moon's mouth, I represented a Creator's hand, Grandma's hand, that's beginning to peel the cedar bark from the tree. I've drawn the five crescent segments of the cedar tree so that it reflects the different aspects of our selves to balance male and female. It is the beginning of rutting season, when all beings (including humans) come into a very strong sense of themselves. I wanted to represent this in a lighter way. The stars are represented in this moon's mouth because there are different formations of stars that happen in the springtime and I wanted to tell of these changes.

The Season of Gathering ... Collecting ... Socializing–Summer

Camas Moon

In the fifth moon, our year has progressed enough that we are able to go back out on our canoes. We are able to start harvesting and collecting some of the things that we need. In this mouth, I represented SQIȽI~small sea urchin and camas, the purple-flowered plants whose roots provide nourishment. ḴENI~ seagulls and others like to lay their eggs around this time of year, too. On this moon's mouth, I represented SQIȽI being crab-like, because to me, the part you eat of the urchin tastes like a sweet crab. The canoe tells that this is a good time to start travelling again. It's calmer, without strong storms. The summer change happens around now, then turns back towards winter.

Sockeye Moon

The sixth moon is the moon when ȾEḴI~Sockeye salmon generally are welcomed back into our area. They hang out off our beaches but are not in the rivers yet. They're starting to think about coming home, so this is a good time to net them, and that's what I drew here. First of all, there are the HÍSW̱ḴE \0/ hands being really thankful for the return of that which nourishes us. The hands are moving. They're actually dancing and being very, very thankful for the return that has come because this means that we can replenish our stores. The salmon design is very "round" because ȾEḴI is very rich and very big-feeling. ȾEḴI does not last through our winter, but it's a really good, big feed that gives us our strength. There are many ways to take in these salmon, but I have only drawn one. This net could be made of cedar rope (spun like wool) with stinging nettles. A combination of fibres can make a very, very strong rope, too. It's important to remember that we've moved now into the busy time of summer.

Time for Visiting Moon

This seventh moon is our busy time, a joyful, cool sharing time where we would be travelling and doing much feasting. We would be playing S'LA'HAL~ bone games, having canoe races, and journeying by canoe to see family. Because the season is very abundant with food, it is really good for travelling; you don't put hardship on your relatives. As you're travelling along, you might stop to gather more things and you might trade Sockeye. This moon is about different family connections and large gatherings.

Have you ever seen some of the old pictures where massive amounts of canoes are all lined up on the beach? That would be this time of year. There would be temporary shelters made of cattail mats, your homes just filled to the brim with all your guests, family from many communities. This mouth also has Pinks, the humpies salmon. They have come back, swimming around by our coastline. It's also a time for collecting different medicines such as KEXMIN~seeds. It is a time where you're at the beach, doing all kinds of travelling and collecting and trading, and getting prepared. While visiting and gathering, we never took more resources than TEṈEW~Earth could easily recover from.

The Season of Preparation–Fall

Berry and Little Rain Moon

In our eighth moon, we are starting to have some rains. This is the starting of the spawning cycle as lots of fresh water begins coming down the creeks and rivers. I've represented that by the little tiny raindrops coming at the top. This rain encourages the berries to get ripe and plump enough for fixing, collecting, and preserving. We smash them up and dry them out like fruit leather. This is also when the Coho start to spawn. We fish differently for each kind of fish, and hooks are important. Remember the SQIȻI of the fifth moon? In this moon, you'd be spending a lot of time looking for cod. So you'd be going out with your hooks. There is a very elaborate system of how to get a piece of bait to go down to where the fish are. The line has a twirly piece with hooks on the bottom, and when you pull up your line, you've caught your good fish. It's a really rich fish. It's a time to start getting your body ready, beefing it up a little bit more, because you're getting close to a season when you're going to start having to be quiet. These fish are not necessarily going to keep very well, so they are for nurturing you in the now.

Salmon-Spawning Moon

During the earth fibres class, we were moving into our ninth moon, and it's somewhere around this time, depending on the year, when we are going to celebrate our change going into fall. In this moon, we are going to be having lots of big rains. This is when our creeks and our rivers fill so much that the big fish can now go upriver for spawning. I represented the bigness of the rain by really big teardrops. And I also included our dog salmon that are going up, the males with the big curved nose. This salmon was always smoked because it is one of the best fish for keeping. It is a really important supply to be gathering up, because these fish can be hung in the rafters in your home, or they can be put in one of those big storage boxes. I have one of those boxes at home that no longer smells like fish, so I put my books and other things in it.

The heads of the salmon are really important, and this is the only place I could figure out how to include them in the year of moons. I wanted to show that the fish heads and other pieces were all used for different things. The head was considered a big, important food; it made our heads brilliant and was made into soups quite a lot. This could also have been in the springtime moon. There is the hand bringing up and holding the fish head to show it has significance.

Leaves Turning White Moon

In our tenth moon, we are moving definitely into fall time. Our leaves are starting to turn white. That means we're starting to get frost and some cold time. It also means it's the perfect time for hunting SMÍEȽ~deer. If you take their skin before this moon, you can't reuse all the pieces that you might need to use. If you had need in the summertime, you could go hunt a SMÍEȽ, but it's very hard to make a summer skin into a good drum. There are many parts – the hooves, antlers, fat, and meat – that are used all the time. And incidentally, one of the best medicines is the fat that is collected from around the tummy to help with eczema.

There are many other animals that people might have chosen to honour, but I wanted to acknowledge the SMÍEȽ. One of its really cool attributes is its ability to be very agile but also very strong. It has a big heart so it can run a long time. That's an important thing to know because in order to hunt the SMÍEȽ, you have to be very agile and strong yourself. This is a way for us to talk about how important it is to have really good health through collecting and eating the foods and medicines that are in season. There are generally things that everybody collects, and then there are things that only people with certain gifts would be collecting. They are the caretakers of that medicine for when somebody needs it, and I want to acknowledge that.

The Season of Going Inside–Winter

The Beginning of the Storms Moon

Into the eleventh moon, we're moving into a huge storm season. And where we might have had storms before, these are bigger. Somewhere between the ninth and the eleventh moon, there is a way of defining approximately how many storms will be coming through our wintertime. After we have our change of season, between there and the next moon, there will be clues as to how many deaths we will have and how many storms we will have and to what severity. You can also tell these things by looking at some of our different plants, how things are spaced, and how the animals might be behaving. Our brothers and sisters might be making a really big home, or they might be taking off. This will help you to know how cold your year is going to be and give you an understanding of how much to prepare.

We have light seasons, and we have really heavy seasons. It's so interesting that this year we went through huge, big winds and storms. I pictured here the Creator's face, blowing the wind. The wind is blowing tree branches, blowing leaves, blowing a whole bunch of things. It is said that this is the time of the year when some of that heaviness we might have been feeling from other times will be taken away by the winds, making things fresh and new again. It's a time for clearing out old – the winds take it away. We're also making ourselves really ready for being inside, which is why the longhouse is pictured but doesn't have a fire started yet.

Put Away Your Paddles Moon

When we get into our twelfth moon, we are looking at putting away our paddles. Not only is the wind blowing, but the water has big waves! It's getting to be quite dark now. We have very little light left during the day. The fires are started, and it's time for our inner focus. Our houses are waking up for our winter ceremonies. And on this mouth, I've acknowledged the HÍSW̱K̲E \0/ hands with the two paddles. The two paddles are very different; one is an egg and dart design, and one has a blackfish, killer-whale design. That is because I wanted to show great appreciation for the differences in each one of our homes.

Again, we might be having relatives visiting from another place. This house is really much more emphasized and decorated because it's the main focus during this moon. We have started to send our thoughts and prayers out with our winter ceremonies. The smoke is travelling out through the roof. Somewhere between here and our final moon of the year, we have our change of season again. We're in the darkest part of our days. In earlier moons, with the journeying and gathering and trading, we had time to gather supplies to now make Giveaway items. For example, we would have traded for the mountain goat wool, combed our dogs throughout all of the seasons, and now we sit at our stationary weaving looms and make blankets like wisdom keeper~ Grandma May showed us how to do in the earth fibres class.

Elder–Grandma Moon

The thirteenth moon is called the Elder–Grandma moon. It's a time of gathering together and being only inside. Travel could only be in small bits, to get to winter ceremony happenings with the neighbouring relatives or community. While we were strong people, travel out on the open ocean would have been way, way too much to consider unless absolutely necessary. This moon shows a little bit of winter ceremony time. Nowadays there is much more public acknowledgment of some parts of our ceremony.

The Creator's hand is actually holding up the long house. And there are two figures inside, one on either side of the fire, and both have their WEM~ tears, which is the prayer. And both are different, because that represents each individual within our winter ceremonies; we all have our individual gifts. And this is especially the time of year when those things might be acknowledged. You'll see that there is smoke inside the longhouse, and the smoke goes out of the longhouse through the smoke hole. The smoke goes to the Creator, and the needs come back to the people because the Creator is blowing back towards them. That completes our year cycle. The year will start again, and we would now go back into the newness.

~ ~ ~

The stories of the moons are not linear or logical. It is possible to be born into them or to leave them at any time. In the past, before the Visitors came here, visiting often happened. You might stay a week, a moon~month, or even a whole season. Life had a bigger cycle. Things were more drawn out, more relaxed than how we are in the quickness of today. At different times of the year, it would be important to gather what it was that you would need ahead of time, because it wasn't like today when you can just go to the grocery store. You had to plan ahead and you had to always be busy. You would have people come and help with gatherings for different things. For instance, your family might plan ahead for a memorial, or maybe there was going to be a joining of two families with a marriage. That's why some of the teachings are about always having good hands, about always being productive and busy and helpful towards the whole of the structure.

Remember, part of our culture from this area and other places on the coast is about Giving, and so you prepared ahead of time to have enough to be able to Giveaway. If it ever came to it, you always gave absolutely everything away. You would never be SA'UCE~poor of spirit/judgment or not willing to share, because there was enough around and enough people that, even if you had given everything away, it would've been their honour to give back to you. So in turn, I have done my Giveaway by sharing some of the teachings that I have been given the responsibility for. This keeps the cycles turning and moving. My hope for this sharing is that both your great, great grandchildren's grandchildren and my great, great grandchildren's grandchildren live with appreciation of all that holds us up, with all that sustains us. \0/

In closing, Michele and I gratefully acknowledge the support of UBC Press, Lorna and the University of Victoria, all of the Aunties and Grandmas (also known as wisdom keepers), fellow learners-students, faculty members, the Curriculum Library staff (caretakers of XAXE SIÁM SILA), the many hands that helped to raise XAXE SIÁM SILA to her current home, all the community, family and friends, and our great, great grandchildren's children. Together we have brought this life-altering, paradigm-changing opportunity of XAXE SIÁM SILA to life.

\0/ \0/ \0/ \0/

Author's note: When Charlene first saw her oral story in print, she asked me to place a tilde (~) between SENĆOŦEN words and their English translations to show that they are approximate. For example, the SENĆOŦEN word *TEṈEW* can be roughly translated as *Earth*, yet, according to Charlene, a true translation would involve many pages to explain accurately and with cultural integrity; hence, *TEṈEW~Earth*. She also asked me to use an image created with text to represent the gesture that usually accompanies an offering of thanks \0/ – uplifted forearms framing an oval head. More importantly, she requested that these explanations wait until after the story of the moons was told, thus keeping resonance with an indigenous pedagogy that requires us to be patient, listen, and learn from the subtleties of experience.

1

Orienting to Place and Pedagogical Purpose

Early in the course, kQwa'ste'not Charlene led us through an especially poignant activity using two large cattail mats, woven by kQwa'ste'not Charlene's father's grandmother, who carried the name previously. Over a hundred years old and measuring roughly one and a half by six metres, these tightly woven pieces had been in Charlene's family for generations. Charlene asked us to move in a circle towards the centre of the room, while the wisdom keepers wrapped the mats around us. We stood tightly together, and Charlene then asked us to concentrate on our heartbeats and on our breath. Breathing in ... breathing out ... we listened. Afterwards, I wrote:

> Older than my great grandmother would be if she were alive today, the cattail mats call to me. Their presence is soothing and a sense of wonder arises from my being. I feel a great connection that I cannot explain. I sense the embodied spirit of things that came before – both in the physicality of the cattails and in the stories of those who have sat on the mats around fires of long ago. I listen to the voice of Charlene. She is telling of how the cattails no longer grow so tall. I try to listen through the meditative opening of every pore of my skin. What is this knowing? What is this place? What are these stories that I am honoured to hear? For now, it is enough for me to sit in the presence of these mats, listening. (Field notes)

Traditional cattail mats made by kQwa'ste'not~T'Sou'ke (c.1920)

Standing shoulder to shoulder in the mats, we found ourselves acknowledging the centre of the wheel. This provided us with a rare opportunity to take a moment to breathe, to gather thoughts, and to scan for location within this particular time and place. You might try it now. Close your eyes and ask yourself: Where am I within surrounding physical, spiritual, intellectual, and social sites? What is my intent from this particular location? When we centre in this way, we pay attention to who we are and on what ground we stand. It is a meditative kind of place, requiring careful attention. Breathing in … breathing out.

In her interview, Chelsea (PST) talked about how this experience with the mats gave her a sense of place: "I don't have the family connection of hundreds of years … I know [my ancestors] are from England, but that's all I know. So, I like the history in the mats, and there must be so many stories that those mats have heard. All those different bodies sitting on them, and that they were made by people's hands." The experience gave the pre-service teachers a heightened sense of being part of a real community. As Garrett (PST) said, even though they were packed "as tight as sardines," when the mats were removed there was a sense of having "touched base with everything around us."

Right in There in the Dirt

The wisdom keepers brought a wide variety of earth fibre materials into the course and saw them as being central to understanding the knowledge of a certain place. The wisdom that resided in the natural fibres was often demonstrated through stories. On the first day, Charlene pointed out how the cattails in her Grandmother's mat were much longer than the ones she had brought in for us to weave that day. That visual confirmation of how things had changed was striking. Kevin (PST) shared with me how the course was a unique learning opportunity, where "examining the plants, seeing the working knowledge in action" was "almost seeing a history." His comment points out the usefulness of this direct interaction with a physical place as a way to gain knowledge about the changes in our physical environment.

Another kind of wisdom belonging to the earth fibres is centred in the culture of the people whose lives intermingle with the fibres of a certain place. Carolyn (WK) talked about the depth of connection with cedar in her Hesqiaht traditions: "We use the roots, we use the wood, we use the bark, we even use the branches and the greens when we pray … It's such a part of our culture … It's like your right arm or your left arm. It's a piece that's always there." Carolyn went on to say that "if there was one essence that could be captured" for the mural project, it should be cedar because of its cultural importance.

The significance of cedar extends beyond its physical usefulness, and the wisdom keepers felt that the students in the earth fibres course grasped these deeper understandings. Courtney (PST) spoke about learning beyond the surface of a place:

> We learned what I wrote down on my paper, like, names of plants, all the different things we can do [with them]. But we also learned to pay attention to the plants that we walk through and [about giving] tobacco and the thank you. And [wisdom keeper Della] was singing before pulling some of the plants and being respectful. There was that whole experience that you can take a lot more from than just simply, "This is rosehip and it helps with blank."

Both the wisdom keepers and the pre-service teachers often mentioned this deep connectedness to nature as being important.

The wisdom keepers were very clear in their goals to help students see patterns in nature and connect them with their everyday lives. Charlene, as lead instructor, often discussed the seasons, the moons, and how certain things happened at specific, cyclical times. Many of the wisdom keepers spoke of the importance of experiencing the full cycle of the earth fibres lifespan in order to really understand a reciprocal connection to Earth. For example, Carolyn felt "forlorn" that her group couldn't "process it from start to finish" by going out to strip the cedar bark right from the tree:

They would have had a more profound awareness if they had been able to get that bark themselves. So, I was trying to explain to them … that although we were not able to take them out to get their own bark because it was not the season … if they could maybe go out and find some forest, and offer up a little prayer, whatever they felt appropriate, a little gift or tobacco or something that they felt, you know? I just wanted them to have that, at least. But it was hard to reiterate everything about the whole process just verbally. So that was the one drawback [of the timing of the course].

Gay (WK) spoke about how she noticed a disconnection with nature in her own community:

We had brought children … to the lake to cut fish. Within five minutes, I think, three of the students fell in the lake. And I said, "My goodness! This is our surrounding, this is where we live for all the time, and yet our children can't function in what should be normal for our children to function." They don't really grasp how to respect the fish; they don't really grasp that it's connected. The fish isn't only connected to us – we are connected to the fish. And you can't put that into them unless they live it, unless they do the whole process. And that's what I [would like to see] for education.

And Nicole (PST) pondered a similar need in non-indigenous students:

It just doesn't have to be First Nations culture; you don't have to teach it in that way. But why not take your kids on a walk and tell them some things about the plants, or ask them to sit under a tree instead of in the classroom when you're teaching them, or things like that, you know? Why not? Why isn't it that way? Why are kids watching TV instead of going outside? I guess this class has got me thinking about that.

For the pre-service teachers, the experience brought to the fore questions about how they could help students to appreciate the environment more fully and feel a connection to local place. They spoke frequently of how novel it was to interact with nature and how they enjoyed taking time to be aware of the environment right outside the classroom doorway. As Courtney said, "Can you believe that we've gone through so many years of school and we've never learned what the plants outside the window are and all the cool things they can do?"

The pre-service teachers worried about the institutionalized settings in which children spend so much time. Garrett recognized that "the environment that we learn in has [a] major impact on what we learn and how we use that knowledge." They were also aware of the difficulties of implementing nature-based programs in schools on a practical level. They cited time constraints, pressures of curriculum expectations, and liability concerns as some of the limiting factors they faced as classroom teachers.

Both the wisdom keepers and the pre-service teachers expressed concerns about the overall health of the planet. For example, Gay articulated how consumerism plays a role in damaging nature and said that "getting along" with nature would leave us "better off, instead of destroying so much of it and, in turn, destroying ourselves, possibly … It seems like there should be a better way."

It was disconcerting to me, however, that there wasn't a stronger awareness of the role that a consumerist mentality might play in this regard. Our dominant culture's patterns and habits of consumption play a significant part in how we take care of the planet, yet in the interviews, the topic was rarely brought up. Of course, the intent of the course was not to address such concerns head on. Rather, it was to immerse the participants in direct experiences with the indigenous ways of relating to nature.

The following dialogue with Chelsea elucidates her process of getting in touch with nature, and how that might transfer into her teaching in ways that counteract a disconnection from nature in her students:

CHELSEA: I loved the second class when Della took us out to the garden and taught us all the plants. And just the fact that she was actually in, right next to the plants and trees and stuff, whereas other teachers might have stood with us on the path, but she was right in there in the dirt … And at first, I noticed that we were all on the path, because we don't walk on the grass here. I think, "Oh, I don't want to wreck the gardener's hard work." And then I noticed after a while, people were walking through the garden … So I think we realized that it was okay to be in there, like a part of the whole thing.

MICHELE: That's interesting. I didn't notice that, but now that you say it, I wonder why that is. Do you have any sense of that?

CHELSEA: I don't know, I think it's that there's always signs to stay off the grass, or don't pick the flowers, that sort of thing. So, for me it seems like nature or gardens, or whatever, is just there to look at from a distance. So it was nice to really know that we could get closer to it. Because I think it's more healing than probably I realized.

Chelsea's description of her realization that she could actually be right next to the plants illustrates how disconnected we can be from nature. Her sense of well-being in nature echoes the experiences of other pre-service teachers who spoke of a different sense of energy when they were connected to nature or were working with natural materials. This attachment to physical place within the surrounding environment became a cornerstone for the course pedagogy. It nourished the participants' need for close contact with nature and gave them embodied touchstones for how connections with nature might be incorporated into a classroom.

A Jumble of Teaching Beliefs

This and the following section expand the notion of place to include finding location as a teacher through examining one's personal beliefs. Charlene pointed out the importance of teachers having an understanding of personal positioning through a sense of what has been learned from relationships with people:

> [Learning to connect with your students] has to come from a real deep under-standing of your own self, from where you came from, from where your siblings might have come from. Because whether that was a created family or a physical family, you are in that family structure, so what did you learn from that? What did you learn from looking at those other people? What did you learn from feeling from all those other people?

To locate the participants in their perceived positioning as teachers, it is useful to understand the beliefs that they held on the topics of learning and teaching at the beginning of the course. Overall, the pre-service teachers saw themselves as being actively involved in a process of developing as teachers. They acknowledged that learning and teaching were complex endeavours, requiring them to try to make sense of what Sara (PST) called a "jumble of teaching beliefs." During the first interviews, they were consistently hesitant when asked to explain what the concept of learning meant to them – they had not thought about it much before the course, and saw the question as huge and complex. They welcomed the interview process as a chance to explore the topic, as Courtney expressed: "It's not every day that you sit down and question teacher roles and where you are in your life."

The beliefs expressed by the pre-service teachers consistently revolved around notions of constructivism, in which the learner needed to be engaged and hands-on in a lifelong learning process. As Chelsea said, "It's like building blocks in your brain or something, always adding to things." Sara expanded on these ideas:

My teaching beliefs, or philosophies, are still really developing, but for the most part, I want to bring the world into my classroom. And I think in order to do that properly, I have to get as much experience as possible ... I'm not into rote learning. I don't believe in kids sitting at their desks doing math sheets and spelling sheets. And I've been in classrooms like that teaching, and it's just not me. I want kids to have fun – I want kids to enjoy life. And hopefully those kids who aren't enjoying life at the time that I meet them, that maybe I can help them in some ways to appreciate what they have and learn how to go on with life in a positive way and become lifelong learners.

The pre-service teachers believed that some learning was fact-based and required transmissive approaches to teaching, but they also were looking for ways of engaging learners in, as Nicole said, "interesting methods that aren't really out there yet." They talked about how, in some of their courses, they were asked to put kids in boxes to categorize their learning. However, Courtney felt that "you can't separate teaching and learning from life in general, and we know that life's an awfully complex thing." The pre-service teachers believed that many of their classes were narrow in scope, and they wanted to take more diverse courses that were not limited to a particular subject area. Many of them chose the earth fibres course for this reason, believing that it would add to their knowledge in important ways.

The pre-service teachers saw the process of learning as a vehicle that gave the learner power through knowing, and freedom to follow their passions. Learning was also seen as a social endeavour, where social skills and peer learning are fundamentally important. Jade (PST) speaks to this:

Learning? In a classroom setting it's kind of taking up ideas, and building on your own background experiences, and adding to that. Not only from the teacher, but from your peers, and just getting a broader sense of what the world's like, as well as the content area. But I think the social skills and the life skills are the most important things to be learning in the classroom setting ... I know no kids are blank slates – and I know they go in with some knowledge, some notions that may not be fully correct, but they are their ideas, their beliefs. And they just build on that through experiences that they're exposed to and the other people they are exposed to.

For the pre-service teachers, learning was also tied to social responsibility and making the world a better place. Many of them believed that learners get more out of learning when it happens in community, citing that it was important to have a positive environment where, as Jade said, "people feel comfortable sharing their ideas and there is respect." However, this belief was seen as problematic by some who felt they might be crossing a fine line into being more like a counsellor than a teacher – a role for which they felt unprepared. Leanne (PST) thought that she could take on that role "maybe if I had more qualities, like training in how to talk to [students] like that. But really, my job is to motivate and inspire them and get them excited about learning." Our conversation continued:

MICHELE: What are the skills that a counsellor would have that a teacher isn't taught?

LEANNE: I think what a lot of counsellors do is kind of echo back people's feelings in an articulate way that [shows] they understand ... But, I think it's so sensitive for teachers to be in that role, even though we may feel like we have the insight to do that role. But that's just not our job. And it's just an area where we really can't go into ... We can't allow children to be opening up to us and to have this confidentiality because it just causes a different dynamic in the class.

Paradoxically, despite holding these feelings of being unprepared to deal with emotions that come up in a classroom, pre-service teachers felt that teachers should promote "compassion and empathy" in their classroom and take the lead to "establish guidelines" around respectful socio-emotional environments.

For the most part, the pre-service teachers also felt unprepared to teach students who were culturally different from themselves, particularly Aboriginal students, despite having indigenous content in some of their other classes, as Courtney described:

I think there's a need. I mean, this morning we watched a movie ... about residential schools. And it was exploring some of the social issues that surround Aboriginal education in BC today ... And I thought, gosh, I'm glad I'm in [the earth fibres] class because ... this class will provide just a small insight into a culture that is so complex and so different and diverse that perhaps in the traditional curriculum we have simplified and not ... given it the respect or the understanding that maybe it needs, [in order] to be able to bring it into the curriculum. I mean, it's listed in our curriculum; it's there. We as teachers are coming out, supposedly ready to teach it, but it's by no means something I feel ready to teach.

Many saw the course as a way of learning practical methods to meet the needs of crosscultural classrooms, and the experience gave them an embodied understanding of an indigenous worldview.

During the initial interviews, I asked the pre-service teachers to give me an image of what they believed the roles of the learner and teacher might look like. Images they gave for learners included (1) a vacuum sucking up information; 2) something growing, such as a flower or tree; and (3) a sponge absorbing knowledge. The teacher was seen primarily in a gentle directive role as tour guide, leader, manager, role model, guide, helper, friend, learner, coach, instructor, giver of knowledge, and facilitator. Chapter 5 describes important shifts in these images as the course progressed.

The role of teacher was understood to be a complex response to the many responsibilities of the classroom that require, as Courtney said, a "career sort of mentality" that can juggle different expectations. In addition, the pre-service teachers often acknowledged that it was their job to help learners find passion in learning, as expressed by April (PST):

I think there [are] many forms of teaching for the many types of learning that there are. So you could have your factual teacher who just covers the basic facts, the facts of life, the facts of textbooks. But then you can also totally go beyond that and be aware of where your students' sponges are located, and what they're ready to take in, and that all students are different so try and connect things to all their learning levels – [which is] kind of difficult, I'm sure. But try and teach not just to those facts but to deeper meanings and things that are going to really intrigue and make kids passionate about learning.

After the first round of interviews it was evident that this was a group of deeply committed and caring professionals. Yet I wondered if our teacher education programs might have done more to help them deal with today's diverse classrooms. Adding to my worries about the lack of understanding about consumerist perspectives and a disconnection from nature were my growing concerns over how the pre-service teachers could truly teach compassionately without counselling-type skills that address the emotional nature of learning and tap into, as April said, each learner's passion.

Bringing the Teachings Forward

In response to my questions about the nature of learning and teaching, the wisdom keepers were much less hesitant to speak than the pre-service teachers. Charlene was clear in her intent to "bring the strength of the old teachings into the modern," and the other wisdom keepers reflected this aim as well. They wanted the course participants to pay attention to natural cycles such as weather and to think about how these things may have changed since colonial contact. Charlene spoke of how these teachings were often subtle, "internal learnings" that took time to be absorbed after "seeds" were planted. Gina (WK) said that "sometimes the lessons are so subtle, you don't realize you're being taught" until it cycles back, sometimes years later. May (WK) spoke about the importance of these lessons embedded in unconscious learning, saying that often they are "learning but not knowing it. The teachings that [we] have passed on have taught our children how to be."

The wisdom keepers talked about how the teachings had been misrepresented, persecuted, and destroyed since colonization. They described their struggle to find the ways that things used to be done. Charlene mentioned that some of the teachings were private and couldn't be shared in the context of the course in order to protect their integrity. At the same time, wisdom keepers were excited to share what knowledge they could with the learners in the course. They saw the times they worked with textiles and ate food together as good opportunities to share teachings. May explained how "part of our teachings is [that] we're teaching while people are eating and swallowing. They are swallowing what they're learning, and [they] remember it."

Conceptually, the wisdom keepers saw learning as an organic yet focused process embedded in the practical usefulness of getting to know how things work within a relational context. The process of learning is rooted in the simple act of observation. From there, as Gay said, "you can learn just because you're around it all the time," and you "do it hands-on only later." Gay described that the learning process is embodied as the learners "[absorb] the information into [their] whole being so that it's there without consciously thinking about it." Gina described her own process of learning from her elders:

I would watch them, whatever they were doing. Whether it was learning to fillet salmon, or hanging the salmon in a smokehouse, or making jam, picking berries, making bread. Both my grandmothers made their own bread for all their lives, and I do that today. And I can remember saying to my one grandmother, "What recipe do you use?" And she said, "I don't have a recipe. I've been doing this all my life." And I said, "Well, I'd like to learn, but I need a recipe. I need to get the measuring cups out, and I need to know how much flour to put in, how much yeast to use." And she said, "I'll write you out the recipe." And so the next time she made a batch of bread, she measured everything, wrote it all down.

And then, it wasn't until I was probably in my thirties, and I had my own children, and I'd been making bread every week for many years, that I realized where my grandmother had been when she was trying to teach me how to make bread. Because I don't measure anything anymore, and my daughter had the same problem. You know, "How am I going to learn, Mom, if I don't have a recipe?" And my grandmother taught me that making bread is a very personal thing. You get to feel the dough, and you know the texture, and you know when it's just right. And you can only learn that by doing it.

This story describes the process of watching followed by doing, as well as giving an example of how the "seeds" of the teachings may not be recognized for some time. The notion of watching is so important that some of the wisdom keepers were concerned that the adult learners in the class would be unable to pick up the work with the fibres because they had not had the chance to first observe the craft skills over time.

Another concern of the wisdom keepers revolved around questions of learner intent towards sustainability. This happened to the extent that Gay even wondered if her efforts in the course would be worthwhile:

> That was the other thing I was trying to sort out ... Do I want to teach someone that just wants to do it the one time? Do you know? And that was difficult for me because most of the time, the people that I like to teach are the ones that are not doing something for a living, but they do something for themselves.

The notion of the learners doing something for themselves that is sustainable is tied to a common belief among the wisdom keepers that the learner must intrinsically want to learn and that each learner also has an intuitive sense about exactly what learning is appropriate for him or her.

In addition, many of the wisdom keepers spoke about how, when a learner creates, for example, beadwork or a button blanket, the process is connected to spiritual knowing. James, the husband of Lynne (WK), was present in my interviews with her and wholeheartedly participated in our discussions. He carefully described how, when a learner is fully engaged in activities such as beading or weaving, the learner becomes "the creator creating." Reminiscent of the concept of "flow" (Csikszentmihalyi, 2007), the idea James was describing is that of a meditative merging with the earth fibres where learning direction comes from the relationship between who is creating and what is being created. From an indigenous worldview, this autonomous and endogenous process of the learner is seen as opportunity, as Janet (WK) explains:

> It's like being a photographer and knowing that the perfect picture is out there just waiting for you, and it's your job to recognize it. The learner is the photographer, knowing that what they need to learn, want to learn, is out there for them ... It's the job of the learner to recognize the opportunities or the instances where they can learn.

In fact, for many of the wisdom keepers, the very term *teacher* is problematic. As Lynne said,

> You don't teach anybody; people learn. And they learn what they're willing to absorb because example is the only real teacher. You can share your knowledge, you can share your awareness, but you can't teach. I don't like the word *teach* because I don't believe anybody teaches anybody anything. I think people share knowledge and awareness, and that's what you're doing with the children. And as soon as you stop teaching them and start sharing knowledge with them, you'll reach them better.

Many of the wisdom keepers held this attitude of loving the sharing of knowledge. As Carolyn expressed, "I'm not a master in [weaving cedar]. I'm just here to show you some simple ways of manipulating the bark so we can make something. But I'll tell you a little bit about what I know." Other wisdom keepers talked about how this process was simply a natural place of sharing how to do something. The teacher was seen as being open to learning and on the same level as his or her students in many ways. This attitude ties into issues of trust in the learner, a topic discussed further in Chapter 3.

Learning in the earth fibres course was an organic process, where there was an emphasis on watching followed by doing. The wisdom keepers sought to bring the strength of the time-tested teachings into the modern world but did not see themselves as "teachers." Instead, they relied on each learner's intent to develop sustainable skills. The learning process was closely tied to spiritual knowing, and the love of sharing knowledge and learning was often seamlessly embedded in the typical activities of the day.

How Am I Connected?

The participants spoke frequently during the interviews about the overall theme of community. From the perspective of locating oneself in place, the poignant stories about community revolved around the idea that the course became a learning community that differed from that which the pre-service teachers typically had experienced in university and in the K-12 schools of their youth. The experience was a conscious act of re-storying, or redefining, the possible ways of being in a learning community. They felt welcomed and included within the non-judgmental environment created by the wisdom keepers and became unusually engaged and committed to the learning community. This redefined space played an important role in entering into crosscultural understanding.

The pre-service teachers perceived the wisdom keepers as having a strong sense of personal culture that was embedded in an equally strong sense of community. They also were aware that community was structured differently for the wisdom keepers. The term *family* was used often to refer to the large group of participants as well as the smaller groups, and took on new meanings in the context of the course. Nicole explains:

I heard Lorna [WK] calling all of us a "family" a few times. And I know
cousins and sisters and brothers aren't defined as I define them, which is neat.
It's anyone who you love and care about in that way. It can be your sister, or
your brother, or your cousin, or your auntie. That's kind of neat, how family
is a broad spectrum instead of this little, tight-knit group [*laughter*].

Lynne talked about how, in her community, this notion of extended family has more of a group consciousness that begins at birth as babies are passed from "grandma to grandma" and never put down. The wisdom keepers often brought family members with them to the class, including children, siblings, aunties, and partners. The pre-service teachers were impressed by the fact that some of the teenaged visitors were interested and/or willing to go to school with a parent. As April said, "I couldn't imagine sitting in that room with my mom right next to me, you know?"

The pre-service teachers were conscious of not wanting to idealize the relationships they saw, but expressed that it was refreshing to be around that kind of intimacy across generations. Some felt that, while they were close to members of their own family, things seemed to be more of a production or an obligation when they got together.

This extended sense of community was evident throughout the course in the way that the wisdom keepers included and acknowledged the pre-service teachers in many aspects of the decision-making process. Heather (PST) explained the importance of an extended community to her:

> I really like the aspect of having leaders from the community come in. I think that is something that is so crucial and it's such a powerful connection ... because it really helps create a sense of place and a sense of belonging ... Where are we, and why is this my community, and how am I connected to it? And I think that that's something that is so important for anyone to have, that sense of "I belong here." You know, this is somewhere where I'm welcome, where I feel comfortable.

The pre-service teachers spoke about how important it was for them to hear the stories of others as they introduced themselves at the beginning of the course. Some were impatient about this initially, as they thought it would be a superficial activity, but they changed their minds as they listened. They soon found it to be one of the most useful and enjoyable parts of the early class meetings in terms of building community across cultures. Garrett observed:

> Hearing everyone's stories, especially the stories from the people that are from First Nations cultures, was pretty impactful for me because I want to learn so much. I feel so disconnected from other cultural ways of learning, that it's kind of neat [hearing] why they're in this class and what they'd like to get out of it ... For [some] people, it was a long journey to get to this class ... You know, I don't see this much in classes here, in my program anyways. Giving other people the chance to speak their mind, and not always feel like they're being graded on it or anything like that. I've enjoyed that.

Many of the pre-service teachers felt that their stories were not as interesting or as important as those of some of the other participants, and Kevin wondered if "that would change significantly if we were to introduce ourselves again at the end of the course."

The pre-service teachers understood that the stories told in families and within community were significant in the passing down or articulation of cultural beliefs. They were struck by the depth of this type of knowledge transfer that happened for the wisdom keepers. As Danielle (PST) shared,

> Hearing everybody's experiences that they've had growing up, and their grandmothers and their aunties and sisters and moms, and passing down the knowledge, I thought it was really neat ... They can just tell story after story of sitting with somebody, and their learning by doing and telling in stories, and that's a really important part of learning. And yeah, it's really missing in my family and in my culture. I thought that was really neat though, just to stop and be with somebody and learn like that.

The wisdom keepers' typical ways of being in community gave the pre-service teachers a re-storied sense of what a learning community could be. In this particular community, the pre-service teachers felt welcomed and became thoughtful about their personal sense of place in the larger context of their own community and culture.

Experiencing It Yourself

This last section about orienting to place and purpose has to do with the conscious intent of the participants to envision the earth fibres course as a site for making schools better places for learners (both indigenous and non-indigenous) through an experience that deepened pre-service teachers' cultural knowledge of indigenous ways. Both the pre-service teachers and the wisdom keepers acknowledged that in Canadian classrooms indigenous children won't always be taught by indigenous teachers. Non-indigenous teachers need to know more about possible ways that these students learn as well as possible ways they live outside of the classroom. The intent of the course was to provide a direct immersive experience that would enable the pre-service teachers to holistically experience and gain understanding of indigenous ways of learning and teaching. As Sara said,

> I think it's so important to teach kids about the world and that we're just this tiny little place in this huge universe ... And I think I can't teach that

understanding unless I have experience with other cultures ... You can read about [places in the world] but it's not the same. I think actually being in this class and working with things from the Earth, it just sort of starts that experience, if that makes sense.

In addition, there was acknowledgment by both groups that indigenous students can have particular learning styles and learning needs that should be attended to and that it was problematic for schools to measure all students by only one standard. They cited examples of important issues to consider in the classroom, such as learning and telling through stories, observing before acting, and using eye contact so that listening is heightened.

Charlene also saw that developing an understanding of a physical, natural place was tied to understanding and working better with students crossculturally. She hoped that the course would give the pre-service teachers a "flavouring" of awareness about nature that would then help them in the future with any "Native student that they might have in their class or a student from a total other area of this whole planet." She also looked at the course as a way to encourage awareness about the planetary changes that are occurring, saying that "people still stick their heads in the sand for the most part. They don't want to stand up and have a look."

The wisdom keepers were conscious of creating a space where participants could experience ways of learning and teaching that were congruent with learning dynamics in indigenous community settings. They made a conscious effort to pass this awareness on to others who could support the work they were trying to do. This attitude fit into the teaching philosophies of the pre-service teachers who were aware of, and upset by, the ways in which Aboriginal students and indigenous pedagogy were marginalized in the schools. Courtney articulated the need for a university experience that directly addresses these concerns: "[I] would like all children to see something of themselves in the classroom environment. And that goes with any child from any culture. So as an outgoing teacher, the more I can experience different cultures and get an idea – and just have different teaching strategies and different learning experiences – the more I can create that diverse classroom, too."

The pre-service teachers wanted a hands-on, authentic environment where they felt like they were experiencing the actual pedagogy that they were hoping to go out to teach. They were tired of being in classes where the instructor asked them to "do as I say, not as I do." As Leanne (PST) said, "It's hard to create that ideal classroom without having experienced it yourself." The course gave the pre-service teachers hope that they could gain insight and understanding into how they might work to change the more prescriptive practices they often observed in schools. Courtney shared that "to be able to experience this classroom environment and then for us to be able to take that experience and bring it into the classroom is priceless."

The pre-service teachers spoke about noticing a deliberate effort on the part of some of their peers who weren't enrolled in the course to avoid learning about Aboriginal culture. Based on my observations while teaching the required indigenous education course in our program, I would speculate that this might reflect a general feeling of being overwhelmed with the extensive requirements of the program, along with a reluctance (and lack of time and space) to look carefully at one's personal beliefs, values, and attitudes. On the other hand, the wisdom keepers were conscious of providing a space within the university environment where the status quo was actively being disturbed. The pre-service teachers felt that the course reaffirmed values that they held about education and that the class set an example that helped them put their teaching goals into perspective. This aspect of the course experience was often described in contrast to experiences they had in other courses, some of which they perceived to be outdated, conventional, and unhelpful concerning the issues they expected to face in the classroom.

The pre-service teachers also saw themselves as needing experiences that would help them feel more comfortable as advocates for their indigenous students and wanted more understanding so that they could share indigenous ways with non-indigenous students, as Nicole expressed:

> I'm hoping to take [what I learn] into the classroom so I can teach … children this wonderful culture that's all around us, really. Even if they're not indigenous people, I think it's a part of them. This is the land where they lived. And I hope to get a sense of that more, and a sense of the culture more. Because like I said, I never learned that. I don't know a lot about the culture in terms of being able to say they value this and do that.

Initially, the pre-service teachers expressed discomfort about not knowing what was politically correct language and behaviour in indigenous contexts. The earth fibres course gave them a safe place to explore those issues.

Both the wisdom keepers and the pre-service teachers saw the importance of interacting with each other to develop deeper relationships and understandings about indigenous ways, so that, as Carolyn said, the pre-service teachers "didn't feel so weird when they start[ed] to teach" students who are Aboriginal. Gina stated: "One of the problems we have in this world today, the reason we don't have peace, is because we're not taking the time to learn about each other. We're not giving each other the respect that is due." Both groups were excited about the possibilities of working together and were eager to learn together.

The pre-service teachers saw the course as a chance to have authentic conversations with people from another culture and, as Garrett said, to "hear straight from them the experience that they had been through and their perspectives on everything." They felt that very quickly an atypically strong sense of community was forged in the course and that it happened both crossculturally and among themselves as a peer group. Many talked with surprise about how, even though they had spent three years together as a cohort, they were just really getting to know each other in the context of the course. Kevin believed this was because "we were united towards common goals, and we were invited to help each other explicitly."

Many of the wisdom keepers talked about how encouraged they were by the level of interest in indigenous ways that was expressed by the pre-service teachers, and Janet observed that the learning was done in a way in which "there was just an equal amount of respect on both sides for everybody. Everybody came as a student willing and open to learn, whether they were Native or non-Native. And so that was beautiful to see." The participants frequently acknowledged that all students, indigenous and non-indigenous, would benefit from the types of indigenous ways of learning and teaching that were presented in the class. Many of the pre-service teachers expressed their gratitude that the class was helping them to grow and expand personally.

Leanne, like her peers, was aware that this course was unusual and important:

> You can see that it's just so much more than a class ... This is something that's
> hopefully a step in a more positive direction, as opposed to getting my grade
> out of it or whatever. I just see everybody there has so much more invested
> in it, and there was so much more meaning behind it. It was really [*pause*]
> necessary to have something like this.

This realization of relevancy gave the class an air of excitement and most participants were very committed to putting in energy beyond what they would normally do in a more typical university-level course. From the beginning of the course, the pre-service teachers were thinking of ways to incorporate indigenous pedagogy into their upcoming final practicum experience. They were aware that the type of changes that needed to happen would involve hard work.

Simple stitching and beadwork

The course became useful for them to be able to act more immediately on the topic.

Aside from the course's main goal of developing cultural awareness, there were two other intentions that should be noted. First was the intention to teach textile skills. While a few of the participants were drawn to the course because of their interest in working with fibres, most of the pre-service teachers felt that they knew little about the making of textiles. Some had never used a needle and thread and were intimidated by the challenge. Others who were more familiar with working with fibres opted to participate in groups that presented unfamiliar textiles so that they could learn a new skill. The wisdom keepers talked about the importance of teaching basic skills so that the pre-service teachers could continue to interact with the materials creatively and share this knowledge with others.

Second, there was a conscious intention to honour the work of women through the creation and display of the mural within the MacLaurin Building. It was, as Janet said, "giving honour to the women who did this work before, and before, and before – generations ago, and bringing it in this institution here and saying, 'We validate this work; we honour this work; and we honour those women who have brought this work [and] helped it to survive into this day and age.'"

The sense of place embodied in the course was exemplified as Gina spoke extensively about her personal experiences as a learner in university courses. She described what being a good teacher meant to her in the context of cross-cultural understanding:

[Good teachers] have the heart to reach out and try to understand where [Aboriginal people] are in our location. And from those people, I try and learn ... I think it means an individual who has no judgment, who has no preconceived idea about what a First Nations person should be, who simply accepts them as they are, where they're at, and strives to meet them where they're at without asking a lot of questions, or wanting explanations, or [asking] "Well, what is your view on this?" They have an idea of our history and our culture, and they understand a lot of things that are not said when you're in a classroom. But because they are so sensitive to where you are at, they are good people to be around ... It's a balance, and they're not pretending to be the experts. While they might be very learned people, they are open to what you have to say. And so it's a learning-teaching for both of you. They are very honest about who they are. They know who they are ... [They are people who] sit quietly and listen. And they have no motivation other than they respect the culture, they want to be in it, and they want to learn it. Those are open people. And I have no problem sharing with those people.

I believe that her words, in many ways, summarize the overarching intent of the course and speak to the qualities and dispositions needed in teachers who want to have more inclusive, socially healthy classrooms that acknowledge and thrive on diversity.

2

Opening Oneself to Indigenous Ways of Being-Knowing-Doing

It is in the East of the medicine wheel that all journeys begin.

– Phil Lane and colleagues, *The Sacred Tree*

Moving from the centre, the eastern direction of the wheel opens to spirit. It is a place of birth, illumination, renewal, hope for the people, courage, vulnerability, belief in the unseen, uncritical acceptance of others, trust in your own vision, concentration, and devotion to service to others (Lane et al., 1984, p. 72). In our conversations, the wisdom keepers spoke often and openly about how, for them, culture was inseparable from spirit. They saw culture as holistically inclusive of the interrelated aspects of spirit, emotion, physicality, and mind, and felt that dominant society placed an over-emphasis on the latter. The wisdom keepers repeatedly spoke of how spirit was embedded in everything they did, and how it was experienced both consciously and unconsciously. For the wisdom keepers, spirituality had to do with respect for all life, reciprocity with nature, remembering connections with ancestors, and a belief that everything is connected intimately within creation and therefore has its own place and purpose.

Carolyn (WK) explained further as she spoke about the process of her small group having used cedar bark to create the ceremonial shawl for the mural:

> Sometimes when carvers get wood … they wait a while. They wait until the tree speaks to them about what it's going to become. And that's very true. It's how totem poles are born and masks are born. It's the same with the bark. So you know, maybe that bark made up its mind a long time ago and gathered that was its purpose. And that's how I feel about it, you know? Because, like I said, everything has an energy, and that's what it was born into.

The wisdom keepers spoke about how important it was to learn the skills of working with a given material, and then the necessity of letting go of the skills so that the spirit of the piece could be represented.

For the wisdom keepers, spirituality was tied to natural place, as with the cedar, and it was also connected to the bringing forward of wisdom from the past. Janet (WK) explained:

> I think that it's within context to apply the word *spiritual* to what we did [in the course]. And I think what that is rooted in is the fact that these artistic practices have come from such a long time ago. And the fact that we are participating in perpetuating these artistic practices is spiritual. It's many things. It's multifaceted, but spirituality is definitely one of them. It's political, it's cultural, it's educational, and it is spiritual, you know? … The measure of that is [that we are] going back out into the [larger] community, recognizing these people you've had this experience with, and feeling, "Ah, I know who you are because of what we've done together. And I know that you're okay. I know where you're at mentally and spiritually because we've had this experience together," you know?

This quote also points out the communal nature of spirituality, and the sense that acknowledging and experiencing spirit together is a way of knowing how you are related to another person at a deep level of authenticity.

While the teachings brought forward were inherently spiritual, the preservice teachers saw spirituality as unfamiliar and unpredictable territory within the university setting. This caused them to feel disoriented, unsure, and emotional at times. However, in the interviews, they were very interested in talking about spirituality, even though I had not specifically asked them about the topic. Three of the twelve spoke openly, repeatedly, and with relative comfort about their own spirituality. Another said that she wasn't spiritual at all, yet the course experiences made her feel surprisingly intrigued by it. The remaining eight pre-service teachers talked about the spiritual experiences in the course, with varying degrees of uncertainty, worry, excitement, and awe. Jayne (PST) described her feelings after some visiting drummers had shared a powerful song acknowledging the recent death of a friend:

> It's a really beautiful culture. They're very interconnected, it seems, a lot more than my culture is, with the here and the now, and the land, and that sort of stuff. But it's [also] with the things that have gone and the stuff you can't see – people who have passed away. I find in my culture, it's a lot of "if" and guessing and, you know, *if* there is a heaven, then this is what it would be like. Or, you know, *if* grandma could see me right now. But, it seems with the people that I've been introduced to here, they *know*. And I would *love* to know. I'd love to be that confident that life is always happening and continuous and that this is just a small part of it.

Jayne's clarity expressed well some of the concerns that the pre-service teachers had around their own cultural sense of being out of touch with spirituality.

Choosing to Come

Despite the unfamiliarity of a spiritually oriented learning environment, the pre-service teachers actively chose to enrol in the course. Their initial decision to join the class revolved around issues of practicality, past experience, and passion. Overall, they enrolled because they wanted to know more about indigenous pedagogy and culture, in order to be better prepared for teaching indigenous students. One came because of convenient scheduling, although most felt that it was an inconvenient time but came anyway. In addition, some of the pre-service teachers said that while typically they would consult their peers before signing up for a class, in the case of the course, they made the decision on their own.

Some pre-service teachers had had experiences with indigenous cultures in their personal life and realized that they had only surface information about cultural beliefs. Others had classroom experiences with indigenous youth that piqued their interest. Two of the pre-service teachers heard about the course from peers and decided to register late. Two knew of Lorna and felt that they could learn a lot from her. The novelty of the course was appealing to some, and the chance to be involved in a class that let the pre-service teachers be passionate in a learning environment was important to many. Overall, they felt that the course was not a class that was another hoop to jump through, like many of their other university courses, but that it would hold deep pedagogical value.

Putting Down the Notepad

Beyond the initial choice to be a part of the course, the pre-service teachers had to choose consciously to walk into unknown territory that often cut to the core of their personal cultural beliefs. Many spoke about how the course was more of a listening class than a place to talk. They described trying to con-sciously stop the chatter in their heads that naturally and continuously critiqued what was happening. Instead, they explained how their internal monologue was replaced by more holistic and embodied processes of listening and observ-ing. But paying attention in these different ways was not always easy or comfortable.

Many spoke in-depth about their experience in the course of having to put aside familiar university habits, particularly around the act of taking written notes, a rote process in which they felt they did not fully engage in listening. It was a habitual way to take down information that could be memorized later on. They felt that note-taking looked impressive but often saw it as a waste of time because they really didn't have to think about what they were writing. As Leanne (PST) said, while taking notes she was "copying down what's being said, but ... not actually processing what's being said." In letting go of taking notes, they were pushed beyond their academic comfort zone and their reliance on written notes to pay attention and watch the actual experience. Sara (PST) described it as follows:

> I found that, if I just let go and just listened and just took in what [Della] was saying for what it was, and not worry so much about [how] I really, really want to remember all these things that she's saying so I'm going to write them all down. I left my book in the classroom, I left my pen, and I came with just myself, which is hard for me because I'm a perfectionist. You know, if I'm learning, I want to learn it; I want to remember it. Otherwise, I sort of feel like I've failed a little bit ... And I think I got past the fact that we're learning different plants and their names and what they're useful for. [I was] actually learning a new way to learn. So, I think that was a big difference. I was letting go of that notion that I need to learn exactly what's being said – but more, learn from the experience.

Paying attention without a notepad

Sara's anxiety about perfectionism was shared by other pre-service teachers and, as a common theme, will resurface again in the weaving of this story.

Setting aside the act of note-taking left pre-service teachers feeling like they weren't just getting ready to regurgitate information for a test. They found the process hard to describe but said that they were learning more through all of their senses and that it happened in a more effortless way. They spoke of how taking notes in a lecture hall required lots of energy to stay focused, while the course experience let them absorb information without having to categorize it somehow mentally. In addition, they felt that listening without note-taking was more respectful and had more of a give-and-take feel that was more congruent with a reciprocal indigenous orientation.

The Sky Is the Colour of Snow Coming

One day, Charlene spoke of how she often had to find ways of translating the language of the dominant culture into her own indigenous cosmology. It was a process of grasping the deeper constructs of culture that are reflected in verbal language. She remarked that for the pre-service teachers, the course was a chance to feel the sense of unknowing that comes from being immersed in another culture. As non-indigenous participants, the pre-service teachers could be the ones who struggled to understand. She spoke about how this would be useful for them when they became teachers in multicultural classrooms: "[The course] was a culture shock for them, a total cultural shock … [But] once you have a basic understanding of a cultural setting, it doesn't matter from whose, then you can make comparative changes and understanding from one set to the next, and bring that with you." The oral indigenous language that the wisdom keepers shared in the course became a portal into their ontologies, and many of the wisdom keepers were conscious of choosing their words very carefully, especially when they were sharing specific cultural teachings. Gina (WK) said that participating in the earth fibres course

> has taught me to be very aware of the words that I'm using – which may
> sound strange, but if [learners] don't know a culture, it's important to use
> the right words to describe what you're trying to teach. And in our class in
> particular, I've been sharing the stories, the legends that go behind some of
> the figures that we use on our button blankets, for example, in our dances,
> and why we do certain dances when we do them. I think it's important to
> not just do the hands-on craft, but to give meaning behind that craft.

In order to articulate what the deeper constructs of language looked like in the context of the course, Gina spoke about describing the sky:

> Maybe it would help if I said something like, we can teach a child that the
> sky is blue. That sentence I've seen in books: The sky is blue. But, we would
> say, the sky is the colour of the water after the wind has blown for three days.
> The sky is the colour of snow coming. Or the sky isn't blue today it's gray, the
> clouds are covering the blue, but it's still a good day. It's just a different way
> of looking at things.

For the pre-service teachers, understanding a different way of looking at things at this deeper conceptual level was often an exciting, but also scary, endeavour. They worried about saying or doing the wrong thing in a cultural situation, but April (PST) spoke about benefits of the process:

> I really enjoyed learning about the words of the Lil'wat language last night. It
> was so powerful. And just the fact that the culture has decided that we need a
> word for this because it's something that's important to them, it's something
> that exists, you know. And … there are like eighty words to translate this one

word. So that kind of learning just blows me away. I really loved hearing how other people interpret the world. And how sometimes you've had a feeling, and all of a sudden there is a word for it.

Many of the pre-service teachers spoke of how certain experiences in the course had the effect of articulating feelings or intuitive knowing that they felt but had been unable to put into words. Charlene said that for her the process "gains, for me, much more appreciation of the ones who came before me. It's so cool. It brings it down to the simplest form. Here is the concept, but it applies to all of these things. And it's a simple concept, but in its simplicity is its incredible largeness." Charlene's statement is reminiscent of Aluli Meyer's (2008) notion that specificity leads to universality. Looking under surface culture to what lies closer to the heart ultimately connects people to each other through a resonance of knowing on a non-intellectual level.

Opening Circles

The opening circle time at the beginning of each class session served as a potential doorway into a spiritual realm of knowing. Charlene spoke of how it was necessary to find spaces away from the dominant culture in order to be able to do the work that spirit presents: "I think so many people just go through stuff without waking up every day and having an awareness about, 'Let my eyes be open. Let my heart be open,' and having that gift of thought and openness through the day of just taking [time] and paying attention."

Sitting together in circle gave the participants a chance to regroup from their busy day and connect with the focus of the class. It set a tone of expectation that the work ahead should be done in a mindful way. This quote from Courtney (PST) describes the community feeling that was developed in the circle and that moved throughout the rest of each class session:

There is a certain warmth to the entering of the classroom, and something new and exciting and unexpected occurs. But it's [also] common, in the sense that we're in a circle, we are welcomed, we have that touching base of how's everyone doing. That doesn't occur, perhaps, in the more traditional classes. You know, how are you doing *really*? And if someone's having something that is bothering them, or if something sad has happened in the community, it's addressed. We don't just pretend that it's an outside world ... And then you plan for each week together as a group. You know, what do we need to have done? Do we want to get together and do it? Half the time we shared food

One of many circles

together, so it's a totally different experience ... There is that sense of being known, and the warmth ... and sense of bonding because we're in this community family together. We're all working towards the same gigantic chunk of canvas, and we all have our little piece to put on it.

The wisdom keepers appreciated that the course truly incorporated cultural components and saw the opening circle as being very important in this way because it respected spiritual beliefs.

The pre-service teachers said that being together in a circular formation was a good thing because they could see everybody equally, and people could see them as well. They saw the circle as being inviting, inclusive, and safe. It didn't feel like a class anymore; it was more real. Garrett (PST) talked further about the sense of realness:

It just didn't feel manufactured. Like, fake, you know? ... I want my students to feel comfortable and supported in the classroom, and you do that by sharing and getting to know each other. And you do activities that you hope would allow for that to happen. And sometimes you don't mean to, but you sort of force that upon the students, and it ends up not being really real. I've had that happen to me where I've had instructors that would have get-to-know-you activities and such things like that, where it just seems forced. But this was different. It didn't feel like that. We all came together and – it's hard to explain. I don't know – it just didn't really feel fake in that sense. It just sort of happened. I think a lot of that had to do with there [being] lots of Aboriginal [participants] in the classroom, and it was second nature to them. They knew how to share and how to come together as one family. And I just sort of watched them. It's hard to explain.

The pre-service teachers thought that the circle times were useful, in part, because of the fact that they were taking time to be thankful and to recognize that it was a privilege to be at university and to be taking the course. They felt that it was an important time when they could collect their thoughts, reflect, and share whatever they wished. It gave them a sense of group bonding and common focus that felt more real than the group work they had done in other classes. Courtney shared thoughts on the difficulty of putting the experience into words:

I think that goes back to the feeling of acceptance. It's such an interesting feeling, and I really would like to get into that more. It's literally that it doesn't feel like a class. If somehow you could quantify feeling ... if you could put a little barometer in the classroom, it would be a totally different colour or something ... I don't know if it's open-mindedness or acceptance. I think its acceptance and willingness to learn maybe, or something. I don't know. It's a very different feeling.

Despite confusion about how it was happening, the pre-service teachers believed that the circles changed their mood, making them feel more alive, renewed their energy, and made them want to return to the class. They felt less anxious after the circle and more willing to participate in the activities. As April said, "I don't really understand how it changes feeling. I guess it's because it's things I believe, and other people are saying them, maybe? And maybe it's like everyone feels good all at once, maybe it's something like sort of healing, I don't know. I definitely don't understand it, but I like it." April's comments resonate with my own feeling of contentedness during the circle times. There was a sense of acknowledging previously subconscious beliefs in a simple yet profound way. This was similar to Chelsea's (PST) feelings around the healing qualities of stepping off the path to "just be" in nature right there in the dirt, and also to the feelings of connectedness, described at the beginning of Chapter 1, experienced when we were wrapped in the cattail mats. During the course, wisdom keepers often suggested that taking a walk, sitting in the forest, or going to cultural celebrations and ceremonies might be useful ways to get outside of daily life and let go of deeply held beliefs for a time being.

For many of the pre-service teachers, this feeling of connectedness carried through other times in the course. This was demonstrated in a conversation that I had with Kevin (PST). It is revealing in that it gets at the heart of a different, more indigenous way of understanding the notion of spirituality.

> KEVIN: Every class basically started with a prayer. So I've been trying to think about what the significance of the prayer is. Is this – and I don't mean it to demean it – is this a mundane thing? Does it occur on a regular basis, or is it a sacred thing? So is everything that we did in our crafting – working together, being together – was this sacred spiritual, or was it normal?
>
> MICHELE: What's the difference?
>
> KEVIN: The mundane is an everyday, normal occurrence. And not that it's any less, but you know, sacred is a special event usually held up above others as ceremony, a festival – something that's held in reverence by many people … And I don't mean to meander all about, but not all the students that I see were completely comfortable with it … There were kind of a few laughs so I'm not quite sure how to interpret that but … [the prayer] provided context to me, towards how important the event was, how important it was [for] my instructors, my teachers, some of my fellows or counterparts …
>
> MICHELE: So were you comfortable with the prayer happening?
>
> KEVIN: I wasn't expecting it. I knew that prayers were part of an Aboriginal custom, but I was not expecting it in this course, nor at the beginning of every class … I mean, my perception of spiritual, as I said in the first interview, is pretty much kind of different.
>
> MICHELE: What is it?
>
> KEVIN: Different in the context that – and this is going to be very difficult to explain – [for me] spiritual is not necessarily a religious feature. It doesn't have to tie in to a god or gods, and it's maybe pretty much agnostic. It's a reverence for everything.

After this conversation with Kevin, I remember feeling very intrigued by his emerging understanding of spirituality. The earth fibres course seemed to reinforce his belief that spirituality was not tied to religion; rather it was embedded in the commonness of everyday life.

3

Rethinking Learner-Teacher Relationships

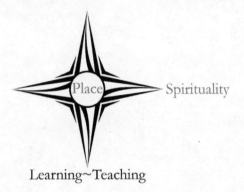

Place ⟷ Spirituality

Learning~Teaching

[The course is] more of a learning with your whole self versus learning with just your intellectual side I think. So, deeper learning that guides your soul almost, and makes you interested in certain things, and want to learn more about them. And [wanting to be] passionate and caring towards people, or aspects of life, like wanting to make the world a better place and stuff like that. I think when you learn things that you're intrigued about, that you care about, it will drive your life in a certain way, versus when you learn things that you don't find important [and] you kind of say why am I learning this? And you stop there. But if you are like, yes, I should be learning this, you start to travel in a certain direction with your thoughts and sometimes with your actions too.

– April, PST

The south direction of the wheel focuses on developing and refining feelings, loyalty, fullness, the heart, sensitivity to the feelings of others, anger at injustice, ability to express feelings, idealism, control of the appetites, and passionate involvement in the world (Lane et al., 1984, p. 72). In our conversations, the pre-service teachers repeatedly spoke about how the environment of the earth fibres course and their relationships with the wisdom keepers were conducive to nourishing their own learning spirits (Battiste, 2009). I now offer a description of the learner-teacher relationships that I observed, engaged in, and had conversations about with the participants. I want to remind the reader of the circuitous and interwoven nature of the stories in the course; they are neither linear nor discrete entities.

Watching for Gifts

The wisdom keepers believed that each learner comes into this world gifted with unique abilities. Adults should never try to shape a child; instead, adults should watch children and wait to see who they are becoming. Janet (WK) said, "It really is [that] there are gifts. And I think ... people are gifted with different things." From this perspective the wisdom keepers recognized each learner's potential, grounded in who the learner was what he or she knew; they did not rely on external sources, such as their own experience or public curriculum documents. Lynne (WK) described how the learner-teacher relationship looked from this worldview, using a musical metaphor:

> [Learners] each have their own note or vibration. And for me, someone who's going to share with them their knowledge, is somebody who is a musician enough to know the notes and give them what they need to create what music that they need to make, with the tones that they have to play with ... What you're giving is the safety to let all of what they feel happen. So, what you're really doing is creating a safe world in which they can live, and that they can have fun and learn things by. Because kids want to learn. All of us want to learn. Everybody has a curious mind. That's not the problem. It's finding out what note they're tuned in to.

This type of learner-teacher relationship requires the teacher to be very open-minded about the possibilities of the learner in terms of what direction the learner might take, and what his or her needs might be. As Lynne said, "You don't teach anybody; people learn." Supporting this notion, Charlene (WK) said it was important that teachers ask themselves: "Is it my need that's being filled, or is it the student's need that's being filled? You know, if we were a real educator, it [would be] the students' needs that we are trying to fill and not ours and not the system's."

The wisdom keepers were concerned that learners were being harmed by the typical pedagogy that is prevalent in today's schools, and that such practices

Wisdom keeper May watching for gifts

were in part responsible for disengagement in school and even extreme reactions to life challenges such as violence and suicide. Gay (WK) advocated for a more hands-off, child-directed approach:

I don't think you should criticize children because it's not going to help them. To give them what they need, you need to encourage them … They already are who they are, and they've already got different talents beyond what you know. Our concept is that we're teaching them and a lot of times I find that children are teaching me! Because they're all different, and they all have different ways of expressing themselves, and they've already got all kinds of talents, you know?

The wisdom keepers believed that nourishing the learning spirit was about helping the learners to actualize the gifts that they had in whatever way they wanted to pursue them. The learners determined the direction of the learning, and the wisdom keepers actively supported that learning.

Finding Space and Place

The learner holds great responsibility in the process of nourishing the learning spirit. April noted that at the beginning of the course, "there was no sign-up sheet of duties and things like that, so you ended up finding your own space and place." It was up to the learner to find his or her own path through the learning process, to recognize possible learning opportunities (similar to the photographer metaphor that Janet presented in Chapter 1), and to decide what matched personal learning needs. This type of process happened at different rates for different learners and was unpredictable.

After having the opportunity to find their own place and space as learners, the pre-service teachers began to think about how learners have to manage tensions between freedom and responsibility, as described by Sara (PST):

> I think what stood out was the way that we were given the opportunity to take responsibility for our learning ... It was really refreshing because you went in there and you got to enjoy it more because there wasn't sort of that pressure to have certain things done by a certain time. And you know, I think I personally learn better that way. If there's not that sort of deadline, then I actually get it done faster and better because it means more to me ... So I think that, for me, really stood out the most, just that freedom, but also that expectation that you're taking responsibility for your learning. And I think it's an important skill for everyone to learn.

This type of freedom as learners gave the pre-service teachers opportunities to find what learning situations and learning content were meaningful and relevant to their real-life experience. For example, some pre-service teachers were able to remember details about the medicinal uses of plants (without writing them down) because they could use that information to influence their own lives in positive ways.

Many of the pre-service teachers reported that being in control of their learning motivated them to be more productive, as Nicole (PST) discussed with me:

> NICOLE: The way we learned stood out. It wasn't regurgitating; it wasn't tak[ing] notes on how to make moccasins. [Instead] it was, "Here's the material. Work with your hands and give it a try" ... I learn really well

that way, and I've never really had the opportunity to learn that way before, so it was neat ... [It was] learning through experience and by doing instead of passively sitting there and getting your head filled up with the information. You're the one that's kind of creating it, and you're in charge of learning. It's up to you how much you learn; it's not up to someone else ...

MICHELE: And how did that feel, or how did that work for you?

NICOLE: I was much more motivated to do the work. I stayed up three hours – I'd sit there and bead at night. And I really wanted to do a good job, too. But it was for myself; it wasn't for anyone else, for a change. When I was in school, I worked because it was more for my parents. If I didn't get a good grade, I was in trouble. And for my teachers. It was never for myself. I didn't really care if I learned anything about English literature. But this one was for myself. It was something I really wanted to do.

Despite the importance of finding their own space and place, some of the pre-service teachers had difficulty adjusting to this new terrain. They looked to the wisdom keepers to guide them, as they would in other courses. But, as Gay said,

I always like people to create their own beading and pattern making and how they would fit, because all your inner expressions will come out in the beadwork ... And [the students] always want to know, "Is this the way?" And I kept on trying to tell them there's no set way to do it. Because it's actually in you coming out, so I can't say, "This is the way to do it" ... They're going to develop their own way, and that will be the proper way for them.

Having control and responsibility over their own learning in this way was a new experience that began to become familiar and enjoyable for the pre-service teachers as the course went on. They began to recognize the opportunities for being nourished by being able to decide what to learn and felt motivated to go out of their comfort zone despite past experiences to the contrary.

The Teachers Were with You

One aspect of the course that surprised many of the pre-service teachers was the feeling that the wisdom keepers and the pre-service teachers held more equal positions in the learning environment. As Nicole explained,

I found just the act of sitting in a circle brought you together a lot more. And ... the teachers, you felt that instead of being superior to you, they were with you almost, guiding you. They weren't this figure to be feared or afraid of. You felt just fine going up to [any of them]. And that's a bit different; usually you see profs as you have to walk on eggshells around them. But it wasn't the same, which changed the dynamic of the class, for sure, from what I'm used to.

The wisdom keepers also saw themselves as equal partners in the learning process, and Carolyn (WK) shared:

It didn't ever occur to me, that they felt somewhat apprehensive simply because they felt that we were teachers and they were students. I really ... wanted for them to feel like we were all equal and to feel comfortable, and that we could learn together. And I think once they became aware of that fact, I think everyone felt far more comfortable ... I really wanted them to just let it flow and experience something come alive through their hands.

The wisdom keepers acknowledged that they often felt passionate about textiles, or called to their work with them, and it was a natural extension of that interest that motivated them to share their understanding. They frequently spoke of how they didn't consider themselves to be experts or masters with a given textile. Instead they described themselves as people who simply knew about certain things and were willing to share that knowing. Garrett (PST) observed this in Della (WK) on the nature walk:

Della was really interesting. When we were out on the plant walk, she didn't really say that she was an expert in anything ... What she knew, she just knows it. And there were some times there where she picked up a plant and she didn't really know the name of it. And you know, if that was anyone else, well, usually the students would question the teacher [and say,] "Oh, they don't know anything. They don't know what they're talking about." But with Della, I believed her. I mean, I knew that she knew what it was. She may not have known the name of it, but I could sense that she knew what it could be used for, and it definitely made me respect her and [indigenous] ways of learning a lot more.

Garrett, like many of the pre-service teachers, was rethinking notions of expertise. As April tried to identify what made the course so different, she further disrupted the learner/teacher bifurcation: "I'm trying to observe to see what it is. But I feel like if there was one thing it could be, is that [the course] allows everyone in the class to be a teacher. And that the ... professors ... are just like guidance for the [instructors] that add their own words that allow you to self-direct where your learning should be going." The wisdom keepers and pre-service teachers were becoming comfortable partners in the learning process. The emphasis on self-directed learning helped reframe the notion of teacher as expert and gave space for a new type of pedagogy.

Gentle Offerings

Charlene spoke about how "a cultural learning is only a gentle offering out there ... All it is, is little gifts that are being offered ... So, let [the learner] find wherever that is for them." In fact, the very way that the course was first discovered by the students was done as a gentle offering. Courtney (PST) said, "We were so excited when that email came ... It was like, you know, 'Attention year-five students. If you would like ...' And it was worded in the way that, ah, you might, you could, look at taking this course. And I remember just thinking, 'Oh, yes!'"

The wisdom keepers felt that it was their job to set a table, or show what they knew to the participants of the course in ways similar to those described by Gina (WK) in Chapter 1, when she learned to make bread. They did this by showing ways of patterning bark and beads, how to use tools and what tools were proper for different projects; they showed shortcuts that might be useful with a textile, such as basting or marking out a design. And after that, they just let the learners go at it on their own. As Gay said,

> there is a proper way to handle the scissors and how to use it and everything.
> But more than likely, they're going to develop their own way, and that will
> be the proper way for them ... I never, ever tell them what colours to pick
> because their colours that they pick appeal to different people than my
> colours that I would pick.

Gay continued to talk about how the wisdom keepers were accepting when the students made mistakes:

> I told them to be careful on how you're sewing a moccasin together because
> there's a wrong side and a right side. And somebody was careless, and we
> ended up with two same sides! But nobody will ever notice; we're not going to
> point it out! ... But, I'm really glad, because normally those people will learn.

Setting a table

I mean, even though they didn't succeed on doing what you tell them, they'll be more careful when they do it next time … It's not always the ones that are doing good that are doing the best.

Gay went on to say that she was pleased that her students often get better than her at certain textile skills, and this view was shared by many of the other wisdom keepers.

The wisdom keepers acknowledged that the gentle guiding process took lots of energy mentally and emotionally, and was tiring at times. They also talked about the importance of being aware of what offerings they made. Lynne likened the process to setting a table filled with healthy foods: "That's why there is so much power in being a teacher and there's so much of a gift that you can bring, because you're setting that table. And what's on the table depends on what the teacher has put there."

Gentle offerings were sometimes so subtle that the pre-service teachers missed opportunities to engage with them. After class one day, Charlene talked to me about a visitor who had come that day and who, in the context of a more formal talk to the large group, offered to share later with anyone who was interested in learning more about her teachings. Charlene was frustrated by the lack of response: "People just didn't get it. And then, finally, there were two students who came and wanted to learn and grow … They made the effort to be there and … wanted to hear those other things. So those are the ones that got more [teachings]."

The pre-service teachers spoke of not always being certain how to interact with the wisdom keepers and guests, and one talked about feeling excluded at times. Some spoke of wanting more background information about what was going on, and more clarity on instructions on how to engage. Many spoke of how they were used to lots of direction in their coursework and felt that they needed to learn to engage with the wisdom keepers consciously in ways other than how they would typically interact with instructors. This created a subtle tension that emerged off and on throughout the course; deep-seated beliefs around the nature of knowledge and learning came into play. Overall, the pre-service teachers said that, while it took some time getting used to, the gentle offering approach became more comfortable and enjoyable for them as learners and the wisdom keepers began to see their growth.

Faith in the Learner

The wisdom keepers believed that once learners knew the basic skills, they could then come up with their own interpretations and ways of creating. Carolyn had a student tell her, "I really appreciated the way that you taught. You had so much faith in us. You guys just said, 'Okay, here it is. Now you do it' ... I just felt that you had so much faith that I could do it that I just had to keep going and do it because you believed in me" (unnamed PST quoted in Carolyn's interview).

Many of the wisdom keepers spoke about how their own first experiences with a particular textile came at times when an adult needed their help and put the tools in their inexperienced hands. When her granny first handed her a moccasin that needed to be finished, Gay said, "She knew that I had the capability. It was just me – I never had attempted it." But Gay had watched, and was pleased by her own relatively quick success.

Leanne (PST) spoke about how she transferred her beginning skills of watching and trying into thinking differently and being creative in her learning:

> There's just a lot more things that I had never even really considered to be learning but were things that I picked up and then they came second nature to me ... There was a large difference from when I started just stitching and sewing and everything, than to when I ended. It's just a lot more natural. It's a bit more fluid. And it allows [my] creative juices to go more because I could see different avenues I could take with it.

The wisdom keepers said that it was important not to put limitations on children in terms of imagining their potential because it was impossible to know

Unique beadwork created by a learner

what a child might be able to do and how that knowledge might be useful for either the child or the community. The pre-service teachers felt that their opinions were genuinely valued by the wisdom keepers, and that they were trusted to put their own signature on things. For me, as a participant learning in the course, this faith in the learner felt like an ebbing and flowing of intuitive understanding between the wisdom keepers and me. They would show me something, and I would choose whether or not to engage. They would show me something else, and the decision would be transferred back to me.

The pre-service teachers also expressed feeling as if the wisdom keepers genuinely cared about them as learners. As Courtney said,

May [WK] ... took so much pride ... and joy in seeing us succeed ... She would do anything for us, before she even learned my name properly! You know she was just so behind me and getting our group to succeed in what we were doing. And we would knit dreadful, dreadful things [*laughter*]. And she would say that they were just amazing. And that's a big thing.

Some of the wisdom keepers went out of their way to give learners their attention outside of the class as well, through email and phone contact, acknowledging the continuous nature of the teaching and learning process. Throughout the course, the back-and-forth aspects of show-choose, practise-appreciate, trust-care continued. This faith in the learner removed limitations on the creative energy of the pre-service teachers in ways they were not used to and gave them much to think about in terms of their own teaching practice.

Teach Them in Four Different Ways

Along with being open to many possible ways of learning, the wisdom keepers spoke about how it was important for teachers to be a bridge that helped students express and understand intuitive and holistic ways of knowing. The wisdom keepers were concerned that schools overemphasized academic learning (mental) at the cost of other significant knowledge and ways of knowing (spiritual, emotional, and physical). The wisdom keepers said that it was important for learners to put their whole selves into learning through hands-on engagement in relevant activities. Charlene spoke about how learners need to experience things four ways before they develop a fullness of understanding:

> That's a cultural teaching, that's how you teach ... Whether it flourishes now or it's a seed for later on, they will get it ... There is such a lack of respect for understanding that you *should* offer teachings in more than one way, instead of just one way, that's it ... Each person is an individual and they learn very individually ... You teach them in four different ways. You make offer of that understanding, of that knowledge, of what you're trying to teach [through the] physical, emotional, spiritual, and mental.

The wisdom keepers felt that the holistic experiences in the course took pressure off the pre-service teachers as learners, and that it would encourage them to try new ways of acting as teachers. As Carolyn said, "I felt like they learned something in a way that maybe they hadn't learned ... before. And maybe it [would] encourage them to try something new later on when they become teachers – just to approach it from a different angle."

April spoke about how the wisdom keepers' holistic way of teaching would be good for learners who might be anxious in the classroom: "This seems like the way that education should be going: more focused on educating the whole self and creating people who feel welcomed in the world and know they have a place. And then *that* I think in turn will make them more relaxed in the classroom and let them learn better, you know? Let them learn more deeply."

The pre-service teachers felt that the learning styles of other students around them in the education program were not particularly diverse. They were excited to be around community members and students from other areas of interest who had different ways of looking at learning, as it opened up another type of knowledge community to them.

The pre-service teachers spoke about how learning in the context of the course was more unconscious and harder to explain than in other settings. They said that it was a different way of focusing attention that took effort and practice, but that they liked using more than their brain in the learning process. They were very enthusiastic about engaging in hands-on learning that was highly experiential and involved other ways of knowing such as smell and taste. They said that it was a more natural way to learn. Garrett gave the following description:

> It was more of an experiential sort of learning rather than somebody telling you what they know, and then you absorbing that. There were people that taught us, but I learned it in my own way, my own process. So, it wasn't like somebody passed on their knowledge to me in a direct way. It was sort of an indirect way where it allowed me to gain that knowledge in the way that I felt comfortable in doing so. Just almost like an unconscious sort of learning. Yeah, it's sort of hard to describe, I guess, because it's nothing that I've ever really experienced before.

And Kevin (PST) spoke of how he began to be aware of knowing through the sensations in his hands:

> As I progressed through the craft, I began to rely on my fingers, my hands a lot more. I mean, I could feel things that I wouldn't necessarily have noticed in the past. And so I was becoming more aware of a sense, perhaps, that I've took for granted. I didn't need to use my eyes so much, as I could feel with my fingers, feel the texture of the fabric or string, know how far I could go ... As my crafts grew, I think part of me grew too – something that I was not familiar

Paying attention through hands

with before, or had very little experience with ... If I were to have been taught directly or had been prepared through reading on how to do the craft, my experience would be not the same. It would be drastically different, because of the exploratory [element in hands-on learning].

The wisdom keepers and the pre-service teachers spoke repeatedly of the importance of getting to know something through modes other than the intellect. These other ways of knowing gave them a deeper, more authentic and meaningful understanding of the work at hand. As Kevin said, as his crafts grew, another part of him grew as well. His willingness to practise focusing his attention within Charlene's style of four ways of knowing led him to embody and become aware of new ways of learning that could later be transferred to his teaching.

A Collective Community

The opening quotation of this chapter points out how the nourishing of April's learning spirit was connected to her sense of community and her increased sense of social responsibility. The actions of the participants demonstrated that the learning spirit of an individual was intimately tied to the wellness of the community at large. There was a back-and-forth awareness of self in community, and community in self, similar to the ebb and flow between learner and teacher. The pre-service teachers would alternate between paying attention to their internal learning and paying attention to the needs of the group.

The small groups within the earth fibres course often worked together to find their focus and decide on what they would be creating together for the mural. For the cedar bark group, this was a complicated process embedded in the context of the larger community. Carolyn explained:

> I figured whoever was meant to use this bark would gravitate towards our group. And they did. It was funny, actually. And ... my mom and I ... sat with them and we talked about ideas about how to contribute to the whole mural, as a group. And one of the things that occurred to me was in that video about ... the totem pole [project from the last course. The carver] kept referring to the totem pole as the "Old Man." And it made a lot of sense to me because, honestly, it is ... And then for me, the bark was the old woman because they go together. So, we talked about it with the group. And we talked about ideas about how to personify visually, in a three-dimensional sense, the old woman.

Carolyn went on to describe how the group had to go through an initial stage of getting to know and trust each other. They had long discussions on the best way of representing the female aspect of the cedar. At one point, Carolyn and Fran (WK) suggested doing this through weaving a burden basket. Some of the pre-service teachers worried that this represented a negative image of women's work, despite assurances by Carolyn and Fran that men also used the basket. This idea was eventually discarded when the wisdom keepers offered the idea of weaving a ceremonial shawl. Once that idea was accepted by the group, the creation of the piece, as Fran said, "just sort of flowed out of them ... They got excited once they realized that something was growing, and they really enhanced it. We gave them tools as we went along, just little things like shells or whatever. And to see their minds were working about, 'Hold on, this is how I can be creative with it.'"

Working on the cedar shawl

At this point in her story, Carolyn brought up an issue of tension in her group, brought on by expectations of the larger earth fibres course community. In addition to making the shawl, her group was asked to make some cedar rope that could be placed along the border of the mural. Carolyn described this as a special task that was "not to be taken lightly" and said that the weaver "needed to have some level of peace to do that type of work." Carolyn felt that making rope would be stressful, in terms of the group not having enough time and resources. She believed that her responsibility was to honour what was emerging from the group as they worked with the cedar. She spoke of protecting her group from what she felt was an overemphasis on product rather than process by those requesting the rope, saying she appreciated the vision that others had, "but I'm glad we kept to task for what felt right for us."

Learning and Teaching Together

Members of the button blanket group also felt particular pressures to produce. They had extra responsibilities for the overall mural production, such as the intricate moons across the top. One pre-service teacher was particularly distressed by this and said:

[In the beginning] I felt that I wanted to do the work and, more or less, that the work was for me. I was inspired. In the last portion of the class, I felt like the work was for an external person [or] thing. I feel like UVic wanted to show their interconnectedness with different cultures so they decided to rope a bunch of students into making something. The work asked for in the end lacked meaning for me. Not that they weren't meaningful to someone or something as a whole, and the ideas behind them were meaningful ... It's just the process, I think, that lacked the meaning. Also, when the pieces were initially discussed, I was motivated and inspired ... but as the time grew tight ... it was less about the piece and more about getting it done ... Our group lost a sense of connectedness to each other and the piece. And even seeing the whole piece together set up in the library does not give me the sense of meaningfulness and pride that I think the piece initially deserved.

In a follow-up interview, Gina verified that some of her button blanket group felt anxiety similar to that expressed above. During my observations, I noticed the pressures that the cedar and button blanket groups had felt on occasion. External pressures that emphasized a focus on product instead of on the learning process were disrupting the internally defined rhythms of each group. In a later conversation, the pre-service teacher quoted above reiterated how important the first few weeks were, saying that the course "really did change the way I think about education" in a useful way. However, it raised concerns for me about how easily pressures to produce crept into the course experience. This theme, like the aforementioned anxiety around perfectionism (see Chapters 2 and 4), shows up repeatedly in the telling of this story.

Despite the pressures described, the pre-service teachers felt overall that a very unusual and positive type of community was created in the course, saying that it was not so much the "what" of community, but the "how" of going about community that mattered. Compared to their previous experiences of group work, this was different. Courtney talked about the inclusive feeling she experienced that extended beyond the students in her small group:

It should be qualified [that] the *we* is inclusive of the teachers as well. I don't want it to seem that, you know, the teachers came but then we just took off and did it ourselves. We couldn't have done it without them. So we, as a collective community, through the scaffolding that the university, and the planning, and the wisdom keepers gave us, created [the mural].

Many of the pre-service teachers spoke of feeling that they were working side by side in this way with their small groups and with the wisdom keepers.

In addition, the collective project of the mural took pressure off individual achievement. The pre-service teachers saw the small groups as being very helpful to creating a feeling of safety, as described by Nicole:

I think the relationship that you form within your small groups stood out. It was, like, a little family. Every week you came and we worked so hard together, and we really fed off of each other. And I was one of the weaker ones in terms of sewing; I'd never sewn before, so I really needed the help. And I didn't feel bad asking for it. And we took and we gave, you know? And everyone was helping each other; I don't think anyone felt that it was on them. That was really neat.

Leanne added that it was like the pre-service teachers had "turned our brains on to a different way of thinking" that was more inclusive and community-oriented. Pressures were there but the overall experience was of a healthy learning community that honoured each member's learning spirit in relation to the larger group.

Opening Up a Safe Place

At the beginning of this chapter, Lynne suggested that teachers give learners "the safety to let all of what they feel happen." The pre-service teachers spoke repeatedly and in depth about how important it was for them to feel safe in educational settings. As Heather (PST) said, safe spaces affected the learning spirit:

In my experience, there have been a lot of times where I personally haven't learned as much as I could because I'm not in a place where I feel comfortable or I feel safe. And so creating a learning environment is more about opening up a safe place, and then pursuing passions, or interests, or things that catch your eye, and then going deeper into them.

April wondered what it was that the wisdom keepers did to involve everyone and make them feel "really special and worthwhile, and not scared, and not all those bad things that are often associated with academic learning." Some of the pre-service teachers felt that they had developed anxiety being in the teacher education program and that being in the earth fibres course made them feel calm. This was partly because it was a choice for them to be there but they also talked about how the nature of the learning environment was different.

The wisdom keepers spoke about wanting to create a safe environment where learners could be themselves and explore new ideas. Charlene likened the pre-service teachers to marbles – all going off in different directions to learn – and said that her role was to give guidance:

> [It's a] a gentle guiding process ... I see it as a spiral, but it's a spiral that touches and grows. And a marble is a very good equivalent [for the learner] because we need to have an outside boundary of ourselves. And sometimes that's hard like a marble, and sometimes it's much more soft and malleable. When it gets to the soft and malleable stage, it means that there's much more willingness to have things coming into that space of growing and learning.

Charlene added that safety is especially important when change is happening within all aspects of a person, including mental, physical, emotional, and spiritual change. She felt it was important to "create a space where it's safe to allow some of those boundaries to become less structured, less hard," and that the artistic process of the fibre work was a safe place for these internal kinds of learning to occur.

The different structure of the course and the uncertainty about what would happen left the pre-service teachers uncomfortable and wary at times. However, they also spoke of feeling welcomed and accepted. There was a heightened sense of social equality and a sense of being able to bring what they felt like bringing to the experience, rather than trying to meet external expectations. Because the work was sometimes personal and emotional, they genuinely appreciated that learning could be more relaxed and happen more at its own pace.

In addition, the pre-service teachers felt that they were a part of the creative process and that it was okay to make mistakes. Chelsea (PST) shared:

> At the end, we had gone in to do the finishing stuff [on the mural], and Charlene would come around and show us how to do the cutting or the

tracing and that sort of thing. I was so worried that I would mess everything up. And then she would just come and help me fix it, and it wasn't a big deal … I was so worried that I would wreck it. But you just fix it. And she would say, "You're the artist; this is your work."

Most of the pre-service teachers talked about how significant it was that the course was offered as a pass/fail instead of a graded course. They spoke about many benefits that this ungraded situation offered, saying that it increased their feelings of safety and that it made them more relaxed and less anxious. They saw each other taking pride in the work and experienced less competition with their peers. They believed that people were there for the right reasons, which helped them to focus on the similarities between people rather than the differences. This factor also increased their feelings of safety.

Nicole describes how the pre-service teachers enjoyed that they could just be there in the class without worrying about taking notes and tests:

I love the fact that I don't have to worry about how good my little cattail mat is going to be and if I'm going to get an A on it. I just got to experience doing it without worrying, and it made me enjoy it so much more than being so stressed out and worried about it. I think that learning for the sake of learning is so important. And I think that that's what we need to instill in the children, too – is the love of learning and learning for the sake of learning, instead of learning because I need to get a grade, or learning because I need to let my parents know that I'm doing well in school, or things like that. I think that's very important.

As we leave the southern territory of the wheel, I share a story about Garrett that highlights the process of nourishing the learning spirit. Garrett chose to be in the course because of the feelings he got from a previous course he had taken with Lorna. As he said,

Every time I leave a class with [Lorna] – and it may be all First Nations classes, I don't know – I always feel more connected to what I know. And I always feel like it's a more supportive environment, and I don't feel as stressed to learn what other people expect me to learn. I enjoy being in an environment where I can choose what I want to learn.

Garrett told me that he was drawn to the smell of cedar and so decided to be in the cedar weaving small group. Unfortunately, it was hard going for Garrett

Learning and Teaching Together

Cedar rose (Photo credit: Emma Tanaka)

as he often struggled with preparing the bark. After many sessions, however, he became inspired as he became skilled at making cedar roses:

> It was a really good feeling, *getting* something, because I struggled a lot with the cedar. You know, it was such an intricate process, trying to strip it, and making those long strands. Most of the time, I'd end up stripping it half way and then it would break, and I'd end up with something that I couldn't really use. So, it was frustrating a lot of times. So the rose thing, it was really good, because it was simple for me to understand, and it wasn't something that I could really screw up on. I mean, it's something that I felt like I could contribute to something. So, I just sat there and made roses. And it was something that I really felt satisfied about.

Garrett was nick-named "the rose man" from that point on. In his interview, I asked him if he could share more about the rose-making process, and he spoke about the gentle and trusting role of the wisdom keepers:

> Well, Carolyn showed me how to do it *once*. And I watched her do it, and then she just kind of left. And then I tried to do it, and I know that I didn't get it the first few times, and I just kept on picturing her doing it. And then I finally got it. And it wasn't like she stood over me and watched me do it and watched me struggle. It was [more like] she left and sort of had confidence in me –

knowing that I would get it eventually. And I did. It wasn't like there was that pressure, you know, that somebody is *there,* waiting for you to succeed. It was like, she knew that I would – it was just that I needed to do it on my own, you know?

Although the specifics were different for each individual, others spoke about going through similar processes where they were finding their paths as learners in ways that guided their souls.

The tone of the learner-teacher relationships set by the wisdom keepers supported the pre-service teachers to learn with their "whole selves," as April said earlier. Within the particular style of the course, the pre-service teachers were able to gain autonomy as learners as they found their own space and place within the learning community. The wisdom keepers behaved differently from traditional teachers, as they walked alongside each learner, watching for gifts, teaching in multiple modes, and collectively joining in on the work at hand. This created a safe space that was undermined to some extent, however, by the external pressures of institutional expectations of the course and the tight timeline for completing the work. Despite these challenges, the overall tone of the pre-service teachers' comments suggests that they felt their souls were being touched in unexpected ways, and they became interested in creating similar learning-teaching relationships within their own teaching practice.

4

Invoking Good Intention and Conscious Action

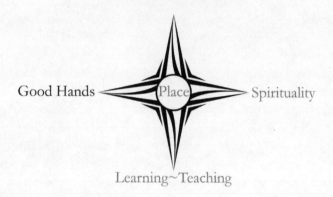

Good Hands — Place — Spirituality

Learning~Teaching

Learning to work with my hands was definitely something that I've never really been a part of. And it's a different way of focusing your attention than if you're just using your brain for essays, or anything like that. It does take a lot of focus, and it takes repetition, and it takes practice, like everything does, but in a more natural way, you know? If you think about it, it's almost more instinctual to be working with our hands and to be creating than it is to be writing and [things] like that, so it felt like more of a connection in a way.

– Leanne, PST

The western direction of the wheel is about perseverance, the unknown, management of power, going within, dreams, reflection, silence, sacrifice, humility, awareness of our spiritual nature, respect for others, commitment to a path of personal development, commitment to struggle to assist the development of the people, clear self-knowledge, and vision (Lane et al., 1984, p. 73). As we move in this direction, I remind the reader once again of the overlapping and intermingled nature of the stories. The themes of the western direction emerge momentarily from the tapestry for examination, only to return to the entwined nature of the experience. Weaving out, weaving in ...

Good Hands

During the course, the wisdom keepers often told the pre-service teachers that work should be done using good hands. For the pre-service teachers, including April (PST), using good hands was about the attitude and the energy brought to their work: "The 'good hands' was something new to me but I really like that concept, and it's so true when you think about it. It's obvious [that] everything you feel is reflected in your creation." Courtney (PST) shared that having good hands was based in "knowing that what you're feeling inside will come out in the work that you do with your hands." April also described how having good hands included mental engagement: "You have to have a positive attitude about it, kind of having good hands, but with your mind ... positive thoughts so you're not frustrated, you're not shutting things out, you are open to learning new things." For Sara (PST), focusing on having good hands was a practical way to be present with the task at hand: "I think back to my other classes and a lot of the times I was there physically, but I had a hundred other things on my mind. So I wasn't really there, you know? But this class, I really tried to focus on what we were doing." The pre-service teachers also saw that invoking the use of good hands was a way to connect with the other people with whom they were working. It gave them a sense of peace and focus, even when there was much work to be done.

Leanne's comment at the beginning of this chapter speaks to the importance of getting out of a mental framework and engaging in more holistic, hands-on action with your good hands. As Charlene (WK) told me, it was important to act in a good way, getting "out of your head ... letting go of judgment ... working hard and work[ing] until it's finished." The wisdom keepers noted that the hands-on learning seemed to relax the pre-service teachers. As May (WK) said, her group told her "how nice it is to do something different than what they do in most of their classes ... It's like a different kind of learning for them. And they're just really excited about it and appreciative to be here." Danielle (PST) spoke of how the work had a meditative quality: "It's taking a step out of our [normal life], because we're so focused on just graduating and writing these tests. And it just made you stop and appreciate even working with your hands. And they talked about that calm that would come from it. It's so true – you just get mesmerized by the work. You keep going and going and going."

Good hands preparing cedar bark

The pre-service teachers got caught up in the process of working with the earth fibres so completely that it was as if the fibres themselves led the way in the creative process, reminiscent of James's description of the spiritual process of the Creator creating (in Chapter 1). Entering into the spirit of good hands led many of the pre-service teachers to work with the earth fibres above and beyond the normal time expectations of the course.

One concern brought up by Charlene was that, due to scheduling and shared space, the university environment at times "interrupted the groove" of the participants and caused breaks in the work just when things were at the height of engagement. Charlene spoke of how helpful it was to have a more permanent space, as was the case during the final week of the course. She described how this allowed for the natural rhythms of the learning process to occur and supported a good hands approach:

> To open up into work intuitively, emotionally, and spiritually within the university setting was a difficult thing to do. So I was so glad we actually had that room for a whole week. We didn't have to pack up and put back together again. I think that would be much more respectful from a cultural perspective if we could have a space that was designated our space [for the whole term]. It would also have allowed the students to come into that space more regularly, instead of just once a week.

While Charlene expressed the importance of having a space that would support the learning rhythms of the group, she also saw that "on the other hand, it was cool for the university, because that ... creativity, spirit, and emotional part was allowed to be built within" and embedded in the university structure as the course occupied various locations in the building. Hence, the qualities of good hands and of being positive, calm, focused, engaged, and committed travelled outwards like the ripples in a pond.

Giveaway

Throughout the earth fibres course, there was an expectation on the part of the wisdom keepers that the good of the community and the act of "Giveaway" should be kept in mind. The pre-service teachers picked up on the first of these quickly: as Chelsea (PST) said, it was important to "do your best work for the community's benefit, not just your own. So make it better for everyone." Work in the course was focused on the energy and intent of good hands for the good of the community and for the common goal of improving educational settings. Carolyn (WK) pointed out that this type of work was exciting and exhilarating "because you really are a part of each other's vision."

Working together towards a common goal gave the pre-service teachers a sense of group work that differed from that which they had experienced previously in the university setting. They talked about how common problems, like learning to thread a needle, brought them together and led them to support each other. They saw their individual work as clearly being part of a meaningful group project, which motivated them to do their best work and to take pride in that work. Chelsea, though she did not think of herself as artistic, said, "I had to make it look nice for the whole. It was my individual work, but it counted for everybody's in the final outcome, which was nicer because, I think if it was only my piece of work going up somewhere, maybe I wouldn't care. But because it was contributing to everyone's, I didn't want to let them down."

Another significant aspect of the group work was that, although there were high expectations, it was generally not a competitive environment. Leanne noticed "the energy and enthusiasm, the participation level, and the awareness in everybody. You almost leave everything else at the door when you come in there. It feels [like] it's just a different learning environment. And it's more of a community and everybody's there to help each other. It's not competitive." The pre-service teachers felt that people were taking the work seriously and that it was their job to help fellow classmates if they were struggling.

Although connections were strong within the small groups, some of the pre-service teachers felt disconnected from the other groups and wanted to have more contact with them and what they were doing. Overall, however, there was a sense of community, well described in this comment by Janet (WK):

> The Native and non-Native participation of the students was a beautiful thing to see. And [they were] just like little worker bees, you know? Having the opportunity to stand back every now and then and watching all these little hands go at it, and everyone's chatting, and sometimes they're sharing collectively, and sometimes just two people off to the side sharing, but they're still doing the work.

Within this busy context, the concept of Giveaway as part of the larger social context presented challenges for both wisdom keepers and pre-service teachers. The wisdom keepers spoke of how some indigenous people still have a "Give-away room" in their home, where things are kept until given away as needed or through ceremony such as potlatch. Wisdom keeper Lynne's husband James shared:

> Native ... teaching says that ... a wealthy person is not a person who has great wealth, who has stored all these things, is holding on to them. The wealthy person is a person who gives things away. The generous person is a wealthy person. And that really separates the Native people from the cultures that say your importance in society has to do with how much you have and how much you own, instead of how much you have to Giveaway.

The wisdom keepers spoke of not being sure how to share this teaching with the pre-service teachers. At one point, a wisdom keeper who had brought cups of tea to the other elders shared with me that she was "tired of modelling"

Giveaway types of behaviours. Lynne reiterated this weariness by saying that at times there was frustration around, for example,

> how to try and make the white people understand the Giveaway, and the need to *really* Giveaway. [The whites] are thinking, "Oh, I'll just Giveaway one thing." And I'm pushing everybody to at least have two, right? And ... I said, "I've done three or four because I want to be sure that at least we have five belts separate from the one we hang, because at least that much should be given out ... If we had our way ... we would have three hundred gifts, you know. Go buy three hundred bowls or something, and put them out."

Lynne believed that one of the reasons the pre-service teachers did not understand the concept of Giveaway was that they didn't realize that what they gave away would come back to them in some other form at some other, often unforeseen time. For example, the members of her small group were later invited to a pipe ceremony to honour their work in the course. At this ceremony they were gifted with many teachings, as well as an unexpected beaded medicine bag lovingly handcrafted by Lynne. To some degree Lynne may have planned this reciprocity of giving, but I sensed her deep faith in this principle beyond her offerings, as she recollected, "Native people are measured by what they Giveaway, not by what they have." The concept of good hands is about generosity, not about individual gain, and this is often a difficult concept for Euro-Western–oriented people to understand at its deepest levels.

In the wisdom keepers' culture, it is common to start teaching the concept of Giveaway at an early age, but the pre-service teachers did not have this experience. They struggled with the Giveaway concept in several ways. Some were surprised by the expectation that each group would make numerous items to set aside for the ceremony and at the quantity of gifts given out at the final mural unveiling. Some wanted to keep their creations for themselves as they had become attached to the product of their work. Some worried that their work wasn't good enough or that it would somehow detract from the work of others. Gay (WK) explained why, from her perspective, the pre-service teachers' concerns were unfounded:

> It's a real honour to get somebody's first thing ... It's a more special thing because we're not looking for perfection. And that is really hard to get across to the group because they kept wanting to be [perfect]. Like when they would see that work that we showed them – some of those moccasins ... are really

master craft moccasins ... – and I was saying, "We're not going to get that [level of skill]. That's just to show you where you can go. And those people have been at it for years. I mean, if you watch those ladies, it will take them less than a day to bead that moccasin that we were looking at, hey? But it is not perfection you're after. Because you're just learning and, as you go along, you get better and better and better."

Some of the pre-service teachers recognized that the wisdom keepers were more accepting of mistakes than they were used to in other learning situations. April thought that the expectation was to "just do your best, you know, not anyone else's best," and Sara understood that the focus should be on working with good hands: "You know, it's not the final product. And Charlene, she stood up there and said, 'Mine's not great but, you know, I put a lot of love and a lot of thought into it.' So I pondered over that for a while."

My own experience of true Giveaway work is that it can be extremely personal. As Carolyn pointed out, "You give so much of yourself." As Jade (PST) said, the pre-service teachers felt they were giving away a part of their lives in both the things they made and in the oral teachings they passed on:

> At first I was embarrassed to Giveaway what I had created, or even the skills that I had learned, because I wasn't really sure what I was doing myself. But in working with someone else, you kind of refine your skills, and it helps you ... The things I gave away, I was pretty embarrassed about because it's your first try, and you have to give that away. How many people Giveaway their first copy of an essay or anything like that, right? But the people who received it last night [at the ceremony], I hope they took the time to look at it and appreciate it for its beauty, even though it has flaws in some places, and, I don't know, just for the time and for good thoughts that went into that.

Jade went on to explain the complex layers of meaning in her first piece:

> I think that one piece that I created, that first finger weaving had *every* emotion you can possibly think of in there. It had all the frustration. And I think that's the best feeling I've ever felt to complete something, because I did have the struggles and I *did* have all of those feelings that you don't have very often, usually. I was glad to have it finished, but I was kind of sad that it was finished, because the second piece didn't evoke all those raw emotions I had the first time. It did, but not in the same way.

Gifts for the Giveaway

Another issue that came up was the idea that the pre-service teachers would not be able to control the direction of what they were giving away. It was disturbing to some that the gifts they had put all that energy into would be placed in a box and passed out randomly to the guests at the unveiling ceremony. They worried that the time and energy invested in their gifts would not be appreciated, and some said that it was easier to give something away to a specific person.

For the pre-service teachers, a deeper understanding of Giveaway was gradual and not fully embraced by all. This situation reflected the recognition of the wisdom keepers that the course was only a glimpse into the wider world of indigenous ways. Pre-service teacher Kevin's remarks about what he learned by giving away his creations suggest a deepened understanding of this concept:

KEVIN: These are things that I had more than a material interest invested in. They had some sentimental value attached to them ... [I was] giving away something that had ... not just a material value but also an experiential value. *That* is a learning opportunity.

MICHELE: What did you learn from that?

KEVIN: [It was] a departure. I mean, in life we have to deal with departures. Giving things away, giving up, and it's experience that you gain from that. You gain an expectation of what to expect of yourself and what you expect of others. It's not the same thing as giving away presents. Perhaps [it is] giving something of yourself away to other people ... Let me try to put it in this way – it was a part of my life and in that sense, it was significant and meant something of my life, so *that* I was giving away.

What Kevin described was a deeper giving away that actually altered who he was in a way that was profoundly intimate and reciprocal, keeping the good of the community in mind. This raises a very interesting issue in crosscultural understanding. Deeply held values such as Giveaway are difficult to communicate and difficult to embrace for those who have a very different worldview.

How Am I Using My Energy?

Within the context of the course, the pre-service teachers used both deep reflection and the practice of reflexivity to focus on being community-centred, learning from their soul, using good hands, and incorporating the idea of Giveaway. As Charlene said, if teachers "understand that change is from within themselves, they can then help other people to make that change." Through their other coursework, the pre-service teachers had been learning to be reflective practitioners. They acknowledged that, as Jade said, "The things that you grow up with aren't necessarily completely accurate," and that the process of reflection helped them to see that different people hold different beliefs. As well, they saw that a good teacher stays open to learning and that increasing their reflective skills would help them to become lifelong learners, to conceptualize better, to understand themselves as learners, to sort through their emotions, and to make sense of the jumble of teaching beliefs that Sara mentioned in Chapter 1.

Nicole (PST) talked about how, prior to the teacher education program, she had always learned by rote memory, without reflection:

I was ... not really encouraged to go outside the box, so to speak. I'm starting to learn for the sake of my own learning, now that I'm in the university setting, and because I'm becoming a teacher. It's part of [my] professional role ... I think being a teacher is what pushed me out of the box – realizing that if I want my students to take control of their own learning, I'm going have to take control of my own learning as well. So it was more of that role that's appearing in me as a teacher that pushed me outside the box, not the classes themselves, although I have had some very good professors that have pushed the limits.

At the same time, Garrett (PST) felt that within the teacher education program he was not given full independence in his struggle to find his way as a teacher:

GARRETT: [In the earth fibres course] I spend a lot of time thinking about ways that I would like to teach … It's ironic, but I don't really do that in my other classes. Even though they are education courses, I kind of feel disconnected. I kind of feel too much like a student in those other classes, and not like a future teacher, you know.

MICHELE: And do you have any sense of why that is?

GARRETT: I think it's just how our society works, that there's still so much emphasis on competitiveness and grading, and social hierarchies, and all of that. I think that's just the way it is and I would like to think that there's a better way out there. But it's a system, and I think it's just kind of a [hoop] that I'm feeling that I have to get through. You know, I'm just waiting for the day that I can sort of have my own classroom. But then again, I'm thinking that I'm going to be in the school system and there's still going to be limitations there.

Finding a balance between the dual roles of learner and teacher is difficult. At the beginning of the course, many of the pre-service teachers did not know how they should act or how they fit in. Nicole describes it as follows:

At first … I was confused, and all the students in my program, we were talking amongst each other like, "Well, what's this? What are we doing? What is expected of us? What are we getting graded on? What do we have to hand in?" And that was the main focus. And as we got used to it and shifted, it was more, "What are you working on? What does that look like? How did you do that? Was it difficult? What have you learned from the elder in your group?" We were talking more along those lines, instead of "What grade do you think you're going to get?"

Through engagement in the course, the pre-service teachers shifted their focus more naturally to the processes of learning. As Courtney said, "It's a teacher-student role that's created there." This is a subtle but important difference for the pre-service teachers who are often seen as "student teachers."

Teacher as learner, learner as teacher

The pre-service teachers felt that indigenous education was a more reflective kind of education and that the reflection was somehow embedded within the process of learning. The pre-service teachers appreciated how the unhurried pace of the earth fibres course gave them time to reflect in meaningful ways. One of the ways this was done was through keeping a personal journal. For some, it was a welcome time to sit quietly, think about things, and keep a written record of what had happened in the course. Sara explains the importance of the journal assignment and how it was appreciated because it was done differently from how it had been done in other courses:

> I think a big part of it was that the journals in the other classes were being checked every week. So it was kind of like, well, I'm going to write what my teacher wants to hear – quite honestly, right? And this journal [for the earth fibres course] was going to be summarized in a paper at the end, but it was my own thoughts and I didn't have to share them with anybody else. And so

I felt like I could write both positive and negative things. So that was really powerful for me because journaling, for me before, was just, "Well, let's write the good things, and the teacher will be happy, and I'll get a good mark," and everything was great, right?

The pre-service teachers felt that the final paper gave their journal a purpose and that they were actually excited to be writing it. Jayne (PST) shared the common feeling that the assignment was a more honest way of reflecting as it was tied first and foremost to learning: "It's more for me. And if I ever use journaling again, I hope to do that for my kids – that it's theirs, and it has nothing to do with grades or nothing to do with what you're supposed to say, or what I want you to say. Just reflect. Just learn and think about it."

Another type of reflecting happened in relationship with others, often through spontaneous and frequent conversations with peers. The pre-service teachers shared with me that these conversations helped them sort out what they were experiencing in the course and to discover different perspectives on the group work. The interviews for my study also became a vehicle for reflecting in community. They talked about doing some thinking before our meetings and that this process itself was reflective, as described by Sara: "A lot of stuff that I'm telling you is honestly coming out as you're asking the questions, you know? Like, I hadn't necessarily thought about all of these things before. So that's kind of neat too, for me. I think this has been another reflection opportunity for me, definitely."

A third type of reflection was embodied in more holistic experiences of doing. Charlene described the importance of engaging ways of knowing beyond thinking skills when reflecting:

That's the part I think is missing. [It would be good] if it was built into some of the courses, like, how do you go back into your heart? How do you get out of your head? How do you take and learn from all aspects of yourself? When do you take up the physical time to go move and walk? When do you take up the emotional time of, okay, yeah, that stuff really triggered this part here and now I can take that out and have a look at it? And then how do I close that down, and how do I integrate all of that back into being the whole of me? And what do I really want to focus on? And then go back to their regular daily lives.

She describes a process of opening to reflexivity and then closing down that reflexivity in order to continue with daily life. This is akin to the process of walking the medicine wheel, where one always returns to centre in order to move forward.

For the pre-service teachers, this recursive type of reflection was employed specifically at times when they were frustrated or anxious with their work. They consciously returned to the notion of using good hands and paying attention to the energy that was being used to produce something. Reflecting on how they were actively engaging a concept such as good hands was sometimes hard to do; they said they couldn't always find the words to describe what they were feeling. Gay pointed out that reflection sometimes meant paying attention to the outward signs that might suggest inner feelings:

> I don't know what my mom would call it in her language, but when you pick up a piece of work, you only work on it so long, because you don't want to get sick of it. So you put it down and then you don't force yourself and say, "I've gotta work on this for many times of the day and finish it by this time." There's no real deadline ... And most artists, you don't work when you're in that funny space. There's all kinds of signs, like when you break your needle. And that one girl [in my group], she had to break the needle three times. It was trying to tell her, "You're not in a good space to be doing this. You shouldn't be doing it." And it took the third needle breaking before she would figure it out.

The pre-service teachers had different stories about reflecting on their frustration, particularly regarding the cattail mats. They felt strongly that the crafts on which they worked were somehow physical extensions of themselves; as some of them wrestled with the earth fibres, they began to look more closely and reflexively at themselves and their role in the frustration they were experiencing. Leanne explains:

> It's a confusing thing because it's obviously just my perspective on something. But, when you're working on homework or something, and that frustrates you, then you can kind of dismiss it and [say,] "It's just [the] homework ... That's the reason that I'm mad ... *That's* the problem." But then when you're working with something with your hands, and it's something more artistic, and more of a therapeutic something, if that frustrates you, then you really have to think, "Okay, it's not like it's this piece's problem." You know what I mean? Because you just have to think, "Okay, well what about this is making me frustrated? Why am I getting angry right now? ... If it's my homework and I'm frustrated with that, I really put it on the textbook ... And maybe my

frustration level is something that I should be looking at and not be pushing it off onto something else."

Leanne went on to say that she needed to embrace patience and use it as a reflective tool to look inward at her own beliefs and ideas and emotions.

For Sara, reflecting on the difficulties of the cattail experience was a way of paying attention to how she was using her energy to produce her work:

I found myself so frustrated with it. And I just put it aside. I thought, "I can't do this. It's too hard. I don't know how to do it. I need more guidance" or whatever. And then, we had another class, and they talked about putting good thoughts and good energy into your work and turning that frustration into something positive. Like, okay, I'm frustrated, but I am learning things. So, now I've taken that frustration, I've put it into good energy. And amazingly, I went home and I finished [the mat]. [*Laughter*] So you know, I think it made me reflect on [how] something like that can be such a powerful learning experience, you know? Whereas before, I probably would have thought, "Oh, this is a fun art project. Great." But, I really did think about my learning and how I was using my energy to produce something ... and I thought, "Okay, now it comes back to taking responsibility for my own learning."

Underlying the frustration about the cattails was a sense of overall impatience, which many spoke about in our conversations. Danielle mentioned how this was tied to a personal feeling of pressure to produce efficiently:

One big thing [that stood out for me] is how impatient I realized I am ... especially towards the end of the course when we were trying to get it wrapped up, and [I found myself saying] "Oh, it's in a week, and we have to get everything done." And I was like, "Okay, come on, let's go, let's go, let's start working!" And, you know, they're taking time to pray and think about their hands and everything. And I was like, calm down. Like, I'm totally always on time and always go by my watch. So I learned how impatient I am. And just to stop. And you know, the quality is more important than getting it done on time.

The wisdom keepers were aware of the pre-service teachers' need for speed and tried to explain to them that they would miss other significant teachings besides the importance of quality, if they didn't slow down. Gay would say to her group:

"No, no, no! I know we have to be finished; I understand that. But you can lose the enjoyment of the whole thing and that will partly alter your learning. And I can't explain it otherwise because in order to get that far, you want to also absorb it. If you speed along, you might be missing something and you may not even realize it. It's nothing I can teach you even. It's the process you have to go through." And that was the difficult part, trying to tell them, "No, no, you don't have to be speedy!"

Being witness to the patience of the wisdom keepers was a graphic reminder of how to embody patience. Many of the pre-service teachers talked about how the wisdom keepers took time to show them how to untangle their knots and how to fix things they felt weren't right. In my conversations with the pre-service teachers, I noticed how their increased awareness of patience was transferred into patience for themselves as learners. Many of them narrated examples of undoing and re-stitching work that they were unhappy with, and as Danielle described, some applied patience to their practice of reflection:

Having the patience to reflect ... is absolutely useful. It's huge. It helps so much. It's been a task for me, though; I've had to learn how to do it. I don't do it naturally. I just do something and then I move on. So actually having to sit down and think about it, you learn so much about yourself especially and how you do things.

Along with gaining more patience, some of the pre-service teachers talked about their tendency to be perfectionists. Most of them had always been top students who held themselves to high work standards. The course helped them to think carefully about what perfection meant to them. In an interview with Sara I suggested to her that she seemed to be re-defining what perfection meant. She replied:

Yeah, definitely, that's a good way of putting it, which was huge for me because I'm one of those people who wants to be the best at everything. And I want mine to be better than everybody else's. And when you say it out loud, it sounds so immature and silly, because it should be trying to be the best for

A unique cattail mat

yourself, not for other people. So, it sounds so silly, from a little project, but I was amazed at how much I did learn from it.

Sara's reply indicated that she was moving towards honouring her endogenous processes as a learner and that she was driven by internal motivation instead of an external sense of perfection.

Ceremony

From the beginning of the course, many of the pre-service teachers and wisdom keepers commented on how little they knew about what the finished mural was going to look like. Despite this not knowing, they showed incredible commitment and perseverance to the huge task before them. Jade spoke about how things began to come together shortly before the piece was unveiled:

Once we finally had most of our pieces together ... Charlene laid out the canvas for the first time, and I realized how huge it was going to be and how much work everybody did put into that. It was amazing because, working

The unveiling of the mural

in your group, you're like, "Oh, this little sash, it's not going to be much to display." But [the whole mural] turned out beautiful.

Many spoke of being surprised and pleased to finally get to know XAXE SIÁM SILA~Honoured Grandmother of Many Generations: Wise, Learned, and Respected as Mother Earth. There is an interesting counterpoint here between individual works and the equally important need to be accountable to the relationships of the group. There is a delicate yet powerful balance to be struck in following a personal path while at the same time trying to be mindful of the larger picture. It is an ebb and flow, breathing out ... and breathing in ... a different definition of perfection indeed.

For the six pre-service teachers in my study who could attend, the community unveiling ceremony of the finished mural was a full-circle experience. It was a chance to show off their hard work, celebrate, interact with the community, connect with the stories of the ancestors, and tell the story of their

Attending to detail

experiences in the course. This took place with important family members, friends, and the community at large. They spoke of being nervous and proud when they stood in front of the larger audience to share their part of the story. As they spoke and listened to each other, the pride and dedication the pre-service teachers and wisdom keepers felt towards the mural was evident. As Heather (PST) said,

> It was just an amazing dedication of a lot of people's time to make the project go, especially with the delays and everything that happened. It's really phenomenal that so many people felt so passionately about the class and about the project that they put in all those hours and did all that really good-quality, great work. I think that was really powerful for me.

The pre-service teachers were also proud of the work that they did in the earth fibres course in ways that differed from their pride in their work for other classes. They spoke of how they were excited to do their homework, go to meetings outside of regular class hours, and re-do work that wasn't quite right. This was due in large part to their feeling of creative ownership. In addition, they felt that the course gave them a place to be able to put in the care and attention necessary to nurture pride in their work rather than just get the assignment done. They were also affected by the fact that the piece would be displayed in the MacLaurin Building. Leanne talked about how her dedication brought out her undivided attention and seemingly limitless effort towards the goal of the group:

Learning and Teaching Together

I helped stitch some of the hands that were on the bottom [of the mural] and so at first I did hand stitching. It was so tedious because I had a crappy little pin that wouldn't go through the two fabrics together, but I did them all. And I looked at them, and they didn't look good, you know? And I was, like, this is going to go up in UVic and yeah, sure, I spent three hours stitching these, but they didn't look good. And so I unstitched all of them and I started over, which was another three, four, I don't even know how many hours. But, it doesn't matter. Time didn't matter.

The ceremony had a sense of stepping out of time as well. Many of the pre-service teachers spoke of having to actively engage their patience as the long evening unfolded. Before the guests arrived, there was much excitement and anxiety while the finishing touches were placed on the piece. The ceremony protocol was unfamiliar to the pre-service teachers, and some felt anxious about not knowing what would happen. They also worried that their lack of knowledge might somehow ruin the ceremony. They talked about adjusting to the slower pace and getting used to standing and waiting. Many also noted how patient the wisdom keepers were about the pre-service teachers' learning as things unfolded.

There was some concern among the pre-service teachers as to whether there should have been more explicit information given to themselves and the audience to explain what was going on. Garrett observed:

[During the ceremony] I spent a lot of time looking in the audience and watching people who had no idea what was going on and remembering how I was in those shoes once. I was sort of feeling sympathetic for them because they were getting kind of restless, you know. It was a whole learning experience for them – for me, too, but I sort of knew what was going on. So it was neat to see how there was such a learning gap, a knowledge gap, a cultural sort of gap there ... When they were doing the blanketing and all that, I was thinking that there should be like a play-by-play analysis, giving the audience sort of a heads' up of what was going on. But then I thought, you know, that wouldn't be right.

Garrett's comments articulate his process of releasing anxiety and becoming comfortable with not knowing. Many of the other pre-service teachers at the ceremony were also able to see their own growth as patient participants in the ceremony. Throughout the evening, the uneasy feelings settled and often disappeared as the pre-service teachers lost track of time and relaxed into listening.

The listening of the evening was deep and important. Stories were told about the other small groups, and about the lives of the wisdom keepers. We listened to stories told by members of the larger indigenous community. Members of the university community spoke, and we gained a deeper sense of the effort it took, on the part of both the university and the indigenous community, to have a course like this take place. Danielle spoke of gaining a deeper sense of history and how that might be brought forward to change the sense of ownership within the university setting:

> DANIELLE: I just realized how important this course is, and how different it is, and how nice and refreshing it is than a regular, sit down and study this [type of course].
>
> MICHELE: What do you see as being important about it?
>
> DANIELLE: Learning who came before us. What they are all about. What they stand for ... to learn about cultures that are *so* close to our everyday life but we just don't really see or acknowledge. But now it's starting to come more in the university, and I think [the dean] is doing a really great job of bringing that in. One of the other speakers was saying how I hope [First Nations people] feel more comfortable coming into this environment and realize that we do acknowledge that they were here first, and it is their land. And yeah, we don't just take it for granted that this is the university, and *we're* supposed to be here.

In addition to gaining this type of deeper sense of history, some pre-service teachers acknowledged that they hadn't realized the extent to which indigenous people were forced to adapt in order to be a part of universities and schools. They said that hearing the community stories at the ceremony gave a clearer picture of the reasons people felt unwelcome.

The ceremony fostered within the wisdom keepers recognition of the personal significance of the course experience for themselves and recognition of the work they did as women. In addition to the pieces created in the course, the mural displayed earth fibre textiles from women located throughout Turtle Island (North America). Thus, XAXE SIÁM SILA embodies ancient wisdom passed down, through the creation of earth fibre textile pieces, over time and place. As Jade said,

Learning and Teaching Together

Honouring the wisdom keepers

I just [saw] the empowerment *for* women and, just when they were speaking last night, you could *feel* it, you could feel the meaning and how deep it was. It was just so strong ... And it's not very often that women get a chance to shine like that and have *ceremonies* based around their work and songs written about them, and I thought that was great, too. I don't know, just to show what's kind of been in the background of history, and display its importance and how it's been passed down and remains really prominent in these women's lives, and that *they* were able to share with us.

The pre-service teachers recognized that not only were women being acknowledged but the mural was significant as a representation and welcoming of indigenous cultures within the university. Again, Jade comments:

[It's significant] to display something in the university that's of a different culture than the university culture. I mean, you look at some of these buildings, they have gray walls and there's not a lot of culture anywhere in these buildings – regardless of the culture, there's nothing. And so to have something displayed that's of someone's culture and has importance to them, it's just nice to be a part of that. To help other people feel welcomed – as welcomed as maybe I've always felt at university.

The pre-service teachers who were able to attend the ceremony felt it was a significant event in terms of bringing a sense of completion or of coming full circle to their understanding of local Aboriginal culture. They shared that it was great to end a course on such a positive note of celebration, rather than in the stressful energy of an exam. They felt that their hard work had really been honoured and that the ceremony gave them a chance to step back and engage in further reflection. Garrett said,

> Having the celebration the way we did was a good ending, it sort of wrapped everything up … That's not usually what happens in a typical course here. You know, you hand in your assignments, you say your goodbyes briefly, and then that's it. You move on to the next course … I don't know if I'll ever have a chance to take another course like this. So, it was a good way to end it.

Unfortunately, the other pre-service teachers in my study were frustrated that they were unable to attend the ceremony. The ceremony had originally been scheduled inside of the regular university term timetable. The extensive nature of the work involved with finishing the mural, as well as cancellations of some class and external meeting times due to weather and other issues, caused the ceremony to be pushed back to the month following the end of term. At this point, many of the pre-service teachers were in practicum settings away from campus or had previous commitments; they were disappointed to not be able to help with the finishing efforts or to attend the ceremony. Leanne, who was able to attend the ceremony, expressed some of the intensity of the final days:

> I have so much respect for everybody that pulled it together … in the last couple of weeks … I mean, I went out to Charlene's house [for a work session], but I know that there was a lot of background work, and that not everybody contributed. So that was a small handful of people really doing a huge amount of work. And the little amount of work that I did, I can really appreciate how much more went into it … Charlene had a great vision and was able to pull it off. And it looks spectacular … I wish I could have been there more and I wish that there had been more time that worked with my schedule. And I feel bad for taking credit for something that is so much bigger than anything I put into it … I'm disappointed, in a way, because it wasn't as cohesive at the end

as it was at the beginning, but, I mean, you can't really help that – the snow days and whatever. And now we're on our practicums and that's huge, so it's just hard to give up that time, right?

Charlene was also paying attention to the way in which the course ended, and was saddened by the lack of closure:

I was trying very much to do it in a cultural way. But some of my frustration – although I was willing to let go and just let whatever needed to happen, happen – was that we never got to the end part with everybody working on the main larger piece. And there [were] so many teachings that were to come in that part there, that I had held back ... There were very few of them [at the ceremony], but maybe [they were] the ones that were meant [to be there] and could hear ... My plan had been to have a full end part for them to round everything and tie everything together. And to show how those teachings that they were learning in their smaller groups were actually very much the same as what this overall piece is.

Charlene said that these teachings would be difficult for her to write down and so she had hoped that there could be another gathering where she and the other wisdom keepers could share what remained to be said. There were discussions about having another ceremonial gathering when the mural was installed in its permanent spot in the MacLaurin Building, in order to have, as Charlene said,

one final evening where we can come together and just have even a little bit of reflection time of completion. Yes, our baby's finally in its proper place, in its respectful way, and here are some of the other things that maybe not everybody was aware of, like about what each moon time was. [It would give time for] the rest of the teachings [to be] offered and available.

Almost three years after the unveiling, a simple installation and Grandmother honouring ceremony did take place. It was attended by some of the wisdom keepers and also current University of Victoria staff and students. XAXE SIÁM SILA is now on permanent display in the Curriculum Lab located in the MacLaurin Building. She is a welcome, appreciated, and integral piece of this dynamic location.

5

Focusing on How and Why We Teach

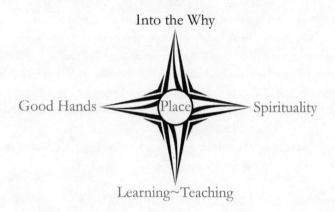

Closer to the end of our time together … it was interesting to watch how
quickly [people] could act from their heart. Turning [their thinking] part
off and just being in their spirit, and in their heart and letting their hands
flow. It took a lot less time to make the quietness in the class and the
peacefulness in the class happen, and it took less pulling, and less of
my energy because … it was already becoming automatic.

– Charlene, WK

The northern direction of the wheel is about elders, wisdom, thinking, understanding, organizing, imagining, interpreting, moderation, completion, freedom
from knowledge, seeing how all things fit together, intuition made conscious,
and the capacity to dwell in the centre of things, to see and take the middle way
(Lane et al., 1984, p. 73).

In this chapter, I draw increasingly from the data gathered in the post-
practicum focus groups that reflect how the pre-service teachers' conceptual
thinking was made more complex in the process of actual classroom teaching.
I have also included some of the oral image data from the interviews, as well as

sketched images from the focus group session notebooks. These images help to illustrate a conceptual movement away from images of the teacher as a facilitative and directive type of personality towards images of learners and teachers entering into a more symbiotic relationship, similar to the ones experienced in the earth fibres course.

Into the Why

The course provided participants with a unique opportunity to see the world from a different perspective. The pre-service teachers said repeatedly that the experience was deeper, more real, and gave them more personal connections than their previous learning about other cultures, particularly learning gathered from textbooks. As Kevin (PST) said, the course "started to unlock a picture" of another culture, where it was possible to "appreciate the actual work that goes into people's beliefs [and] knowledge." This was true even for those who had previous experiences with indigenous culture, as Nicole (PST) discussed with me:

> NICOLE: I had always seen ceremonial dances, and I've been to sweat lodges and things like that. I knew the basics, like the food, the dance, the traditional wear, but I didn't know why those things were important – why salmon is so important in the culture. I didn't know why often things are done slowly and there's not much emphasis on time or schedule. I didn't know those sorts of things. I think I've learned more about that now, and about the history of it and why it's important, that sort of connection.
> MICHELE: You seem to be moving beyond the feasts, festivals, and fashion understanding of culture, into a little bit deeper ...
> NICOLE: Yeah, into the why.

April (PST) tried to explain how she was developing an understanding that indigenous people have a fundamentally different worldview:

> It's more about the spiritual and the worldview of it. Not, like, what did they eat, and how did they catch the salmon in the river. That stuff doesn't blow my mind. I think it's amazing that they lived off the land for thousands of years and that they were so a part of the cycle, and not disconnected like we've done to ourselves, you know? That's amazing, but it's not exactly [what I mean]. It's just the spiritual, and the knowledge side of it, the way it's different.

Like many of their peers, April and Nicole were beginning to grasp, in an embodied way, the existence of cosmologies that differed from their own, and their excitement about this was palpable.

Through the course, the pre-service teachers clarified misperceptions they had of indigenous culture. They also built on knowledge they had gathered from other courses. For example, Courtney (PST) spoke of how her earth fibres experience overlapped with her experience in a biology class on people's use of plants, commenting on how the biology course had not incorporated indigenous uses of the land and plant life. The wisdom keepers also became more aware of other cultures and spoke about their excitement learning new ways of weaving and working with the earth fibres.

There was recognition that the course acknowledged indigeneity and gave it a voice in ways that were deeply respectful and representative of the culture. Heather (PST) said,

> I think something that's important is that it's the point of view from that culture. It's not me looking at a culture and explaining to someone else about that culture. Because, I mean, who am I to say that? And I think that to have all the different cultures come together and be able to share personally what their culture is to them is a real first-hand look, rather than having kind of a second-hand judgment.

Janet (WK) echoed this deeper way of appreciating, saying that she felt the course was successful because

> people have now walked away with a tangible, and emotional, and educational, and spiritual experience that will stay with them ... And seeing [the culture this way] takes the curiosity aspect out of it, when you invite people in and say, "Okay, get your hands dirty, clean this fish," or whatever. And it removes that whole let-me-be-a-tourist-to-your-culture kind of thing.

Many pre-service teachers spoke about realizing the importance of not trying to assimilate everyone into one culture. As Leanne (PST) said, she wanted "to really keep it diverse and acknowledge all of that, not just on a superficial level but on a much deeper level ... to bring pride and to bring acknowledgment, and to bring other cultures in. And just to give that insight into other ways of thinking because I think each culture has such a different way of approaching ideas." They hoped to transfer that positive and deeper way of looking at culture to their teaching and said that the course helped them relate better to indigenous people and made them feel more prepared to teach indigenous students. Nicole said:

> I think learning about the culture helps me understand First Nations people more and appreciate it more and the work that they do. And if there's a child in my class that's First Nations, I'll be able to make those adjustments as well. Like, I know now ... if one of their brothers is having a naming ceremony, they're going to be up all night, and they might not be ready to go to school the next day. And [I know now] to make those adjustments, because it's just a different culture. You know, learning about the culture helps a lot. And I still have a lot to learn, but I think knowing a bit more will really help me connect with those students, too.

The post-practicum focus groups revealed that the pre-service teachers felt more comfortable after the course to share the historical knowledge that they had gained (e.g., the stories behind the textiles on the mural or the purpose of Giveaway). They also felt interested in actively seeking out a deeper understanding of local cultures and expressed being more comfortable asking Aboriginal people questions. At the same time, some pre-service teachers were cautious about this, and spoke of simply trying to be open to when and what Aboriginal students wanted to share in the classroom. All felt it was their role to provide a comfortable and welcoming place for sharing to occur. I was heartened to hear the depth of their ability to be sensitive to the ebb and flow of these relationships.

The pre-service teachers saw that they had increased content knowledge about the cultures of the people involved in the course, but the experience went beyond this to a deeper sense of learning through taking a reflexive stance. Sara (PST) discussed with me how the course helped her to understand the learning of others more fully, by paying careful attention to her own learning process:

> SARA: I see two sides for sure, one side being ... about the content that I will be teaching and the appreciation for culture that I'll be teaching. Not just the different ways to represent animals and what totem poles are and that sort of thing. It's more like, well, what is the whole picture here, and what does the whole culture mean? And I think I can do a better job of that. I think I still need support for that by having people from the community come in, but I certainly can do a better job of it now. Definitely.

MICHELE: So there's a depth of understanding that wasn't there before?

SARA: Oh yeah, definitely. And the [other] side [of what I learned] would be the patience and the understanding for the different ways of learning, and uniqueness, and taking the time to really teach the whole child ... That comes from me getting a better understanding of myself through the course ... So I think they're two different things.

MICHELE: They're kind of related though, aren't they?

SARA: They are, yeah. Because that patience and understanding is a big part of the culture, so I think they are connected in that way.

MICHELE: It seems like you have a deeper understanding of yourself somehow, and you have a deeper understanding of their culture. They're different things, but there is a depth that has shifted on both of them a little bit?

SARA: Yep, definitely. And it was hard for me to accept that because I thought, is that really coming from that course? Or am I just trying to make something from nothing? But I think, part of it has come from the course and part of it has come from the skill of reflection that I've gained from the course ... It's not necessarily [the specific content] from the course, it's the skills and the things that you learn about yourself that allow you to learn more about other things.

Many others expressed similar increased confidence in regard to content knowledge about indigenous culture. Sara's second type of learning about reflexive practice and how others experienced it is illuminated more fully in the next section.

Feeling It Deep Down

The earth fibres course was an opportunity to experience learning and teaching from another perspective in concrete and deeply felt ways. April said the course left her "feeling it deep down, believing it completely," as opposed to courses in which she was told what to do by instructors, rather than being shown the pedagogy in action. Jade (PST) spoke further about how the course involved a deeper sharing of knowledge compared to a transmissive-style course:

The learning process that I experienced in that class was from someone else's heart to my heart, from my heart to someone else's heart. So it was definitely deeper than just, "This is what I know; remember it." It's a different kind of learning for me, so it kind of shifts my whole vision that I had going into this course.

The experience altered the conceptual beliefs that many held before coming into the course. Often, it reinforced their existing beliefs and gave them more confidence about those beliefs amidst school and university environments that did not support the same ideas.

There were five key concepts that the course brought to the fore of the pre-service teachers' thinking. These concepts echo the themes in the wisdom keepers' approach to learning and teaching and were often described through the use of both oral and sketched images.

Teaching the whole child. In the focus groups, the pre-service teachers talked about how, in the contexts of their practica, they were able to observe the holistic needs of their learners. These needs included learning styles and ways of developing beyond the intellect, to include creativity, motor skills, and each learner's unique personality. Sara consciously worked to find a different image of the learner than the vacuum cleaner image she thought of during her initial interview. After the course, she saw the learner as being represented by an image of the Earth because it was more holistic and complex. Heather's post-course image had to do with the learner as a swimmer who could choose one of many rivers, each of which represents a way of knowing:

> My picture is an ocean, and there are all these different rivers, there's a whole bunch. So there are kids swimming and they can pick whatever river. And I guess the rivers kind of symbolize different ways of learning … hands-on learning, or auditory, or whatever … It's going to be different for everyone. And as long as they get into a river and they are swimming, that's your goal [as a teacher].

For the pre-service teachers, teaching the whole child meant teaching beyond the curriculum, particularly paying attention to life skills and social responsibility. Jade spoke about her practicum within a primary class:

> I found that I was teaching a lot of life skills and not a whole lot of content … It wasn't at all what I expected … Kids don't know how to deal with their own issues, … which was tough because you kind of have to throw out your math lesson to deal with some of these issues right away when they are fresh … During centre time, you'll have six kids come up to you saying, "So-and-so won't let me play" or "So-and-so won't let me do this." And you're spending so much of your own energy solving all those problems, so you have to give them the tools and the language to be able to do that themselves.

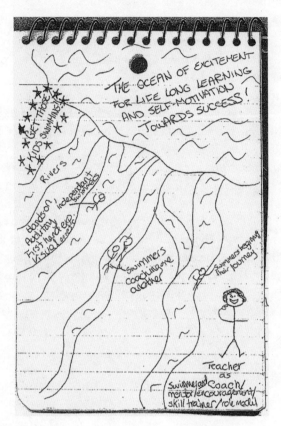

Page from Heather's focus group notebook

Others spoke about similar experiences, needing to address the whole child in this way while following the formal, intellectually focused curriculum.

Interconnected relations. After their practica experiences, the pre-service teachers understood more fully that learning was very much embedded in social processes beyond the learner-teacher relationship. Courtney was unhappy with her original image of the learner as a flower. The following quotation refers to a hand-drawn sketch in the bottom left corner of this entry in her focus group notebook:

> I had earlier in my interviews always talked about the flower and the garden because we use it in our courses, and it's been done. And so I then drew a flower with a cross through it because I've decided I don't like that to use as my representation of learning and teaching. [*Laughter*] But it keeps coming,

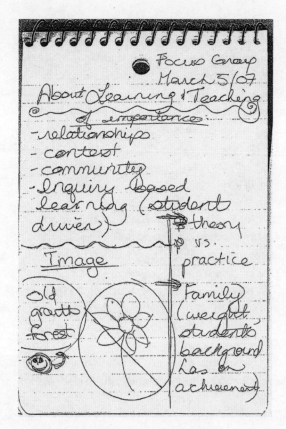

Page from Courtney's focus group notebook

like … this curse in my head. So I then tried to think further, and I came up with the image of an old-growth forest, which I like the image of. And I'll work on that one in my mind for a little bit to try to replace the flower and the garden … I don't like [the flower] because it gives the impression that each kid is their own entity. And it doesn't really represent the interconnectedness that I think that teaching, and just humankind in general, has. So I would prefer to stick to an image that shows those interconnected relations a little bit more.

Leanne spoke of the learner as being embedded in a series of concentric circles, where the learner is situated in the centre within the class group, within the school, and ultimately within the community. Garrett (PST) explained how this embeddedness is more complex within a multicultural classroom:

Children need ... a social context, an environment where they can learn from each other and share their knowledge. And that's especially true when there is a mixture of students, a mixture of ways of knowing. Like when you have an Aboriginal kid in a classroom, like I do, [who is] feeling sort of on the edge and sort of not really feeling in tune with everyone else's learning style and what's going on. I don't think that there's a [supportive] social process going on with her ... I think that needs to be in place ... I think you always need to have people to fall back on. And also feel comfortable and confident that you can step outside your comfort zone and go on your own and discover and explore in an individual way.

In Garrett and Leanne's conceptualizations, the concentric circles became a support system where there was ebb and flow, a representation of the symbiotic relationship between the learner and the members of the various communities. Remembering his experience as the "rose man" (see page 89), Garrett spoke of how teachers can take a gentle offering approach: "What happened with me with the rose and Carolyn [WK] showing me the way, but not staying with me ... I think there's a process there where it's social, and then individual, and then social, and then maybe individual again."

April shared how teachers needed to "create boundaries" so that the learners have guidance about acceptable behaviours because

teaching and learning happens for everyone when you have that space where everyone feels accepted to be themselves, because ... they'll contribute more from themselves, which creates better ideas and thoughts, and a more comfortable sharing atmosphere. And that way you're not just learning with the teacher or one person, but you're learning from everyone around you.

Danielle's (PST) image of a tree supported the notion of symbiosis among learner, teacher, and community, while reflecting Courtney's notion of a rainforest.

The teacher is equal to the students. In one of the focus group sessions, there was much agreement with Danielle when she said, of the learner-teacher relationship, "Learning is a two-way street. You teach as much as you learn, and they learn as much as, hopefully, you'll teach." Chelsea (PST) said that it was common to "think of a teacher as being higher than a student. But I don't think that's really right anymore." In the initial interviews, many of the pre-service teachers did not consider themselves to be teachers within the context of the earth fibres course. After thinking more carefully, however, they all found

Page from Danielle's focus group notebook

examples of how they had moved in and out of the teacher role. In addition, they saw teachers as lifelong learners who didn't necessarily need to be experts to be able to share or teach something.

In their classrooms, the pre-service teachers wanted to incorporate ideas of mutual respect in the learner-teacher relationship, where the student was treated, as Chelsea said, "like an equal human being." Nicole's image demonstrated this equalizing in the classroom: "I did a little drawing of stick people standing in a circle. [*Laughter*] So that the teacher is equal with the students, is part of the circle, and learns as much as they do. And then the students teach one another, as well as the teacher." Many also saw how co-teaching, particularly with indigenous community members, would be useful in their classrooms. As Heather said,

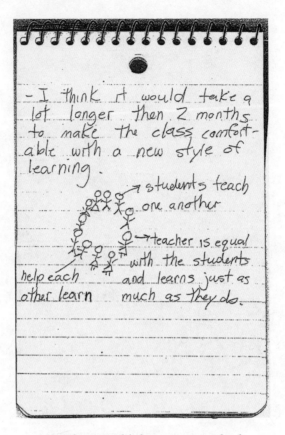

Page from Nicole's focus group notebook

It was really important for me to see how powerful it could be to have other people in the classroom teaching and for me not to necessarily feel ownership for teaching every element of the lesson. To say there are people who can do this better than I can. And that's going to serve my students way more than me trying to do something that isn't necessarily where I am strongest.

Here, Heather was letting go of her need for "teacher perfection," allowing the learner to breathe. As well, there was movement away from a unidirectional and transmissive conceptualization of edication, as Jade explained:

[Learning is] not just receiving. I think to truly learn, you also have to give it to someone else. And I think that's how you learn best and how you realize you've learned something. I mean, if you just take something in, it's not learning because you're not reflecting on it; you're not going deeper. So I think by sharing with someone else what you've learned, or what you've taken in, that helps you internalize it and that helps you realize your growth and reflect on your growth. It's definitely new to me compared to what I've experienced before, which is if you have it down [in your notes], you've learned something. If you can repeat it, you've learned something ... I think you can only remember things for so long, like facts. And ... a week from now, is that really learning if you don't carry that with you? So, I think something that you can take with you and share with people is something you've truly learned.

Jade's comments also reflect shifting beliefs towards a focus on learning rather than content. As Sara said, "It's not about finishing your work and handing it in and getting a sticker. It's about, what have you learned, and how can you use that?"

How does it touch their lives? Many pre-service teachers reiterated Sara's thoughts on the importance of relevancy in the learning process. Kevin talked about how tapping into a student's sense of relevancy could increase learning:

A lot of the students in my classroom, sometimes they just don't [learn] because it's not relevant to them. One little kid, he likes lizards and dinosaurs. If it's lizards and dinosaurs, [*clicks fingers*] spot on! ... So, does the child know what he or she is doing and wanting? Do they want to do it or need it? That's one thing [to keep in mind] in terms of planning and implementing a lesson, and understanding where your student is coming from and where you need to go with them.

The following quotation from April shows some of the tricky terrain that teachers need to navigate to keep learning relevant:

When it's not relevant, perhaps that's our job as teachers to ... show the students how it is relevant so that they can have that same excitement about what they're learning. Because when push comes to shove, we still have content that we're obliged to cover. But I would find it difficult to come up with any content that, when you really look at it, isn't relevant to our lives. So maybe that's what we need to do and work on as teachers, is showing them how it is relevant. A challenge easier said than done, especially when it comes to some of those social studies, history-related outcomes. But it could be done, I'm sure.

Others in April's focus group agreed that it was challenging to engage learners, and that teachers needed to be creative and keep learning hands-on. Heather expressed a shared belief that they would now be able to teach cultural issues in more relevant ways:

> I think I definitely have a different way of approaching how to teach cultural elements, especially social studies. I think to not teach that second-party culture lesson is really important, and to try to go away from textbook and into [the] real world. How is this going to affect you as a person, and how does that touch your life? And is that relevant to you in your life? And I think that applies to every lesson. Because students are going to be way more engaged and way more willing to give of themselves if they can see how it will help them, if they can see how it relates to them.

A more natural way to learn. The pre-service teachers made a number of points about a more natural way to learn. First, they wanted to help each child find their strengths as learners and wanted to do this in a way that resonated with each learner. Jayne (PST) said,

> In the past couple weeks [when planning], I've already thought, "Okay, what's a more natural way to learn this?" I can see that already happening with me … that I will take my Prescribed Learning Outcomes, and my Integrated Resource Packages, and then I'll say, "Now here's the actual kid, not the make-believe kid. Here's the real kid, and how can I make them naturally learn this in a very organic way?" I don't know if I'm saying it the right way but just not in the constructs of what I was taught like.

April's image also addressed student autonomy:

> I drew a picture, I don't really know why. It's an easel, and … a palette, and a paintbrush. I think the picture represents not the teacher, but the learner … I think the learner is the one who has control of what they want to do, what kind of picture they want to draw, whether or not they even pick up their paintbrush, or how detailed they want to do their work, and stuff like that.

Second, the pre-service teachers felt that it was important for teachers to read the learners' needs, as Nicole said, so that learners can learn at their "own pace and time"; even if it takes a couple of weeks, "it should be okay for those kids to take that time."

Page from Jade's focus group notebook

Third, the pre-service teachers said it was important for teachers to assess the learners' needs and maybe play a different role from that of academic mentor. Courtney gave an example of what that could look like in the classroom:

I've seen it actually in other classrooms where the kids have ongoing work, and they figure out what they need to work on. And yeah, that sounds normal at the grade five, six, seven level, but even down in the primary grades, teaching those skills of [balancing], you know, "This is what we need to get through. What's best for you right now? And what do you need extra help on? What do you feel like working on?" Because we're so often with our kids saying, "Nope, now it's social studies time. You all have to do social studies." And there's some kid in the back corner whose brain is racing, and what he needs to do is something that is kinesthetic or whatever.

The pre-service teachers spoke of how, in their future classrooms, they would be more likely to give this kind of space to their students so that they could be more actively engaged in their own learning process.

Jade's image encapsulates the processes of adjustment to incorporating the fundamental complexities of an indigenous pedagogy:

> It's not exactly what I want it to look like. [It is] a Celtic circle, or a Celtic ring, and it represents that everything in life is interconnected, no matter what you do. So … teaching and learning, you can't be learning without teaching, you can't be teaching without learning. Because when I'm teaching, I'm learning so much about myself, about my philosophy and how I feel. As well as learning from the kids … And it's a different picture than what I saw last time … It's just a bit of a different symbol. Before, mine was a circle or something like that, so it's still that ongoing continuous process. It's just that there's a lot more paths involved in my new vision. And just how everything is so interconnected.

After the course, the pre-service teachers' conceptualizations of learning and teaching had shifted. They held a stronger view of needing to teach the whole child and saw teachers as having a more equal and less directive role with the learner. They emphasized the relational aspect of learning and spoke frequently about the importance of making learning relevant and meaningful. The realities of their practicum settings, however, challenged these learnings, as will be discussed in Chapter 10. For now, the first cycle of the wheel is complete; the initial stories shared in the interviews and focus groups have been told. A new cycle begins.

6

Trusting Learners and Remembering Wholeness

The wheel spirals on, into a new layer of attending to the stories. Here, I discuss what I took from the experience of the earth fibres course and begin to take a broader perspective using Cajete's (2009) questions about what educators might do well to focus on: How do we deal with our own souls? How are we going to live with each other? How are we going to deal with the environmental crisis as it is today? These become a useful framework for this next cyclic walk.

Over the next three chapters, I develop the stories of the course into a discussion about what we can learn of significance. The text boxes highlight critical questions I continue to ask myself as I indigenize my own practice. They can be useful starting points for discussion among educators with similar goals. Here, in Chapter 6, I address questions of soul. How do we nourish our own souls? What can we learn from the soul or spirit work observed in the course? What kind of soul tending do learners (and their teachers) need? How might the current context of teacher (education) help or hinder this work?

I continue, as so many of the wisdom keepers did, by laying a table full of possibilities. Charlene explained that all teachings are merely gentle offerings. They can be ignored, sampled, taken up, or left behind. Sometimes they are like seeds, needing time and space to grow into their fullness. My intention is to portray something complex and, in many ways, beyond words. I approach this task with care, my feet planted firmly on TENEW~Earth, remembering that it is difficult to put the knowing of lived experience into the two-dimensionality of written words. I am compelled to write because I believe the strikingly different pedagogy that arises from an indigenous cosmology has a key place in developing possibilities within the realm of mainstream (teacher) education as we have conversations about moving forward in a good way. I proceed humbly to lay this table, knowing that you have a choice in this discussion. I believe what I bring forward is useful, but as King (2003) advises, it will now be up to you to decide how to bring these teachings forward.

The Endogenous Learning Spirit

The organic approach to learning taken in the earth fibres course resonates with what indigenous educational scholar Marie Battiste (2007, 2009) describes as the *learning spirit*. This is an endogenous process, originating from the inside and moving outwards. As a keynote speaker for the 2007 Awâsis Aboriginal Education Conference, Battiste described how nourishing the learning spirit is critical in developing lifelong learning habits and is particularly relevant to learners who struggle in school:

> Being able to connect consistently to the inner forces of the self is one way
> that learners can each seek to achieve optimally their life journey. It is about
> the ability to understand the capacities and lessons needed to learn on a
> life path. It is knowing of the self and the life journey that conditions certain
> skills, talents or propensities like what makes us an artist, singer, dancer,
> teacher, lawyer, architect, service provider, activist, ecologist, etc. The learning
> spirit then is an important, [and also] neglected, aspect of learning in the
> current mind-focused learning paradigm of education. We need then a
> refresher course in the learning spirit to enable us to balance the cognitive
> and physical world in which we live to the inner spiritual and emotional
> journey of our lives.

In many ways, the earth fibres course was a refresher, a chance for participants to reconnect with their own learning spirit, or inner spiritual knowing. The wisdom keepers expressed an overarching confidence in the pre-service teachers' ability to find their own learning direction. Although they used different terminology, the wisdom keepers all referred to the concept of the learning spirit frequently as they spoke about their gentle offering approach.

While the idea of nourishing the learning spirit was strongly embedded in the indigenous belief systems of the wisdom keepers, the pre-service teachers struggled at times to understand what was expected of them in this regard. Much of their previous school experience was based on positivist transmissive approaches, in which the teacher is in primary control of the content being learned. They were used to relying on directives from the teacher in terms of how, when, and where to proceed in their learning. Within the course, each participant experienced a period of adjustment during which they had to discover and practise a new way of learning that was more self-directed. This was uncomfortable and frustrating at times for some, but once they got used to the approach, excitement and engagement in learning followed. Awareness shifted from what should be taught to what might be learned (Britzman et al., 1997), and focus came to rest on the pedagogy of the question (Esteve, 2000; Freire, 1970/2005; Leonardo, 2004). Each person's queries were his or her own. The notion of "student teacher" shifted into that of being-becoming a learner-teacher, in which the learning spirit acted in good relation to both the community and TENEW~Earth.

Rupert Ross (1996/2006), a former Crown prosecutor, describes how this particular sense of being and becoming fits with indigenous ontology and epistemology. With a foot in both indigenous and Euro-Western worlds, Ross spent many years working with the Cree and Ojibwa Nations on issues of restorative justice. His astute awareness about what lies beneath the spoken word led him to observe that many indigenous languages do not use concrete labels, relying on verbs more than nouns. This reflects "an understanding that all of life is a process, that every person is seen as a 'thing-which-is-becoming,' as opposed to a 'thing-which-is'" (p. 104). Indigenous languages assume that people, life, and learning are in flux. English, on the other hand, suggests a very different way of knowing the world:

> First, I never realized how "harsh" the English language is, or how judg-
> mental and argumentative we become as we speak it. Second, I had no idea
> that people could – and do – live otherwise, without having to respond to
> everything around them in such combative and judgmental ways. (Ross,
> 1996/2006, p. 105)

In the course, there were tensions around nurturing the learning spirit when external stress was placed on the learner. One such strain came from time pressures, when the participants felt they had too much to do in too short a time. The indigenous perspective is that learners that are being and becoming progress in their own time, as guided by spirit. This perspective reflects an acceptance of an internal motivation and sense of movement as opposed to movement based on an external schedule, structure, or expectation. When the learner works in harmony with the learning spirit, the rhythm and pace of the learner is an organic process led by intuitive understanding, skill level, and the nature of the task at hand within the context of community. External time structures are in conflict with this process.

Another tension that arose had to do with external requests focused on product as opposed to process. Both the wisdom keepers and the pre-service teachers spoke about how the textile maker should pay attention to the earth fibres for guidance on how to proceed and at what tempo. This process was thwarted when external expectations were imposed, and was complicated by the fact that, well before the earth fibres course started, there was hope and intent that the mural would be a legacy left at the university. The mural was seen as a vehicle for bringing forward the teachings of the female energy in order to balance the male energy of the pole carved in the course the previous year. The mural was an ambitious project that tried to balance the needs of many, including the individual course participants, the small groups, the large group, the university community, and local First Nations communities. This situation is reminiscent of pre-service teacher Leanne's image mentioned in Chapter 5 of the learner surrounded by concentric circles of influence. There was a complicated web of interactions within the course that required constant and careful attention.

It was unfortunate that some participants felt overly stressed by these pressures, which inhibited the endogenous workings of learning spirit. However, this tension brings to the fore the important notion of reciprocity within a learning community (Kuokkanen, 2007; Lave and Wenger, 1991/2003; S. Wilson, 2008). While the learning spirit is a personal, individual process, there is also always a relational tie between the individual and the community. Overall, it was remarkable how the course addressed the needs of both the learner and the community. Despite the time and product pressures, all of the pre-service teachers spoke of their personal learning process having been nourished. As their individual learning spirits were cultivated, their actions moved out to strengthen the community in kind.

Through watching the wisdom keepers, the pre-service teachers developed a deeper understanding of Aboriginal cultures and indigenous pedagogy, and they became more confident in engaging with Aboriginal people. The small groups were, as Janet (WK) said, filled with the busy bee activity of cooperation. As the small groups worked within the larger group, a remarkable mural was ultimately produced. Hanging in the MacLaurin Building amidst the activity of future teachers, XAXE SIÁM SILA continues, years later, to stand witness and give voice to the important story of indigenous ways of learning and teaching.

Learning Is More Than an Intellectual Project

The earth fibres stories strongly indicate that attending to the whole learner is a beneficial practice that boosts the endogenous engagement of the learner. Learning is not only intellectual but also physical, emotional, and spiritual. Learning is cross-disciplinary, crosscultural, cyclical, and circular. Each learner creates a unique sense of what wholeness means as learning extends from the inside rather than being motivated solely by external forces. Processes of embodied knowledge (Lakoff and Johnson, 1999) and emotional knowledge (F.L. Brown, 2004) are engaged as important factors in learning. In addition, spiritual knowing becomes key (Aluli Meyer, 2008; Riley-Taylor, 2002; Tisdell, 2007).

In the earth fibres course, experience began to expand out from a more intellectual orientation. This shift was particularly apparent during the opening circles at the beginning of each class. One of the experiences most discussed in the interviews, the time spent in circles, appeared to impact the pre-service teachers deeply. The circle activities opened access to other ways of knowing through experiential contact with the vibrancy of the drumbeats, the songs, and the herbs, and through the physical experiences such as being wrapped in the cattail mats. These extraordinary activities gave the pre-service teachers "permission" to leave old ways of being at the door in order to access other possibilities. It was within this setting that many pre-service teachers spoke about connecting to a sense of spirituality as enduring knowledge passed on for generations (Aluli Meyer, 2008). It was also in this space that deep-seated beliefs appeared to shift towards more indigenist perspectives.

In what ways can we incorporate other ways of knowing (cultural, practical, and scholarly) into (teacher) education (e.g., through using metaphors, arts, alternative texts, poetry, and/or collage)?

One response to acknowledging learners' multiple ways of knowing within teacher education is to include theories such as Gardner's (2006) concept of multiple intelligence. Gardner argues that intelligence is actually made up of different qualities, such as spatial, linguistic, kinesthetic, and so on. This might be a useful place for discussions to begin, but thought needs to be given to the deeper meaning of these types of frameworks. How do the categories such as those laid out by Gardner mesh with an indigenous paradigm? How do they support the indigenous notion that we are all related? How might they reproduce a culture of self-actualization that is narcissistic and dichotomizing? Multiple ways of knowing must be acknowledged and reflected more fully in both the curriculum and the structure of the classroom. The frameworks we use to describe these notions must be rigorously examined. Indigenous models of pedagogy are useful tools in this work in that they disrupt positivist notions of success and provide alternative models for learning and teaching. One significant example of this was developed through a project undertaken by the Canadian Council on Learning (2007, p. 2), using the organic model of a tree's roots, trunk, and branches to describe First Nations ways of learning and teaching:

> Just as the tree draws nourishment through its roots, the First Nations person learns from and through the natural world, language, traditions and ceremonies, and the world of people (self, family, ancestors, clan, community, nation and other nations). Any uneven root growth can de-stabilize the learning system. The root system also depicts the intertwining presence of indigenous and Western knowledge, which forms the tree trunk's core, where learning develops.

In addition to this First Nations model, similar examples were developed for Métis and Inuit learning-teaching. Unfortunately, a loss of funding for this important project resulted in its being discontinued.

You Can Be Inventive

Within the course, participants engaged in a process of re-membering their wholeness, both remembering and re-embodying who they really are. Re-membering in this way is important for educators because we teach who we are (Palmer, 1998). After the course, from their newly found positionality, the pre-service teachers experienced shifts in their teaching practice. At the end of the course, Nicole talked about how she had to "take hold of the methods" she wanted to bring to her class:

> I guess we all need a system or else it might not work, right? But you can be inventive ... Just because they're learning about soil doesn't mean you have to list the soil on the board, have them write it down and memorize it. You can take them outside, have them dig, see what they see, you know? I forget, I think it's called child-centred learning, the approach where they take control

and you don't necessarily tell them the three layers of soil. You get them to go out and see them, and then you might tell them the names ... And you know, they get it that way. So you're kind of putting the learning into their hands. That's the way I'd like to teach.

In the spirit of being inventive and keeping in mind the holistic needs of each learner, the pre-service teachers left the course and proceeded optimistically into their practica. They incorporated into their classrooms a notable array of experiences that increased student awareness of indigenous cultures. These inclusive practices resonated with indigenous ways of honouring the endogenous processes of the learner. Below is a description of some of the concrete ways in which the pre-service teachers brought pedagogy from the earth fibres course into their classrooms. They saw these activities as being useful in future teaching situations. The activities are listed in no particular order and sometimes overlap.

Steeping the classroom in culture. The pre-service teachers were very aware of including cultural knowledge in the fabric of their curriculum (as opposed to taking a more surface-oriented approach). They accessed the culture of the children in their classes and found out more about the local indigenous cultures of their physical school locations. They rewrote unit plans they had developed in the past to include the deeper cultural awareness that they received in the course. Aware that the overall curriculum was lacking in Aboriginal content, they consciously thought of ways to alter the content, as well as ways to include indigenous perspectives.

In addition, they shared with their students stories from the earth fibres course, such as the story of the moons and the history of the Coast Salish peoples. April added local topics such as residential schools to a more globally oriented curriculum and also made efforts to include indigenous perspectives on issues that her students were studying, such as the use of hydroelectric dams in British Columbia. Courtney (PST) adapted a unit on cultural exchange between her class and an imaginary Inuit child, giving it more cultural depth and authenticity, as well as making it more experiential and developmentally appropriate for her grade 1 students.

Attention to language. Some of the pre-service teachers became acutely aware of the importance of language in the context of the course and discussed how the spoken word held many hidden meanings. They realized that what students in a classroom hear is not always what the teacher thinks he or she is saying. They took special care to choose their words carefully. For example, when addressing her students, Jade began using "friends" instead of "grade ones" or "classmates" to indicate a different kind of relationship and set a different tone within the classroom community.

Good hands. Many of the pre-service teachers incorporated the idea of good hands into their classrooms; Leanne consciously used the phrase "do your best work" because she felt that this inspired the learners to slow down and focus on their efforts instead of a final product, find a sense of internal discipline, and take pride in what they were doing. It was acknowledged that incorporating good hands was based on developing strong relationships with students; many felt that this was hard to do in a short, eight-week practicum, but looked forward to incorporating the concept more fully in their long-term teaching situations.

Bodies involved. The pre-service teachers talked about ways to help students experience learning hands-on rather than just seeing information written on the board. These ways included, as Nicole said, "getting kids out of their seats to do work" through active learning such as a scientific squid-dissection project or having her students work with manipulatives in math. The pre-service teachers also thought carefully about how to incorporate stories, drama, and song in ways that engaged the whole child and allowed for student-led learning processes.

Student choices and variety. Student choice was enacted in various ways, through options with assignments or exams (e.g., written or oral) or opportunities for expression of competency through alternative texts such as music, art, theatre, and recorded oral presentations. Leanne gave students behaviour choices, such as either sitting quietly at the rug or working at a desk. Courtney explored inquiry learning within her practicum placement and felt that it held more merit than she had previously thought. In a similar vein, some of the pre-service teachers supported learner detours as being valuable. However, others worried that too much choice could lead to an inflated sense of self-esteem; they felt it was important to find balance between student-led activities and teacher-led ones. Overall, it was agreed that providing students with choices helped them play to their strengths, tap into their passion as learners, gain comfort with exams, and engage in learning topics that they perceived to be relevant and interesting. A range of activities – noisy or quiet, active or still, structured or hands-on, messy or neat, teacher-guided or student-led – provided variety in the classroom; variety engaged students and gave them opportunities to learn in different ways.

Trusting the Learner-Teacher

Within the course, the wisdom keepers trusted that the pre-service teachers could and would find their own learning direction given enough time and space. They also assumed that the learners would contribute in meaningful ways to the learning community. These innate expectations were different from what others had expected of the pre-service teachers in their educational experiences more generally. The pre-service teachers wanted to be trusted as the intelligent, thoughtful, energetic, and emergent teachers that they were, instead of being placed in a subordinate student role. The stories from the course suggest that when pre-service teachers are looked at as learner-teachers instead of student teachers, they rise to the challenge and exceed expectations in terms of participation and professional growth. This takes time. It is an important yet subtle shift that is worth emphasizing, in that it demonstrates the negotiation and renegotiation of roles and of knowledge required within learning communities of practice (Lave and Wenger, 1991/2003).

Jayne (PST) spoke of how her journal writing in the course focused on her own learning and wondering process, rather than what she thought her instructor or supervisor might want. How can following the learning spirit in this way be incorporated into other aspects of (teacher) education?

The actions of the wisdom keepers repeatedly reinforced the notion that trusting the learner is something that improves learning. Unfortunately, after their practica, many of the pre-service teachers expressed that they were unable to do as much as they would have liked in the context of their placements (see Chapter 10). This was not due to a lack of energy or sense of purpose on their part. Rather, I see this as the inability of the system, and those of us who perpetuate it, to trust in the changes that these competent learner-teachers want to bring forward. It is important that emerging teachers be given opportunities to clarify, articulate, and practise their own sense of direction and intent. As in the course, particular attention should be given to the ebb and flow between individual and community needs.

While some pre-service teachers felt destabilized by the unusual level of trust offered by the wisdom keepers, others expressed their feeling that the experience reinforced knowledge held on an intuitive level. To some degree, changing one's disposition was about reinforcing or recognizing one's existing knowledge. Unfortunately, teacher educators may think of their students in terms of a "monolithic and deficient group" (Lowenstein, 2009, p. 187) attending to what they lack rather than what they are able to do. The wisdom keepers saw pre-service teachers as capable emerging teachers who had the integrity to pursue a deeper sense of personal, social, and environmental agency within educational contexts. What would happen if we adopted this view more fully in teacher education?

Garrett (PST) spoke of how the course helped him feel like a future teacher, not just a student. How might we treat pre-service teachers as both being and becoming at the same time, not just as students?

Typically, teacher education programs focus on how to teach other people to teach, but there are numerous studies on learning to teach from a progressive viewpoint (Wideen, Mayer-Smith, and Moon, 1998). The best of these turn around the central academic question in teacher education, namely, "How do people teach?" to ask, "How do people learn?" (Britzman et al., 1997, p. 15). This focus demands that we consider how we become more holistic learners. This can be an uncomfortable process because it requires us to move into less familiar territory; teachers can no longer rely on prescribed answers and must foster learner curiosity and thoughtfulness about the world that surrounds us (Esteve, 2000). When learning is not given the attention it needs, there can be negative effects on teachers' relationships with learners, teachers' pedagogy, and teachers' sense of professional well-being (Valli and Buese, 2007).

For teacher educators, developing pre-service teacher autonomy in this way requires what Freire calls the "death of the professor" (in Vella, 2002, p. 20). Here, the sage on the stage steps down and creates space where learners can take the lead – a difficult process in these times of accountability through testing and grading, and a consumerist mentality. We need teacher education that consciously builds on the gifts of each learner as directed by each person's endogenous learning spirit. The paradigm shift we are engaging in on a societal level must, at least in part, be informed by intuitive ways of knowing. In our hearts, it seems that we know what is right. Often, however, our (intellectual) ego would rather not listen to or act upon this knowledge.

7

Coming Together in Safe Enough Spaces

This chapter resonates with Cajete's (2009) question: How are we going to live with each other? Social issues abound in educational settings. How did the learning community in the course influence our ability to get along with people who are different from us? How might familiar patterns of relating be re-fused? I use the term *re-fuse* intentionally because it adds many layers of meaning to the discussion. Re-fusing can be about resisting the familiar and even putting aside what we have come to know; we refuse, reject, and discard that which is not useful. To re-fuse can also mean to re-do; we rewire and renew our ways of thinking and being. To *fuse* means to combine, to coalesce; we meld and mingle together, re-fusing crossculturally in new and unique ways. In addition, we sometimes say people have a short fuse, metaphorically alluding to an electrically charged state that can lead to explosiveness; we learn to re-fuse by tapping into and refocusing this energy, lighting a fire and using passion in creative and healing ways. Within the earth fibres course, our sense of community was active in this type of complex re-fusing process.

Dialogue plays an important role in re-fusing and re-wiring; teachers must have courageous conversations in order to understand cultural beliefs and build community across cultures (Hirsh, 2005). It is through dialogue that we create meaning and, through the creation of meaning, that we envision change. The therapeutic process of mutual understanding changes our stories together so that we can move towards a different future. This is why I chose to frame the interviews for the study as conversations, and why I was an active participant observer in the course.

The earth fibres experience became a type of "curriculum as conversation" (Applebee, 1996), in which the participants could intermingle and learn. All participants, including myself, co-created understanding of what it meant to learn and teach at that point in time and in that particular location. Through the voicing of our stories in community we engaged in a process of collective liberation from the existing dominant culture of the university setting (Britzman, 1990/2003). We told stories with each other in different ways – through sharing in the circle, small-group discussions, ceremony, and the simple act of cleaning up and putting away supplies. Our stories were vessels that embodied our identities and reminded us of our existence – together we were re-searching our place in the world and our own sense of culture.

Unfortunately, the dialogic act is rarely made explicit in teacher education studies (Grant and Agosto, 2008). Perhaps this is because the unspoken subtleties of communication are difficult to describe. The earth fibres course was a useful site of study in terms of making the role of dialogue in building community more transparent and finding what contexts are possible and/or desirable for such conversations to occur. I continue to envision this project as part of a broader conversation, beyond the pre-service teachers, wisdom keepers, and others in the course to include teacher education colleagues and the educational community at large.

Choosing to Come

Dialogue is about more than verbal exchange; there are subtle elements worth noting. First is the important act of *choosing to come*, a way of being proactive in crosscultural work, especially when acting from a position of privilege. Two years before the earth fibres course, I was enrolled in another course with Lorna. One evening after a late class, we were walking out of the building, chatting together, when I realized that our cars were in different parking lots. Ordinarily, my inclination would be to say goodbye and head the other way, but instead I felt an internal tug to disrupt this characteristic pattern. I opted instead to take a different (rather long) route to my vehicle so that I could stay engaged in our conversation. On our way together, Lorna told me the following story:

A woman who wanted to learn about the Navajo culture was invited by a Navajo man to live in his community. She settled in, learning that their

custom was for women to stay in one house and men in another. The grandparents of her host resided in a third. On the first morning, the woman woke
up to find that everyone had left to gather at the grandparents' for breakfast.
They returned happy and fed, and the woman felt left out. The next morning
the same thing took place, and then the next. After some time, the woman
became distraught. She packed her things, ready to leave. Her host asked her,
"Why are you going?" She replied, "You went for breakfast each morning at
the grandparents.' I felt so left out. You never invited me!" The man turned to
her and said, "We did go for breakfast each morning. Why couldn't you just
come?" (personal communication, fall 2005)

I have kept this story in my heart. Over time, I am learning that, sometimes,
it is up to me to take the initiative in finding a way to walk alongside people
I don't know. I need to consciously go out of my way. This effort can require
time, patience, and risk. Sometimes it can be as simple as straying from a well-
worn path to the parking lot in order to be able to listen to someone else's story:
resisting old patterns and re-fusing new ones. At other times it is about leaving
comfortable and familiar ways or places, such as the university or the school,
in order to be more fully in the community. Participants in the course chose
specifically to enrol in the earth fibres experience, and made various decisions
throughout the course to walk alongside others, being open to re-fusing new
patterns.

Putting Aside the Familiar

Participants in the course were also required to engage in *putting aside the*
familiar. The act of walking alongside the wisdom keepers to enter more fully
into their world, to do as they do, took specific effort on the part of the participants. They had to notice the energy and intent of the wisdom keepers and
adjust their ways of proceeding accordingly. One obvious example of this
was putting down the notepads, described in Chapter 2. By consciously letting
go of the familiar ingrained Eurocentric practice of note-taking, participants
were better able to attend to the wisdom keepers through oral and other indigenous ways of learning. This created an opening that served to expand the participants' understanding of what learning-teaching could be. From this new
place of understanding, many began to think of how they might incorporate
such ways of knowing into their classrooms.

The pre-service teachers sometimes scrambled to figure out what the unspoken cultural conventions were within the course, especially at the beginning.

For some, letting go of familiar ways of being, patterns that had been held since childhood, was a risky and unpleasant experience. The continuous welcoming, non-judgmental, and supportive environment offered by the wisdom keepers was invaluable in helping the pre-service teachers feel comfortable enough to let go of their worries and redefine what it meant to be successful. Participants were able first to look for personal relevancy and engagement in their learning and, later, to assume that improvement in skill and content knowledge would follow.

For many participants, putting aside the familiar also meant letting go of preconceived notions of success and perfection – notions that had been reinforced over years of engagement with a positivist-oriented curriculum. They were used to being in schools that privileged success based on meeting external markers of achievement. Many were haunted by a sense of needing to be perfect in their academic schoolwork – at the expense of their holistic well-being. Worries about perfection wormed their way throughout the course experience and were closely tied to feelings of safety/danger. This fact reminds me of an experience I had as a graduate student, when I helped paint the image of a singing grandmother on the "Old Man" welcoming pole in the MacLaurin Building. My inattention led me to drip a rather large blob of black paint on a place that was supposed to be painted brown. *Yikes!* I shuddered at the thought that I had ruined such an important piece of the project, and with trepidation told Fabian, the master carver. I'll always remember the way he laughed aloud at my concern. His reaction helped me to realize that my vision of perfection was limited and that, in fact, there were many ways to paint a singing grandmother. Together, we worked to incorporate the imperfection, and it is now a part of the grandmother's beautiful face. In similar ways, the pre-service teachers began to understand other ways of defining perfection, through their personal experiences in the course.

Safe Enough Space

Perhaps the most important theme running throughout the earth fibres course data is the issue of safety. The notion of *safe enough space* is at the heart of building good relationships. It is not only that we need to feel safe when we choose to come or to put aside the familiar. It is also that the transformative work of re-membering wholeness and re-fusing the status quo requires pre-service teachers to engage in the risky matter of negotiating emotional terrain (Tisdell, 2001).

Within the course, emotions were handled differently from what is typical in many classrooms. For example, after a death in the community, the wisdom keepers included everyone in the mourning process by sharing personal stories, songs, and tears. Many of the pre-service teachers felt a mixture of unease and intrigue at this honesty. Some wondered about the appropriateness of an instructor sharing in this way, while others felt honoured to be included. What was striking to me was the way in which the wisdom keepers acknowledged and shared their emotions while at the same time continuing with the coursework at hand.

The apparent ease with which the wisdom keepers brought their emotions into the classroom set the tone for acceptance of emotional expression. As the course progressed, the pre-service teachers relaxed into the possibility of sharing in this way. When I visited the various work groups, it was not unusual for me to observe expressions of tears and laughter. I often overheard snippets of personal sharing as everyone went about creating with busy hands. Conversations about boyfriends, children, other course work, and future career paths mingled with beading, weaving, and sewing; the holistic and complex lives of the individual learners were honoured.

The importance of emotions in learning is increasingly well recognized (F.L. Brown, 2004; Goleman, 1995). The wisdom keepers modelled emotional acceptance for the pre-service teachers, who experienced a comfortable emotional setting first-hand as learners. They began to develop a new sense of how learning communities could be caring and nurturing environments (Noddings, 2003). Then they were able to value the need to transfer this to their teaching. But how do teacher educators help prepare teacher-learners to handle the potential difficulties of such an inclusive approach? The answer may be found in part in how the wisdom keepers also exhibited great support for each other as instructors. By working in community, they found strength and skills to counteract the sense of isolation that teachers often feel in transformative practice (Wideen et al., 1998).

How can (teacher) educators support learners to ponder aloud without worrying about finding the "right" answer or saying the "wrong" thing? What does safe enough space look like? How can a learning community be safe enough for honesty, yet not so safe that we shy away from transformative risk?

I've spent a good deal of time trying to understand what it meant that the participants felt safe within the course. Synonyms for safety in the context of the course include security, protection, shelter, and well-being. All of these resonate with the participants' stories, yet it is the notion of well-being that strikes a particularly distinctive chord; there was an overall atmosphere of contented happiness among participants, a feeling of acceptance and a sense that life was good. Of course, this sense of well-being and safety wasn't always present in the earth fibres course. What is striking is how often it did exist and, when it wasn't present, that there was an assumption that it somehow *could* be. Or maybe the assumption was that it *should* be there. This sense of well-being and safety *belongs* in learning environments at a fundamental level because it creates a space where both learners and teachers are more willing to take risks with their learning.

Dwelling in a sense of well-being and safety within a learning environment does not necessarily ensure comfort. At times, the process of walking alongside each other was very awkward and uncomfortable. For example, when the wisdom keepers used prayer, some participants were unsure about, yet at the same drawn to experience, this other way of knowing. Nicole expressed a feeling, shared by others, that there was safety in "teaching in the standard ways you grew up with"; at the same time, she recognized (as did others) that there was a need to do things differently. Change can threaten or compromise what exists, or what we are used to, yet these points of tension can illuminate our way forward, showing (teacher) educators the location of important work that needs our careful attention as we bring learner well-being into the classroom.

Complicating the issue of safe enough space is the underlying preoccupation with being a *perfect teacher*. The industrial model of education often presents a hierarchical system, with the teacher at the top of the hierarchy as expert and knowledge provider. This became apparent to me during my interviews with the pre-service teachers, who were often hesitant to answer my questions about learning and teaching. As Courtney (PST) said, "It's not every day that you question teacher roles and where you are in your life." Anxiety about finding an intellectual answer that was somehow "correct" contributed to their tentativeness to engage. They were not used to questioning the social and institutional structures that govern the many and sometimes hidden layers of school curricula. We must consciously encourage teacher education to move towards another paradigm, in which our pre-service teachers see themselves as capable of having these kinds of conversations within safe enough spaces.

Protecting Learner Well-Being

The wisdom keepers were persistent and stubborn in their efforts to hold a space within the university that supported the organic processes that arose between the learner-teachers and the earth fibres. The wisdom keepers believed that every participant in their unique state of being-becoming would progress in their own time, as guided by spirit-knowledge. The emphasis was on internal, cyclical motivation and sense of movement, as opposed to learning based on an external, linear schedule, structure, or expectation. When the learner was working in harmony with the learning spirit, the learner's rhythm and pace were part of an organic process led by intuitive understanding, skill level, and the nature of the task at hand within the context of community and TENEW~Earth. There were, however, organizational tensions in terms of protecting learner well-being. Strain derived from various time pressures sometimes left the participants feeling that they had too much to do to meet externally imposed deadlines. External time structures set by the university, which the wisdom keepers were unable to alter, conflicted with the processes that supported learner well-being and safety.

Another tension that arose had to do with requests by others for specific products, which hindered attempts to maintain the emphasis on learning and learner. The wisdom keepers were clear in their emphasis that each creator-artist should attend first to the earth fibres themselves for guidance on how, and at what pace, to proceed. This process was thwarted, however, by external expectations rooted in an overarching culture of efficiency (Stein, 2002). As the end of the course drew near, there was sometimes a feeling on the part of participants that it was more important to get things done than to do them well. This tension grew from the intention of course organizers, firmly in place well before the course even started, that the mural should become a legacy for the university. The immensity of this responsibility left some participants feeling overly stressed, which affected their learning spirits and their ability to proceed with good hands. When this pressure to produce was met with attachments to perfection, as described above, the well-being and safety of the learner was compromised.

How do we let go of the timetable and externally derived goals so that learning occurs at its own pace? How might we move away from a product orientation to support processes that are key to teacher development?

Learner reflexivity was one process that required a kind of space that differs from those typically found within institutions of higher education. As the pre-service teachers moved into an understanding of their personal location within the relational context of the community and TENEW~Earth, they developed processes that moved beyond reflection into true reflexive practice (Dressman, 1998). They went through a decolonizing process that was uncomfortable and unpredictable (Apple, 2008; Esteve, 2000) as they supplemented their understanding of the *what and how* of teaching with a deeper understanding of the *why* (Labosky, 1994; Brookfield, 1995; Preece, 2004). This process was risky (Howard, 2004; Ladson-Billings, 1999; Oberg, 2004) and, at times, became so disruptive that it truly boggled the mind on ontological and epistemological levels (Kremer, 1997). Feeling safe while they were engaging in such critical reflexive practice was essential for the pre-service teachers.

What can be done about the controversial position that reflection and reflexivity hold for many pre-service teachers? How do we create space and time in (teacher) education where students feel comfortable and willing to have conversations about their own personal processes and to take up gentle offerings such as those of the course?

One factor that made a big difference in this regard was the policy of assessment in the course. The pre-service teachers spoke of how using a complete/incomplete assessment format instead of letter grades helped them to relax and experience the course for what it was, not for what mark they thought might be required of them. This format enabled them to focus on their own learning, and they took risks they were unwilling to take in other, graded courses. The indigenous approach took them out of a mode that encouraged competition with their peers, and they relaxed into a co-operative community in which they looked out for one another and for the good of the community. In this context, they reported feeling more comfortable taking the kind of risks needed to support reflexive practice that leads to new beliefs, attitudes, and values.

The pre-service teachers' attempts at reflexivity were quite effective when embedded in the authentic learning environment of the course. Their stories indicate that real interactions with real people in a walking-alongside type of crosscultural community made a difference in commitment and openness to change. Furthermore, the indigenous way of the wisdom keepers, which accepted emotional, spiritual, and physical knowing, gave the pre-service teachers a sense of comfort and increased their confidence in accessing these non-intellectual knowledge resources. This in turn expanded their reflexivity on a deeper, more embodied level.

Power of the Circle

The pre-service teachers frequently spoke about how important a sense of safety was in a productive learning environment and attempted to promote this sense of safety in their practicum settings. They were profoundly thoughtful about this topic and aware of the nuanced approach necessary to make students feel safe about sharing personal emotions, while at the same time considering the needs of the other class members. Many found ways to set up environments where the children could share their stories and have discussions about issues that were important to them.

In particular, the pre-service teachers drew on the opening-circle experience in the course as a model for building community in their own classrooms. Many of them said that the experiences in the opening circles felt familiar. Perhaps this was because, in some ways, the opening circles resembled the practice that pre-school and kindergarten teachers refer to as *circle time,* when children gather on a rug to share important personal artefacts, songs, wonderings, family stories, and news. I believe that many of the pre-service teachers tried to bring the spirit of the earth fibres opening circles into public school classrooms.

The pre-service teachers called their circles by other names, such as "class meeting," "circle time," or "group time," and these typically took place at the beginning or end of the school day. The pre-service teachers saw these times as a way to open up communication with and between their students by creating a safe enough environment where students felt included, could share their feelings, have their voices heard, and listen to and be changed by others. They also saw the circles as a way for their students to re-focus energy, re-connect with each other, build a sense of team spirit, and bring everyone to a better understanding of common goals. Some used the circles to explore problems (both social and academic), to develop communication skills, and to discuss current issues and values, both within the school and within the larger community.

Some pre-service teachers experimented with rearranging desks or classroom space so the environment would be more conducive to a circle atmosphere, acknowledging that it was often difficult to use circles, given the limited space in many classrooms. Some adapted to these constraints by forming U-shaped groupings, two half-circles, pods of four, or other creative solutions. Others thought they would wait until they had their own classrooms to move furniture, stating that it felt too risky to try this in front of their mentor teachers.

The pre-service teachers liked the circle arrangements they initiated because they felt that no one stood out in a circle, everyone could see each other, shy students were encouraged to speak, and the teachers themselves could be part of the conversation. Sometimes their students were surprised to see them participate in this way, yet it was important, at times, for the pre-service teachers to be seen as being on the same level as their students. This practice may have brought up tensions over classroom control, but it also made students more comfortable with normal tensions of group dynamics, helped them get to know their teachers better, and led them to be more willing to participate. It was striking how determined and persistent the pre-service teachers were in including circle activities in order to create a different and deeper sense of community in their classrooms.

The pre-service teachers were apprehensive about including emotions in the classroom. They felt they were trained as teachers, not counsellors, and some felt unprepared to work in what is a potentially intense, complex, and shadowy arena. They were concerned about emotions in the classroom getting out of hand and leading to issues of control. And some felt that this emotional work might put them in a vulnerable position personally.

> How do we navigate the edge of counselling in teacher education so that emotional awareness can be more readily included as a supportive and integral part of learning?

Inviting Stories

The stories each learner brings into the classroom hold experiences, emotions, beliefs, and values. The earth fibres course was a weaving together of different stories that brought strength to the group as a learning community as we learned to listen to the complexity of what each person brought to the group. Time was given to listen to the stories of each person present, and among participants the level of comfort with emotion grew. Within their practica, the pre-service teachers naturally began to emulate this model by looking for ways to include the stories of their students, the community, and themselves within the learning day. They believed that building relationships with students was in many ways more important than focusing on the documented curriculum.

Student stories. One way that the pre-service teachers invited the stories of their students was through the sharing circles described above. Other ways included having students share family traditions and celebrations by bringing food and family members to class, showing photos of students engaged in out-of-school activities, spending time with the students on the playground or at lunch, greeting the students at the door as they entered the classroom in the morning or after recess, and engaging the students in life-story writing. Sharing student stories changed the tone of the classrooms, helped students feel listened to and welcome, and fostered a community-oriented environment that could be less structured and less content-driven. The pre-service teachers felt that the relationships developed by their listening to students' stories helped the students feel accepted and led to deeper student learning due to the higher level of trust in the teacher-student relationship. Knowing their students' backgrounds led the pre-service teachers to understand their students' situations more fully, and to address the learning needs of each student more appropriately and holistically. Making space for learner stories also helped students to establish a better rapport with each other. When troubles arose, such as playground disputes, the pre-service teachers were better prepared to understand the social dynamics of individual situations. There was a sense of trust that encouraged resolution.

Community stories. The earth fibres experience emphasized the importance of community stories, and the pre-service teachers actively sought out ways to invite community stories into their classrooms. Especially when teaching about cultures, or across cultures, they believed that, in these lessons, first-hand community input was necessary and valuable; information could be located in people, not just books. As they listened to community members in the context of the course, they were honing their understanding of cultural protocol (for example, Sara asked whether it would be appropriate before using a Coast Salish design in a classroom project); they brought this new understanding into their classrooms by revising their lesson plans.

The course helped the pre-service teachers feel more comfortable with the idea that various ages could come together in a learning environment in fruitful ways. They saw how powerful it was for students to see other people teaching besides the designated teacher. They developed a stronger sense of how having community members in the classroom might support their teaching efforts and how wisdom keepers were potential resources in their future classrooms. Inviting elders into the classroom was the best way to bring culture first-hand into the classroom. The pre-service teachers now felt more comfortable approaching elders in the community. School staff members (such as Aboriginal learning assistants) were also important resources who could be more fully invited into the classroom. In the focus groups, the pre-service teachers discussed how common they felt it was that members of the dominant culture would disregard elders, and they wanted to model other behaviours for their students by drawing on the wisdom of elders.

Teacher stories. After watching the wisdom keepers share their personal stories with students in the course, the pre-service teachers wanted to emulate this practice in order to build stronger and healthier relationships between learners and teachers. When the pre-service teachers shared their own stories in their classrooms, students often gave them their immediate and undivided attention; the pre-service teachers believed that students saw them as more genuine and honest for having shared their personal experiences. For example, when April told her students she was having a bad day, she admitted in a later interview that it had felt like a risk that put her "on the line a bit," but thought that it also modelled a way for students to do the same.

Many of the pre-service teachers spoke of how they shared their stories of the earth fibres course with family, friends, and students. Some of the pre-service teachers brought friends and family to see the mural and shared personal stories in that context. Some felt that sharing their experience of the wisdom keeper's culture was more comfortable than "teaching" about specific elements of Coast Salish culture. Courtney spoke about the difficulty of taking on the teacher-as-expert persona when the pre-service teachers often didn't believe in this persona themselves: "It's easy to not be genuine ... to try to just work the game." But by telling their own personal stories, the pre-service teachers could stay true to an actual experience rather than speaking more broadly in ways that might generalize aspects of a culture that they didn't fully understand. The pre-service teachers also felt that, by sharing their personal stories, they were more genuine and true to themselves. This benefited their own mental state because they felt more authentic and could be perceived as learners, too. Some mentor teachers made this easier to do than did others. Despite the benefits of sharing their personal stories, the pre-service teachers worried about what might be too much personal information to disclose to their students.

The pre-service teachers made a concerted effort to incorporate their experiences from the earth fibres course in many ways in their practicum classrooms, and the discussion here is by no means an exhaustive list of their endeavours. As a teacher educator, I was impressed that, despite the constraints of their practicum settings, the pre-service teachers were committed and creative in bringing forward the teachings shared by the wisdom keepers in the course. The pre-service teachers recognized the importance of sharing stories in the earth fibres experience and transferred this practice to their own teaching situations.

8

Continuing Reflection towards Sustainability

This chapter is about Cajete's (2009) remaining question: How are we going to deal with the environmental crisis as it is today? What can the course show us in terms of connecting to place? How might this deepen our care for the planet? Can habits of environmental sustainability be learned? One of the most alarming findings in the earth fibres study was the degree to which the pre-service teachers felt disconnected from TEṈEW~Earth. Remember in Chapter 1 how Chelsea was surprised that she could actually go off the trail during our nature walk. She was deeply altered by wisdom keeper Della's simple act of stepping into the dirt, standing amidst the plants, as she caressed their green leaves and explained their traditional use. Fostering connections with TEṈEW~Earth is critically important so that people understand ecological interrelatedness and its effect on our existence and the sustainability of the planet (Chambers, 2006; Orr, 2005; O'Sullivan, 2003). While I listened to the many stories of the course, what struck me was that both the wisdom keepers *and* the pre-service teachers expressed personal feelings of disconnection from nature in their daily lives. Many also noticed the same type of disconnect in the children with whom they worked.

The earth fibres course brought to the fore the importance of paying attention to and interacting with nature; the pre-service teachers gained some reflexive awareness of their relationship to the land they walk on every day. Yet they reported very few times when they took the initiative to include activities that connected with nature in their practicum experiences. Some brought natural objects into the classroom for various projects and took the children outside on walks and field trips. Those with older students held classroom discussions on environmental issues such as global warming. But for the most part, these activities were surprisingly limited in scope, especially in light of some of the pre-service teachers' earlier expressions of intent to focus on the environment in their practica. This lack of connection to nature in classroom settings is worrisome given the sense of urgency expressed by environmental educators to include environmental education in curricula everywhere (Barab and Roth, 2006; Capra, 1996; Fisher, 2002; Stone and Barlow, 2005).

Unfortunately, it was not in the scope of my study to explore more fully why the pre-service teachers' inclusion of TEṈEW~Earth relationships was so limited. It is possible that the structures of schooling within the contexts of the practica were so deeply embedded in positivist notions that incorporating experiences of nature was too difficult (see Chapter 9). It is also possible that the pre-service teachers will eventually incorporate nature more fully into their future classrooms. They did indicate this intention in their interviews; however, little was said about this in their post-practica focus groups. This is not surprising as it is nearly impossible for a visiting pre-service teacher to change the existing and persistent patterns of schooling while a guest in a classroom.

> The stories of the course show a serious disconnect. with nature – how might this be remedied? How do we create educational environments that connect learners more fully with TEṈEW~Earth?

An additional factor that may have exacerbated the relative lack of focus on environmental topics was the lack of closure in the earth fibres experience itself (discussed previously in Chapter 4 and later in this section). As Charlene said, there were many teachings that she was unable to share with the group due to the institutional time constraints placed upon the course. Whatever the case, the course stories suggest that careful attention should be paid to embedding explicit experiences within teacher education that emphasize the importance of a relational acknowledgment, understanding, and healing intent for TEṈEW~Earth.

Indigenous Ways of Knowing

The ancient wisdom and traditions of indigenous ways of knowing are an enacted eco-socio-spiritual awareness (Schaefer, 2006). Cajete's (2009) questions reflect

Learning and Teaching Together

a focus on sustainability that, for thousands of years, has been at the root of indigenous worldviews. This wisdom was severely disrupted, almost lost, due to repeated acts of colonization heavily embedded in the positivist paradigm. This painful and heartbreaking history is important to remember. It is important also to acknowledge that efforts to assimilate, appropriate, eliminate, marginalize, and/or ignore indigenous people and indigenous knowledge are still actively underway. Hence, my intention is to draw heavily on the voices of indigenous scholars to inform my own gentle offerings here. I do this with respect for the teachings and the wisdom of the elders.

Decolonization continues to be difficult work. Battiste (2008) underscores the struggles that current indigenous students and scholars face within the interweaving of Euro-Western and indigenous knowledge systems. She emphasizes the importance of recognizing indigenous knowledge "as a distinct knowledge system, with its own concepts of epistemology and scientific and logical validity, within contemporary education systems" (p. 85). Each indigenous group has its own unique ontology and epistemology rooted in its particular sense of place; caution must be used not to universalize indigenous culture (Battiste and Henderson, 2000). There is general agreement among indigenous scholars, however, that indigenous ways of learning and teaching have basic commonalities (Cajete, 1994; Fixico, 2003). While there is specificity of knowledge that resonates with each individual geographic location, it is a "specificity that leads to universality" of indigenous concepts (Aluli Meyer, 2008, p. 217).

Descriptive models of indigenous epistemology often take circular or web-like shapes and centre on holistic understandings that incorporate physical, mental, emotional, and spiritual growth (Battiste and Barman, 1995; Hampton, 1995; Weenie, 1998). Some of the salient and interconnected concepts of an indigenous worldview include (1) time as cyclical and rhythmic rather than linear and progress-oriented; (2) the interrelated sacredness of time and place; (3) nature as a site of indwelling spirits; (4) a richly defined and enacted sense of relationship; and (5) the use of oral transmission of knowledge (J.E. Brown, 1976).

Altamirano (cited in Alfred, 2005, p. 142), a Zapotecan political scientist from southern Mexico, speaks of the aspects of this web of knowledge that she considers to be commonalities among various indigenous groups:

Indigenous people have a strong relationship with their land and territories: they see them as social space where they recreate themselves, so land and territory are not only commodities. To indigenous peoples, religion and culture are linked to their natural contexts. It is not rare to find animal representations being linked to human beings, as with the raven in cultures from the Pacific or the deer in Northern Mexico. The role of elder is something shared among indigenous peoples too. Elders are seen as those who have accumulated knowledge, who have answers, or who know how to do things according to tradition.

It is important to realize that the basic epistemology of indigenous worldviews is different from dominant perspectives in ways that are rarely acknowledged. This is, in part, because indigenous worldviews need to be experienced through ways of knowing other than the intellectual in order to be fully appreciated. One of these epistemological differences has to do with a deeply lived relationship with nature. Momaday (1976, p. 84), a Kiowa novelist from the American Southwest, explains:

[The Indian] view ... is of a different and more imaginative kind. It is a more comprehensive view. When the Native American looks at nature, it isn't with the idea of training a glass upon it, or pushing it away so that he [sic] can focus on it from a distance. In his mind, nature is not something apart from him. He conceives of it, rather, as an element in which he exists. He has existence within that element much in the same way we think of having existence within the element of air. It would be unimaginable for him to think of it in the way the nineteenth century "nature poets" thought of looking at nature and writing about it. They employed a kind of "esthetic distance," as it is sometimes called. This idea would be alien to the Indian.

This embedded ecological perspective is central to the indigenous point of view. It ties into concepts of ecological balance that extend beyond mere physical environment. As Alvord, a Euro-Western–trained Navajo doctor (in Alvord and Van Pelt, 1999, p. 3), suggests:

Everything in life is connected. Learn to understand the bonds between humans, spirit, and nature. Realize that our illness and our healing alike come from maintaining strong and healthy relationships in every aspect of our lives. In my culture – the Navajo culture – medicine is performed by a hataalii, someone who sees a person not simply as a body, but a whole being. Body, mind, and spirit are seen as connected to other people, to families, to communities, and even to the planet and universe. All of these relationships need to be in harmony in order to be healthy.

Ermine (1995/1996, p. 103), a Cree scholar from Canada, writes that within indigenous thought there is a capacity for holism that invites "those who seek to understand the reality of existence and harmony with the environment" to turn inward. This focus is very different from the positivist scientific worldview based on the "fragmentation of the constituents of existence" through the "division of the universe into neatly packaged concepts."

Despite a growing awareness of the importance of indigenous ways of being and knowing in educational settings (Snipp, 2001), these ideas are often discredited by dominant culture (Grande, 2004; Kincheloe and Steinberg, 2008). Indigenous knowledge is rarely present in school curricula. When it is included, it is often done tangentially as a special class or unit of study. While these types of efforts are not necessarily negative, they are not enough. Teachers who have been educated in typical Euro-Western schooling systems are challenged to expand and alter their colonial understandings of pedagogy to include indigenous ways of learning and teaching in order to serve the learning needs of their Aboriginal students more fully.

The significance of indigenous pedagogy extends beyond crosscultural goals of inclusive classroom teaching. Indigenous ways of learning and teaching *in their own right* have the potential to be important and successful pedagogies for indigenous and non-indigenous students alike. Indigenous pedagogy, for all its diversity among various groups, is a pedagogy that embodies great respect and appreciation for the delicate balance of our Earth's ecology (Fixico, 2003). Increasingly, it is seen as fundamentally important in helping to meet some of the most pressing ecological challenges to sustainability that we face today (Davis, 2009; Hawken, 2007).

In addition, Cajete (1994, p. 42) tells us that

Indigenous education, at its innermost core, is education about the life and nature of the spirit that moves us. Spirituality evolves from exploring and coming to know and experience the nature of the living energy moving in each of us, through us, and around us. The ultimate goal of Indigenous education was to be fully knowledgeable about one's innate spirituality. This was considered completeness in its most profound form.

This attention to the spiritual is described by Aluli Meyer (2008, p. 218), who writes that "[k]nowledge that endures is spirit driven. It is a life force connected to all other life forces. It is more of an extension than a thing to accumulate." Linking knowledge with spirit in this way was a very powerful act that reverberated throughout the indigenous ways of learning and teaching in the earth fibres course.

As discussed in Chapter 6, Battiste (2009, 2007) offers the notion of learning spirit, which resonates with the nurturing tenets offered by the wisdom keepers in the course as they focused on the individual needs of each participant. At the same time, nourishing the learning spirit anticipates relational accountability. Bishop (2008, pp. 445–446) writes that indigenous education within his Maori tradition

> is an education where power is shared between self-determining individuals within nondominating relations of interdependence, where culture counts, and where learning is interactive, dialogic, and spirals and participants are connected and committed to one another through the establishment of a common vision for what constitutes educational excellence.

Building on the notion of culturally responsive pedagogy (Gay, 2000), Bishop suggests that "such a pattern might well be termed a culturally responsive pedagogy of relations" (p. 446). Indigenous pedagogy, then, embraces and exemplifies the principle of unity in diversity (Cajete, 1994), finding resonance with the assertion that specificity eventually leads to universality (Aluli Meyer, 2008).

We Are All Related on Animate Earth

What concepts might a pedagogy of relations be built on? In this section, I respectfully describe teachings gathered from a lecture by Blackfoot scholar Little Bear (2009), when he visited SI,ĆENEṈ. He articulated eloquently his indigenous worldview in a way that resonated with the earth fibres course experience. According to Little Bear, physicists tell us the Earth and all things on or surrounding it – from tiny molecules to the vastness of heavenly bodies – are in constant motion. It is the movement of these things, both large and small, that makes them come into their form of existence.

This notion of constant flux is central to an indigenous worldview. People or objects are merely conduits for energy waves of constant motion. It is the movement of the waves that creates who we are. In an indigenous cosmology, energy waves are known as spirit and are seen as sacred. Within this constant motion, everything is animate and everything possesses spirit. This constant flux places everything in ever-moving relationship. In this way, we are all deeply related. Perception within this constant flux is likened to varied radio waves. For example, from my particular perspective, I can understand certain things; an eagle, from its own particular perspective, can understand other things. Sometimes our perspectives overlap. The purpose of vision quests (a way of learning from spirit), for example, is to expand the range of perception by listening to another perspective that may overlap but also extend beyond what we already know.

Little Bear described how the English language reflects the dominant-culture belief that things can be divided into animate and inanimate entities, continuously dichotomizing and polarizing objects and thoughts. Dominant pedagogy typically seeks to label, place in hierarchy, and examine one thing in comparison to another. Racism arises out of this type of dichotomous thinking, for example, as it focuses on accentuating difference rather than understanding relationships. As a teacher in a multicultural classroom, I might ask, how can I expand my worldview by listening to culturally different students in a relational way? It is not enough for teachers to be aware of content and programmatic knowledge (Hollingsworth, Dybdahl, and Minarik, 1993). Teachers serve their students more fully when they are aware of and engage in a relational way of knowing and understanding learning needs.

The indigenous pedagogy of the earth fibres course was deeply concerned with relationships, as they existed within a non-hierarchical, circular web of being. This perspective acknowledged that everything is a thing-which-is-becoming (Ross, 1996/2006). From a circular, relational cosmology, judgment is inconceivable (S. Wilson, 2008). Within the course, it was just such a process of opening to and acknowledging non-hierarchical relationships that was so significant. The pre-service teachers understood that they were not being judged within the familiar hierarchical grading system of the university and felt, as Chelsea said, that the course was "just a nice place to *be*."

> Wisdom keeper Carolyn felt "forlorn" that her group of learners could not go into the woods and strip cedar. How can the fullness of cyclical rhythms be more completely honoured in learning environments?

From this place of being-ness in relationship with others, the true spirit of Giveaway could be better understood. If we all are truly non-hierarchically related, then giving something away is ultimately giving to ourselves. It is an ebb and flow … breathing in and breathing out. In this way, the lived experience of the Earth fibres course was a culturally responsive pedagogy of relations (Bishop, 2008). As the wisdom keepers pointed out, not only are we all related, but, as humans, we are no more important than any other being that exists. To proceed in a good way, we have to stop trying to fully control our physical environment. Rather, we are in humble relationship with TENEW~Earth.

Along with being profoundly relational, an indigenous cosmology is, at its heart, circular (Cajete, 1994; Fixico, 2003; S. Wilson, 2008). Rhythms, patterns, cycles, and phases matter deeply. The stories of the moons hold a prominent place on XAXE SIÁM SILA because they are integral to the ancestral teachings embodied in the mural. Circles imply a certain sense of continuity. There is a coming back to, a sense of returning and of repetition, a sense that is missing from hierarchical structures. A circle is a place of closure yet, paradoxically, also a place of new beginning. To my Euro-Western–trained mind, this can sometimes feel disconcerting and, at the same time, can give my heart-knowledge a satisfactory sense of well-being.

Throughout the course, the priority of the wisdom keepers was to honour, through good relationship, the essential voice, or learning spirit, of XAXE SIÁM SILA as she emerged from the earth fibres. As discussed above, this process became strained within the context of the university timetable. In the last days of the course, the pressure to complete the piece gradually began to drive the momentum of the group, rather than the pace of the course continuing to follow the natural cycle of the creation of the mural. The significance of the piece was beginning to dawn on people, and this also added stress. Just as things were feeling too hectic, an unexpected snowstorm brought work to a near standstill – for almost a week. Charlene noted that the storm's timeliness gave all of us a chance to slow down and catch our collective breath. Breathing in … breathing out …

While the pause enabled us to settle in to the peace of an exhaled breath, the postponement of the unveiling ceremony meant that, for those pre-service teachers who were unable to attend, the course experience lacked closure. The wisdom keepers felt frustrated that they could not offer important full-circle teachings. For example, Charlene spoke of not being able to share final teachings about specific elements, such as the moons depicted on the mural. The moons tell the story of the seasons and are about new beginnings and coming full circle to completion. Course participants who were able to attend the unveiling experienced a more complete sense of closure. Two years later, those who were able to attend the Grandmother's Honouring Ceremony were able to deepen their sense of closure. With each cycle back, the teachings were revisited and offered new learning possibilities. By incorporating the moon stories in this writing, I continue the cycle of honouring the many stories of XAXE SIÁM SILA~Honoured Grandmother of Many Generations: Wise, Learned, and Respected as Mother Earth.

Does It Grow Corn?

Wisdom keeper Lynne shared with me the following teaching she gathered from an indigenous elder named Sun Bear. As the story goes, there was a woman who thought of Sun Bear as her teacher. The woman was trying to sort through a major life decision. She went to Sun Bear and carefully laid out her choices in great detail and explained her dilemma. After her lengthy and complex descriptions and explications, Sun Bear turned to her and simply said, "Yes, but does it grow corn?"

In my understanding of this story, steeped in the belief that knowledge is spirit, the question of growing corn is a reminder to pay attention to our actions within an eco-social-spiritual awareness. Further, and resonant with Cajete's (2009) questions, the story rests on the underlying expectation that we consider deep sustainability and well-being for ourselves, our community, and TENEW~Earth. I believe that, as educators, it is vital to ask ourselves if we are growing corn. Are we teaching knowledge that endures? Are our lessons about relevant topics that help us get along with each other, nourish the planet, and take care of ourselves?

The course highlighted the vital and ancient importance of having a reciprocal relationship with SI,ĆENEN, the specific place upon which we learned and lived. Our experience was permeated with, and therefore shaped by, our telling of stories of place, sharing herbs in ceremony, crafting the earth fibres, and spending time outside. The course reinforced the indigenous teaching that being aware of our natural surroundings helps us to grow corn. For example, seeing the shorter cattails that were harvested for the weaving project in relation to the longer cattails of the ancestral mats gave us pause. Why where these cattails so much shorter? Was their length predictable within the natural cycle of that particular ecosystem? What was the relationship between human behaviour and the shorter growth of the cattails?

At the beginning of the course, the pre-service teachers were unaware of the origins of the earth fibres used for creating the mural. For example, participants did not previously know that the cedar bark used in indigenous handwork comes from one of the inner layers of the cedar tree. Participants were also unfamiliar with the relational positioning of cedar within the larger knowledge context of indigenous stories, spirit, and generational memory.

Cattails for mat weaving

In an indigenous worldview, spirit is the animate energy of everything that exists. It is in the understanding of the relationship of spirit to all things, through respectful research-vision quest, that knowledge is found (S. Wilson, 2008). The knowledge is *in* the relationships. Knowledge is spirit-driven, and as it connects to spirit-life-energy-relationships, this knowledge endures and sustains (Aluli Meyer, 2008). Thus, knowledge is not static but responds within a universal context across time, as it has for many moons past and as it will indefinitely, into what we call the future. When an elder asks, "Does it grow corn?" it is also the sustainability of *action* that is being referenced. Will our activities be useful for seven generations to come?

Like many indigenous scholars and teachers, the wisdom keepers acknowledged that spirit was in everything and, therefore, every act should be undertaken with a sense of respect. Within the course, this sacred engagement was referred to as using good hands. The wisdom keepers, the pre-service teachers, and the Earth fibres were all expressions of spirit. As spirituality was acknowledged in this integrated and practical way, everything in the course became spiritual and, as Kevin (PST) pointed out in Chapter 2, sacredness was embedded in the mundane.

What is the relationship of place to spirit? How does working with earth fibres feed our souls?

Even though I never brought up the topic of spirit, the pre-service teachers were eager to discuss spirit in the interview process. They were seeking ways to "grow corn" in their classrooms. The course opened up possibilities for understanding and implementing the enduring kind of knowledge that they had witnessed through the stories of the wisdom keepers and the whispers of the 100-year-old cattail mats. They felt this knowledge through their emotional connections to others in the opening circles and through their hands as they worked with the various earth fibres. The pre-service teachers accessed knowledge that had endured in this place, SI,ĆENEN, for countless years.

As they spoke with me, the pre-service teachers wove together the stories of the earth fibres, their experiences in the course, and their own teaching narratives to create a rich description of practice that embedded spirituality at its core and embraced the knowledge of TENEW~Earth. Often they appeared to understand spiritual concepts in an unarticulated way and struggled to put them into words in our discussions. They seemed to know intuitively that what they were doing in the course grew corn for them, both personally and as teachers. Some of their heartfelt questions about educational purpose were being acknowledged and addressed. The course experience and the interview discussions created a space for their intuitive knowledge to grow to include intellectual knowing and articulation. The next chapter looks at how this emerging understanding is thwarted by our current system of schooling, and will begin to address how we can engage more fully in re-connecting with TENEW~Earth.

9

Preparing Self and Community for Dispositional Change

Now we cycle into a third round of walking the wheel, our attention spiralling further outwards into the larger context of education. In this chapter, I address both the course as an act of resistance and the importance of focusing on dispositional change in crosscultural work. In Chapter 10, I look at the challenges that pre-service teachers faced in the implementation of indigenous pedagogy within their practicum settings. Chapter 11 is a discussion about the specifics of re-imagining (teacher) education.

Many educators take a *social justice* stance as an act of resistance against Eurocentric predispositions within education. The term *social justice* is an often-contested term, used differently by different people (Goodlad, 2008), and it can be difficult to define (Grant and Agosto, 2008). Here, I use Bell's (1997, p. 3) definition, to refer to both a collaborative process and a goal that includes a vision of society in which "members are physically and psychologically safe and secure." Multicultural education is one avenue for social justice education, which can be described as "a process of constructing engagement across boundaries of difference and power, for the purpose of constructing a social world that supports and confirms all of us" (Sleeter, in Chávez and O'Donnell, 1998, p. xii).

Common themes in multicultural education in the United States include approaches that focus on assimilation, structural equity, cultural pluralism, and cultural reconstructivism that engage K-12 students in the process of analyzing inequalities and oppression (Grant and Tate, 2001). Multiculturalism in Canada values the "cultural mosaic" and often takes the form of either a "socio-pathological perspective" (the deficit view) or the "relativist model," where all cultures are seen as deserving of equal respect and value (Moodley, 2001, p. 807). Sleeter (2008) suggests that pre-service teachers must gain awareness of four important interrelated issues in order to engage in social justice work within diverse classrooms:

- An increased understanding of institutional racism
- The formation of conceptual frameworks other than a deficit view
- Overcoming the fear and discomfort of facing racial difference
- Increasing a personal awareness of teachers as cultural beings who often hold privilege and power

The earth fibres course offered time and space to explore these four interrelated issues with depth and complexity. Stories of race and racism were often shared with honesty and personal perspective within this intimate setting. Over time, the pre-service teachers came to know the wisdom keepers as competent and complex individuals rather than as a homogenous or stereotypical group of "others," thus moving away from a deficit view of Aboriginal cultures. As participants worked, sang, ate, and created alongside the wisdom keepers, they visibly relaxed and asked questions with increasing frequency, sharing stories from their hearts and demonstrating an increased openness towards cultural and racial difference.

The participants also became aware of their own worry and fears about saying the "right thing" in crosscultural settings. The non-judgmental environment encouraged them to take risks and try new ways of interacting across cultural difference. The course gave them time and space to do deeply reflexive work in which they became more aware of the personal power they held as members of dominant, Eurocentric culture. And, as we will see in Chapter 10, the pre-service teachers grappled with how an externally derived curriculum steeped in Eurocentric values controlled what and how they were able to teach during their practica; this increased their understanding of institutional racism.

A Tender Resistance

Resistance as an act of social justice can take many forms. What happened in the course, a specific context of crosscultural education, was a particular type of resistance, informed by the indigenous sensibilities of Lorna, Charlene, and the other wisdom keepers. I call it a *tender resistance* because it was an act of decolonizing that was simultaneously vulnerable, caring, mindful, and dialogic. Participating in the course required us to recognize the colonization that has occurred for generations, on multiple layers of experience – from the institutional to the personal. Countless acts of colonization have led to a profound mutual inflammation, a wound with an intense rawness that continues to agitate, bruise, and cause pain. This harm has been done not only to people, but also to the four-legged, slithering, winged, swimming beings, the ecosystems, and the very Earth on which we depend.

Within the course, making space separate from this painful legacy was often a fragile, sensitive, and subtle undertaking. It required tender acts of honesty, careful attention, determination, and courage. Resisting the overwhelming presence of colonization required us to hold gently the truths of what has occurred and what continues to occur. It required us to listen without judgment to stories, tears, and injustices and, perhaps most importantly, to listen in order to be changed. A tender resistance is one where we resist the harmful effects of the status quo while at the same time open our hearts to the collective hopes of who we can become.

Those who took part in the tender resistance of the course became vulnerable in unexpected ways. For example, the wisdom keepers had to decide whether or not to share the deeply held beliefs that influenced who they were as educators. This was not always easy in an environment that shies away from, or actively negates, important indigenous beliefs about spirit and spirituality. These unexpected stories sometimes required the pre-service teachers to shift foundational constructs they held dear. In fact, the pre-service teachers were gently asked to reposition themselves actively so that they might see the world from the perspective of another cultural worldview (Apple, 2008) – a tender endeavour indeed. Connecting in this way with deeply held personal and cultural beliefs is what made the resistance so delicate and so effective. All participants in the course were expected to engage in listening that was alert, open-minded, and big-hearted. It was a bare, unprotected listening that asked us to let go of our assumptions and to imagine what might be true of another, and then to imagine our possibilities *together*.

A Note about Cultural Appropriation

Ultimately, tender resistance requires a deep appreciation of indigenous knowledge. In the course, this knowledge was gained through the respectful relationships that developed while participants walked alongside the wisdom keepers in the course. As Shawn Wilson (2008, p. 114) writes, "If knowledge is formed in a relationship, it can't be owned. I guess you could ask, would you own the knowledge or would it own you?" In the course, indigenous knowledge began to own the non-indigenous participants, to be embedded in their visceral fibres of being-knowing-doing. According to Wilson, cultural appropriation occurs when someone uses "knowledge out of its context, out of the special relationships that went into forming it. You have to build a relationship with an idea or with knowledge, just like you have to with anything or anyone else." In walking alongside, participants gained deeper insight that went beyond the just-visiting mentality into an indigenist perspective that could be taken on in crosscultural work.

As indigenous cultures are being renewed and indigenous perspectives are increasingly incorporated into educational settings, there is, understandably, resistance on the part of some individuals to intrusions from outsiders. The course provided an unusual environment in which persons highly typical of the teacher population (the non-indigenous pre-service teachers) were invited to immerse themselves in another culture. They not only left the course with an understanding of some of the details of indigenous culture, but more importantly also brought forward teachings that could be applied across contexts, and internalized these, each according to his/her own set of core values. Typically, these teachings disrupted Eurocentric notions of learning and teaching and supported the pre-service teachers to undergo significant dispositional change.

The Importance of Dispositional Change

Teacher education is dedicated to developing a teacher's teaching capacity, the ability to deal with the complex terrain of learning within a classroom. Typically, three broad and interrelated categories are accepted as describing teacher capacity – *knowledge* (what teachers need to know about), *skills* (what teachers are able to do), and *disposition* (what teachers believe and care about) (McDiarmid and Clevenger-Bright, 2008). Teacher education typically focuses on the more concrete processes of building content knowledge and practical skills, while the more ambiguous, yet equally important, issue of disposition – a person's beliefs, values, and attitudes – is underdeveloped or even ignored.

Freire (1998) describes numerous dispositional qualities he believes to be indispensable for teachers who care about issues of social justice. These include humility, lovingness, courage, tolerance, decisiveness, security, the joy of living, and the tension between patience and impatience. These dispositional characteristics are difficult to describe, let alone measure, within a given teacher's practice. It is no wonder that teacher educators tend to gravitate towards the more tangible focus on skill and knowledge acquisition. In the earth fibres course, the wisdom keepers were open to and comfortable with engaging in the tender emotionality of the dispositional change occurring within the pre-service teachers.

As North America's largely mono-cultural population of teachers works with an increasingly multicultural population, teachers must also develop a *willingness to engage* in issues of social justice (McDiarmid and Clevenger-Bright, 2008). The earth fibres course provided a vibrant environment that supported pre-service teachers as they shifted their dispositional characteristics and became more willing to take on issues of social justice in their teaching practice.

The development of teacher capacity is a fluid, career-long process focused on a potential for growth rather than an ability to receive and/or obtain knowledge (Freire, 1998; McDiarmid and Clevenger-Bright, 2008). The lifelong-learning nature of the process begs for it to be included as a fundamental cornerstone within teacher education. But teaching hard-to-grasp concepts such as humility and tolerance is complicated. For example, van Manen (1991) points out that a teacher's capacity to be tactful may be easier to identify when tact is *lacking* rather than when a teacher is actively being tactful. The role of a teacher's past experience also comes into play: many teacher qualities are acquired unconsciously through observation of previous teachers (Britzman, 1990/2003; Lortie, 1975).

There is little academic work that elucidates the relationship between teacher capacity and matters of social justice, particularly around the issues of white teachers teaching non-white students (Grant, 2008). This unfortunate circumstance exists despite suggestions that research on teacher capacity should consider more closely the effectiveness of teachers who participate in social-justice–oriented programs (Howard and Aleman, 2008). The role of teacher disposition seems to play an important role in this regard. One study by Kanu (2005) on integrating indigenous culture and knowledge perspectives into high school curricula suggests that teachers must value indigenous pedagogical strategies in order to integrate them successfully in their classrooms.

Kanu's work highlights the gap in understanding about teacher capacity. Teaching across cultures requires understanding (knowledge) and strategies (skills), but as Kanu points out, changes in practice are brought about by reflexive examination of dispositions. The pre-service teachers' experiences in the earth fibres course corroborate her findings; as other cultures were explored, knowledge of personal culture (in the case of the pre-service teachers, white, dominant culture) was increased.

Reflecting on Islands of Culture

Research suggests that beginning teachers examine their prior beliefs as an essential first step in learning to teach well (Wideen et al., 1998). In the examination of culture, the image of an iceberg is often employed as a metaphor (Merryfield and Wilson, 2005). What can be seen of an iceberg above the water-line represents the visible aspects of culture, how we behave and act in the world. These aspects are sometimes referred to as the feasts, festivals, and fashion of culture. Under the water, however, 90 percent of the iceberg lies hidden from casual view. It is in these shadowy depths that cultural foundations – the ontologies, epistemologies, and cosmologies of a people – can be found. It is important that teachers understand the nature of what lies below the water – especially in crosscultural contexts.

I have often used the iceberg metaphor with my own students, but my thinking on the usefulness of this image was unsettled when Opaskwayak Cree scholar Shawn Wilson (2010) visited SI,ĆENEN̲ and the University of Victoria campus. Because of our location on Vancouver Island, surrounded by the Salish Sea, Wilson wondered aloud if the image of an island might be a more appropriate metaphor for those of us working from this place, surrounded by and embedded in island-ness. For me, this was a poignant example of the need to understand from the context of a different cosmology. Shawn's indigenous worldview incorporated a deep sense of physical place. His attention became connected to the watery roots of SI,ĆENEN̲, the place on which we were standing.

Understanding the differing worldviews that form the bedrock of our cultural islands is important. These affect who we are and how we act. We use numerous interpretive frameworks to convey how we view the world (Denzin and Lincoln, 1994). Worldviews that have influenced educational traditions typically have been categorized according to three main paradigms (Wideen et al., 1998). *Positivism* stems from the modernist tradition of the late nineteenth century and continues to be the pervasive paradigm in education across North America. *Progressivism*, a post-modern paradigm, and *social critique*, a post-colonial paradigm, are conscious and concerted responses to the hegemonic presence of positivism. Unfortunately, the *indigenous* paradigm is often left out of discussions on what frameworks are useful within educational contexts.

Social critique theorists advocate for teachers to engage in reflection as part of a critical consciousness, in which teachers attend to broader issues of multicultural classrooms (Howard and Aleman, 2008). The inescapable political nature of education requires teachers to have clarity about their ideology and an understanding of their socio-cultural positioning in the world in relation to others (Moll and Arnot-Hopffer, 2005). Richardson (1996) describes an interactive relationship between beliefs and teacher action, suggesting that reflection on action "may lead to changes in and/or additions to beliefs" (p. 104). However, Richardson's extensive survey of research on teacher beliefs sheds doubt on the overall efficacy of teacher education coursework in effecting dispositional change, given the influential forces of previous life experience and experience within teachers' practica and other teaching situations. If the indigenous paradigm is not a part of a teacher's past experience, how can it be considered? In the context of the earth fibres course, indigenous life and teaching experience were embedded within the teacher education context, providing new touchstones of possible beliefs.

> How do (teacher) educators take a close look at the larger paradigmatic intent behind courses that students are required to take?

Reflective practices are often incorporated in teacher education courses in the hopes that they will effect change in teacher beliefs, yet this response may be only a partial solution. Reflective thinking can be limited in that it can focus too closely on the obvious surface of an island rather than on what lies beneath the shadowy waters around it. Theories born of reflection may "do little more than rationalize actions we've taken or would like to take; they are the images of our action, not its source" (Dressman, 1998, p. 120). It is more useful for teacher educators to replace the common emphasis on reflection with the deeper practice of reflexivity.

Towards Reflexivity

For teachers to respond to issues of social justice in meaningful ways, a significant dispositional change is linked to a deeper type of reflection (Leonardo, 2004; Sharp, 2003). As discussed in the introduction of this book, this kind of reflection needs to be dialogic as well as consciously situated in each teacher's own process of learning so that both technical and political content can be more fully understood (Hoffman-Kipp, Artiles, and López-Torres, 2003). Pre-service teachers must "develop a content-knowledge base that is multicultural, come to see themselves as cultural beings with a plurality of identities, develop the type of critical thinking and analytic skills necessary for problem posing, critical inquiry, and reflective thinking, and acquire the skills necessary to help ... students succeed" (Gillette and Schultz, 2008, p. 233). The earth fibres course experience greatly enhanced the pre-service teachers' awareness of their own cultural positioning and what this positioning meant for them as teachers.

To be more fully reflexive, teachers must engage in the often uncomfort-able and paradoxical process of *knowing while not knowing*. As Kumashiro (2008, p. 239) writes, "Quality teachers need certain knowledge, but also need to know the limits of their knowledge. They need certain skills, but also need the skill of troubling whatever they do. They need certain dispositions, but also need to be disposed to uncomfortable changes in these very dispositions."

The wisdom keepers supported a rare, safe enough space in which this awkward but essential process could occur. The inevitable discomfort held much potential as a site for growth, and the pre-service teachers rose to the occasion.

> How do we embrace uncertainty more fully within (teacher) education?

In order to do meaningful social justice work, white, middle-class teachers must reflect on their own auto-biographies (Traudt, 2002). As Delpit (1988) says, "We must learn to be vulner-able enough to allow our world to turn upside down in order to allow the realities of others to edge themselves into our consciousness" (p. 298). Examining cultural beliefs is both a reflective and deeply reflexive experience of unearthing what is beneath our islands, and relocating our sense of self (T. Wilson, 2002). It can cause uneasiness among teacher educators as it asks that they pay attention through silence, deep listening, and observing; it requires openness to exposing personal feelings and the possibility of critique (Hart, 2001). Through this com-plicated and ongoing process, (teacher) educators have to find their own location as well as the location of others in the "topography of power" (Hart, 2001, p. 166) within the classroom. Through this process it becomes possible to see the inter-relatedness and common ground of self and other (Hart, 2001, p. 178) that can eventually shift educational horizons of understanding (Greene, 1978).

Transformative Communities

In the context of increasingly overlapping cultural communities, educators must examine closely the stories we live by (King, 2003) to better utilize their role in promoting classroom communities rich in crosscultural understanding. As Okri (1997, p. 46) states, "We live by stories that either give our lives meaning or negate it with meaninglessness. If we change the stories we live by, quite possibly we change our lives." This transformative work can be done on a personal level, and it can occur communally in conversation with others. Here, I look to the realm of adult transformative learning theory to explain how the pre-service teachers changed their dispositional stances, their awareness of their own culture, within the course.

The current field of transformative learning has its roots in the area of adult education and began with a study by Mezirow (1978) that discussed the experiences of women returning to community college. Over the past few decades, Mezirow (1997) has come to describe transformative learning as a process of effecting change in a personal frame of reference through discourse, critical reflection on our assumptions, and the development of autonomous thinking. The theory has evolved "into a comprehensive and complex description of how learners construe, validate and reformulate the meaning of their experience" (Cranton, 1994, p. 22).

Some scholars in the field have moved away from a personal orientation and see transformative learning as a tool for social change. This view has its roots in Paulo Freire's notion of conscientization, introduced in his seminal *Pedagogy of the Oppressed* (1970/2005). This merging of critical reflection and social action is fundamental to the practice of reflective teaching (Dewey, 1933; Schön, 1983; van Manen, 1977; Zeichner, 1987) and is also tied to ideas of radical teacher education (Gore, 1993).

Overlapping the consideration of personal and social orientations towards transformative learning is a discussion about whether transformative learning is a process of rational reflection or one of engagement on a more emotional level. An emphasis on transformative learning based in analytical psychology emphasizes the roles of receptivity, recognition, and grieving in the transformative process (Boyd and Myers, 1988, p. 277). In fact, too much rationality can hinder the transformative learning process; it must be balanced with an *affective* component of shared vulnerability (Tisdell, 2001).

The safe reciprocal sharing of emotions within a learning community can be a significant factor in changing deep-seated dispositions so that individuals gain a richer, more nuanced understanding of other individuals and cultures (Oosterheert and Vermunt, 2003). Engaging the emotions while in community turns reflection into a reflexive act. As observed in the course, opening to emotional knowing within community offers educators hope (Tisdell, 2001). Hope and action together imbue teachers with a sense of agency and the energy to imagine how their classrooms might be different (Generett and Hicks, 2004), as addressed in the next chapter. Transformative learning, then, becomes a holistic process that includes both personal and social perspectives and is engaged through both rational and emotional connections, where thoughtful, autonomous individuals relate their understandings and actions to others (Shugurensky, 2002).

But transformative learning can be taken to yet another realm – that of an eco-centric or cosmological perspective (O'Sullivan, 2001). In this view, the autonomous is embedded in the social milieu, and the social is embedded in the overall global and even universal ecosystem that is our human environment. Here, the transformative process is defined against the backdrop of a constantly-in-process, formative grand narrative that moves us beyond globalization and its compounded effects (O'Sullivan, 2001). This idea ties into the indigenous perspective of relationality and interconnectivity. The notion that learning is connected to a sense of cosmic awareness is a far cry from the positivist worldview that tends towards separateness rather than our state of *interbeing* (Nhất Hạnh, 1991).

> How do we model and encourage appropriate and useful group work that addresses Cajete's (2009) questions?

Transformative learning becomes a decolonizing process that opens up a sense of relationship between indigenous and dominant discourse, a process that may confuse and disorient pre-service teachers (Kumashiro, 2008). In our conversations, many pre-service teachers expressed feelings of uncertainty at times in the course. When I experienced these feelings myself in the course, the uncomfortable sense of disconnect required that I stay mindful and patient within the recursively transformative process. Eventually, new understandings of learning-teaching began to emerge through reflexive processes of observation, conversation, writing, and so on. This had occurred previously as well, during my experience in the earlier pole-carving course, after which I co-authored an article describing the process of shifting pedagogical beliefs (Tanaka et al., 2007). This sense of knowledge construction through interdependency resonated with the indigenous approach of the wisdom keepers.

The very nature of transformative learning is that it is in constant flux. Nevertheless, it is useful to consider the definition of integral transformative learning provided by O'Sullivan, Morrell, and O'Connor (2002, p. 11):

[Transformative] learning involves experiencing a deep, structural shift in the basic premise of thought, feelings, and actions. It is a shift of consciousness that dramatically and permanently alters our way of being in the world. Such a shift involves our understanding of ourselves and our self-locations; our relationships with other humans and the natural world; our understandings of relations of power in interlocking structures of class, race and gender; our body-awarenesses; our visions of alternative approaches to living; and our sense of possibilities for social justice and peace and personal joy.

Within the course, this shift towards an indigenist perspective was not always sudden or dramatic, but it was deeply felt. It is the type of change that teacher educators concerned with Cajete's (2009) questions might look for in their pre-service teachers. How do we clean up the mess humans have made on planet Earth? How do we live more harmoniously with each other? How do we care for our souls?

Embracing Awkwardness

Teaching for social justice is often described as *dangerous work* (Ladson-Billings, 1999). This is, in part, because engaging in dialogue about uncomfortable and unpleasant issues of race is a difficult yet critical self-reflexive process (Chávez and O'Donnell, 1998) that can bring up volatile emotions and cause us to lose what is comfortable and familiar. In addition, being introspective is risky because it challenges beliefs and assumptions that the individual has previously taken for granted (Oberg, 2004), thus leaving us on uncertain epistemological ground. Within (teacher) education, there can be reluctance about, and at times hostility towards, implementing the institutional and/or personal change required to nurture socially just classrooms because it ultimately requires a shift in the topography of power (Hart, 2001). Teachers must risk redefining themselves in this new terrain, giving up previously perceived power for an unknown new role. The wisdom keepers in the earth fibres course set the tone for safe enough space in which pre-service teachers could ask difficult questions, engage in honest conversation, and explore the roots of their own dispositions.

The earth fibres course experiences also indicate that social contexts influence teaching knowledge and practice. This has significance for how teacher educators work with changing teacher capacity. It suggests that, if our understanding of practice is socially mediated, "changing the social contexts in which teachers learn and develop may be necessary for real changes in their understanding of their roles, the purposes of schooling, and core educational concepts and skills" (McDiarmid and Clevenger-Bright, 2008, p. 145). In this vein, (teacher) education becomes a spontaneous and unpredictable process of teacher-led collaborative cultures with teachers working together for educational change (Hargreaves, 1996). Challenging the dominant positivist paradigm is awkward and uncomfortable for individual teachers, whose ontological and epistemological beliefs will be challenged, and for children and school communities, who will need to adapt as new ways of proceeding are explored, yet somehow we must learn to embrace the awkwardness if we want socially just classrooms. The following chapter will continue this discussion of social justice by describing how some of the changes and hopes for education evoked in the earth fibres course met with the realities of pre-service teacher practicum placements within the public school context.

10

Indigenizing Practice amid Classroom Challenges

The pre-service teachers left the course wanting to embrace a more indigenous approach to learning and teaching. They went out into their practica aware that they were forming their own styles as teachers, and they saw the earth fibres course as having given them practical ideas for improving their teaching. They wanted to increase cultural awareness within their students, and they also wanted to incorporate indigenous ways within their own pedagogical practice. To do this effectively, they believed it was necessary to show cultural acceptance in tangible ways, to consciously create safe spaces, and to embed indigenous pedagogy throughout the curriculum.

Their aspirations however, met with various challenges of implementation. By "challenge," I mean a complex non-binary situation, a predicament that holds, among other things, multiple yet often unsatisfactory and even disheartening choices. For the pre-service teachers, these challenges showed up immediately following the completion of the course, when they began the final eight-week practicum required for the completion of their certification. After their practica, I was able to have one last conversation with these teachers, in a series of small focus groups. In this setting, the pre-service teachers reaffirmed that participating in the course had shifted their conceptualizations of pedagogy towards indigenous ways of learning and teaching. For the most part, they were eager to put aspects of an indigenous approach into practice, with both Aboriginal and non-Aboriginal children. However, the realities of their practicum settings hindered these intentions. Before I share six particular challenges faced by the pre-service teachers, I will remind the reader of the general atmosphere typical of the schools the pre-service teachers found themselves teaching in.

The Culture of Positivism

Picture a fish swimming around in a pond: this fish may not notice the substance that we call water, as the water's fluidity permeates much of the pond's reality. Water is above, below, and running through the very gills of the fish. From our perspective onshore, we can see the water; the fish cannot. Now, imagine a classroom in a typical North American school: like the fish, this classroom is surrounded by an often-undetected element. Not water, but the culture of positivism. *Positivism* is a particular worldview rooted in the theory that knowledge can be obtained only through objective observation and rational experimentation. This notion also permeates (teacher) education on many levels. But unlike water to the fish, an overabundance of positivism may be harmful to our collective health and wellness.

Hutchins (1936/1952, p. 66), a contemporary of early educational theorist John Dewey, articulated one of the fundamental beliefs in the positivist tradition when he stated: "Truth is everywhere the same. Hence, education should be everywhere the same." From this viewpoint, education revolves around what social justice activist and scholar Paulo Freire (1970/2005) described as the banking model of education. This model is based on the assumption that people learn primarily by an additive process, absorbing curriculum content in ways that are somehow detached from individual, social, political, and situational contexts. Within this model, learner diversity is not considered to be particularly relevant to the teaching process. Teacher control and appropriate teacher management of the learners are central tenets. The flow of learning typically moves in one direction: from the teacher to the learner. Strong emphasis is placed on the accumulation of factual knowledge and the development of fundamental skills. The epistemological and ontological underpinnings of this tradition are atomistic and isolating. The universe is separated into its constituent parts, and then these parts – and our experience of them – are examined and understood in isolation from their larger, natural context.

Within a positivist worldview, curriculum content is separated out into units of knowledge to be efficiently transferred to students in a structured and separated, hierarchical way (Hutchison and Bosacki, 2000). Knowledge is organized into distinct, seemingly disconnected academic disciplines. Curriculum scholar Grumet (2006, p. 47) warns us, however, that the disciplines offer only "symbolic re-presentations" of the world: "They are an index pointing to its content (what we sometimes call objectivity) projected from human intentionality (what we sometimes call subjectivity)" (p. 48). A heavy focus on such objectivity within (teacher) education often leads us to "settle for someone else's version of the world" (p. 50). This raises important questions about intent, about whose view of learning is privileged in a course of study, and to what end.

Within the positivist framework, effective teachers are seen as those who excel in *content* knowledge and its distribution. This preference is sometimes privileged over the need for teachers to have *pedagogic* knowledge, such as skills of classroom management, the ability to teach to certain learning styles, fair and effective means of discipline, and so on (Kennedy, Ahn, and Choi, 2008). A response to this tension can be found in approaches that focus on pedagogical content knowledge while recognizing that the domains of subject matter and pedagogy are interrelated and must be addressed simultaneously (Howard and Aleman, 2008).

The highly transmissive approach to teaching privileged within positivism can be useful for some areas of learning, particularly those that focus heavily on content-specific knowledge. However, such an approach can be problematic when used as an overarching philosophy for developing and implementing other types of curricula. Process-oriented or relational learning aimed at responding to the more holistic needs of the learner are not well served by a strictly positivist approach (Miller, 2007; Grauerholz, 2001).

Many educational scholars are critical of a positivist approach (Apple, 1995; hooks, 1994; Kanu, 2003; Liston and Zeichner, 1991; Shor, 1986). Yet despite calls for reform (Ladson-Billings, 1995; Futrell, 2008) and specific suggestions to that end (Wideen and Grimmett, 1995; Britzman et al., 1997), positivism is still the dominant tradition in teacher education. Because the positivist approach is rooted in notions of an objective external truth, where knowledge acquisition is seen as an object more than a process, learning and teaching become bifurcated. In addition, Cartesian beliefs in a Euro-Western tradition presume that thought manifests being-ness, placing emphasis on thought as perception, whereas a more indigenous view acknowledges other ways of knowing. The tactile knowledge that comes from stripping and weaving cedar and the intuitive knowledge of spirit in ritual find little room within positivist thought. The positivist paradigm was the atmosphere into which our newly indigenizing pre-service teachers had to leap. Their comments confirm that they faced a lingering positivism in themselves and in the classroom as they dealt with perplexing and multifaceted challenges. How did they fare? Here are six examples of the challenges they faced.

The Challenge of Pieces

The pre-service teachers spoke about wanting to increase both cultural awareness within their classrooms and their use of indigenous ways within their pedagogical practice. They believed that, to do this effectively, it was necessary for teachers to show cultural acceptance in tangible ways, consciously create safe spaces, and embed indigenous pedagogy throughout the curriculum. The lived reality of the classroom presents a difficulty, as Leanne (PST) articulated: "I think a lot of the time in schools, it's executed completely wrong. It's always these small little activities, where it's, like, 'community building time,' or … 'okay, right now we are going to work together.' So it just shows it as this isolated little thing instead of being implemented into every facet of how we teach." Leanne didn't want to "teach" community building as a discrete lesson or unit. She wanted to embed a sense of building community into the very fibre of her classroom. The existing structure of positivism was prohibitive. (Teacher) education needs to respond better to this challenge, as Futrell (2008, p. 536) argues: "The model of schools as cubicles – in which teachers teach their classes in isolation using the didactic method, or where subjects are taught as though they, too, are isolated disciplines – is no longer the most practical nor effective way to teach and learn."

> How do we let go of our obsessive need to organize, label, and control curriculum? How do we take the time and space required to build community when "the curriculum" as prescription is bearing down?

Rather than upholding positivist traditions, it would be useful for (teacher) education to draw from research on learning in communities that includes multicultural perspectives (Cochran-Smith, 2005; Houston and Clift, 1990). Within the earth fibres course, the instructors intentionally built a very particular kind of community. Pre-service teachers need time and space to understand, articulate, and pursue their own intentions around developing community within classrooms. This type of reflexive space should be enacted during professional development days within schools also.

The Challenge of Ownership

The pre-service teachers were very aware of the limitations of their practica, due to the short, eight-week time period. More importantly, they knew that they were visitors in someone else's classroom and that they had varying levels of support from and/or philosophical congruence with their mentor teachers. As Nicole told her focus group,

> I found, in my practicum, it was quite difficult to put my vision of a classroom into action. Maybe it was just because it wasn't my own classroom and you don't get the same kind of opportunities as you get if you had them for the whole year. But it was a lot harder to implement it than I thought it would be. By implementing it, I mean different ways of teaching and learning. Because you have to focus so much on getting [the curriculum] done and getting those marks in for report cards. And there's all this other stuff that's in the way that you have to do. I found that kind of unfortunate, but I think that as I grow and get more experience that I'll be able to do that part a bit better.

Reminiscent of how Courtney (PST) was "cursed" by the flower image in Chapter 5, Nicole is haunted by a deep positivist patterning. She continued her sharing by saying that she felt one of the reasons it was hard to make changes "[was] because you feel safer teaching in that standard way that you grew up with and that the rest of the classes seem to undertake."

The awareness of needing to do things differently was coupled with a concern about the unknown response and outcome of incorporating unfamiliar strategies into the classroom. Courtney said that "not really knowing where it's going to go" was a risk that teachers faced if they wanted to try an earth fibres type of pedagogy. Unfortunately, many teacher education programs are set up to assess pre-service teachers' abilities to recreate the status quo rather than to try innovative ideas such as building community within an indigenous paradigm.

Who owns curriculum? How might pre-service teachers have more voice in this? How can they be supported to take risks?

Constructivist learning theory is based on the notion that knowledge and meaning are derived from experience (Piaget, 1960). This theory moves away from a view of the learner as a relatively inert vessel to be filled. Instead, individuals are seen as being able to engage personal prior knowledge and beliefs to actively construct meaning. The constructivist view has significant implications for teaching students of diverse cultures as it acknowledges that each individual brings his or her own understanding, experience, and positioning to the learning environment (Villegas, 2008). Should this not also apply to pre-service teachers? What might have been possible if Nicole and Courtney had felt supported to explore implementing the ideas they had experienced and developed within the earth fibres course?

There are many issues of ideological control and privilege at play within the positivist social structures and social practices in schools. Schools are key contributors to ideological hegemony (Apple, 1995; Giroux, 1992), and this is what the pre-service teachers came up against. Teacher education programs have long been seen as potential vehicles for democracy (Robertson, 2008), with the goal of preparing teachers for working with diverse populations (Ladson-Billings, 1995; Villegas and Lucas, 2002). But along with their colleagues from the course, Nicole and Courtney were not fully supported in putting into action their unfamiliar, and perhaps even subversive, ideas about indigenous ways of learning and teaching.

Within teacher education, there is an established appreciation of the need for teachers to act as advocates of social justice (Freire, 1970/2005; Goodlad, Mantle-Bromley, and Goodlad, 2004; Grant and Agosto, 2008; Hollins and Guzman, 2005; hooks, 1994). Within this view, the role of teachers finally becomes that of transformative intellectuals working towards radical, conscious change so that education becomes more socially just (Giroux, 1992). In this case, ideas for changing hegemonic practices stalled as the pre-service teachers were left unsupported in their efforts to effect change.

The Challenge of External Motivation

Within the schools, the pre-service teachers noticed that some learners seemed to have lost their heartfelt inner enthusiasm for learning. Nicole expressed a concern that this lack of excitement was pervasive in the positivist environment:

> It kind of goes in a wave, I find. Kindergartners love learning. You know, they'll do it for the sake of learning and they love it. And then it just goes down, down, down, down. And as you hit about grade twelve or so, it starts [up again]. You want to learn for the sake of learning and for yourself ... It just seems that when they are younger, they love [to learn], and I don't think they realize that they're learning, almost. And then all of a sudden, they realize it, and ... it's pulling teeth sometimes to get them to do their work, or to practise something, or to try hard.

What is happening here? Why do learners lose touch with their learning spirits? Could it be that the externally derived curriculum becomes privileged to the point that the learning spirit is forgotten? Typically, even hard-core positivists agree that play and exploration are great activities for the early years. But by the time learners are in grade 1 (or even kindergarten), there looms a message that it's time to get serious. With vigorous passion, we teach reading, math, and other fundamental skills, forgetting that each child also needs to have his or her will and desire to learn acknowledged and nourished.

We can learn much from observing the habits of early childhood educators in this regard. Play is a lovely vehicle for the learning spirit. What might that look like in primary classrooms, middle years, secondary, and even post-secondary settings?

> If pre-service teachers have their learning spirit nourished, as happened in the earth fibres course, will they be more inclined to try to pass this on to their own students?

Nicole went on to say that learner enthusiasm seemed to really drop after the primary years, when letter grades were introduced, and that she "hates that they get graded at such a young age." The pre-service teachers expressed concern that the external motivation of grades was affecting internal motivation to learn. They acknowledged that it was an issue that they would often be negotiating if they wanted to stay focused on the needs of the learner.

The Challenge of Assessment

The pre-service teachers articulated clearly the tensions between grading and letting students guide their own learning. As Nicole said, "Most times in classrooms, learning seems to be forced. Instead of it being something that you want to do, it's something that you have to do." The pre-service teachers acknowledged that forcing a particular curriculum was driven, in part, by an all-encompassing need to assess. Courtney reminisced about how wisdom keeper May "took so much joy" in the success of her knitting group, but lamented,

> I'd like to think that any teacher wants to have that sense of pride, that joy
> in their students' work, that pure untainted love of seeing a student succeed.
> However, in reality, I think it often gets squashed down by meeting learning
> outcomes, and ensuring that curriculum is met, and getting the assessment
> done, and creating quantitative data that we can evaluate our students on.

As learners in the earth fibres course, the pre-service teachers appreciated that there was no external pressure of marks. They could work together in a non-competitive, cooperative environment that fostered their love of learning. Once in their practica, they thought carefully about assessment and ways that they could make it more useful to their learners. They tried various approaches including the following:

1. Having students work together to come up with assignment criteria in order to build a sense of community in which the students were equal to each other and to the teacher.
2. Including opportunities for combining self-assessment with teacher assessment, wherein the two marks were averaged.
3. Rating effort as well as academic ability.
4. Taking emphasis off grades by giving out check marks and comments on the assignments while keeping the grades out of sight in a grade book. They told the students that a check meant that everything was fine, and had occasional conferences with the students to discuss their growth. This technique forced the students to pay closer attention to the comments and to think about process rather than getting a mark.

For the most part, however, the pre-service teachers maintained the status quo on the issues of assessment and grades.

A significant issue within the positivist paradigm has to do with meeting the pressures of increasingly high-stakes testing and assessment (Valli and Buese, 2007). Transmissive teaching approaches that emphasize knowledge as subject matter lend themselves to evaluation and assessment, and this tends to be the default position in most schools. This approach provides teachers only a partial understanding of what a given student might know (Esteve, 2000). Unfortunately, this expanding emphasis on testing encourages a dependency on the transmissive approach, along with the misguided and potentially harmful approach of teaching to the test (Shepard, 1990).

> How can new teachers find courage to change harmful assessment when there is so much pressure on them in terms of accountability?

The Challenge of Efficiency

Throughout the earth fibres course, the pre-service teachers were aware of the patience of the wisdom keepers and how that affected their learning. In Chapter 4, Sara discusses how her own sense of patience with herself influenced her learning processes, as in the case of weaving cattail mats. Some pre-service teachers also noticed how time pressures such as deadlines and schedules shaped their learning experiences. This understanding increased as learners developed their teaching practice. Many spoke of finding ways to be more patient in the classroom, talking about how patience could take various forms, including giving "wait time" for students to think before answering, being more flexible with deadlines, seeing "tangents" or "detours" that the students took as enriching learning opportunities, and sitting back and listening to their students more often. Sara spoke of a deeper kind of patience that would maximize the learning of her students:

> It's not just being patient, you know, you've got thirty kids and twenty of them have their hands up at the same time needing help. I mean, that's one type of patience, but another type of patience is that understanding of how they're thinking and understanding that you need to take time with each child and have patience for their own development and their own understanding of what you're teaching. So I think it's very different ... I don't think I've really fully understood that [other people learn in different ways] and that I need not only to provide them with opportunities to learn in different ways, but give them more time to just sort of understand what they're doing and why they're doing it.

In this quote, Sara articulates how the pre-service teachers linked increased patience with developing a real and useful understanding of the nuances of other cultural ways of knowing.

In addition, the pre-service teachers saw that patience was tied to focusing on learning rather than on the content to be taught. Leanne said that teaching is too often "just so goal-focused or so answer-focused" and that by "doing that, you can really miss out on a lot of meaningful thought processes." She described how a teacher could instead pursue tangents by engaging a dialogue that might not be in the lesson plan, "[by] letting them go on that [direction] and giving them those couple of minutes where they can form their thoughts. It's a really subtle thing, ... giving that confidence to articulate or to explain themselves. It's really part of the teacher holding back instead of the teacher wanting it this way or whatever." Leanne went on to say that by being patient with students in this way, it was possible to tap into areas of interest for other students as well.

The pre-service teachers spoke of being driven by an underlying sense of urgency in the classroom and were taking a closer look at why that might be so. Many of the pre-service teachers acknowledged that their lifestyle was one that, as Courtney said, was "all busied up." They made concerted efforts in their teaching to slow down and consciously try to create the feeling of calm that was so often present in the earth fibres course. They did this both with their students and with their own growth processes as teachers. The pressures of expectations and time, however, strained their efforts.

We live within a culture deeply wedded to notions of efficiency, where efficiency is often seen as an end in itself rather than as a means to an end (Stein, 2002). Positivist schooling seems to get caught up on this gerbil wheel, as teachers roll forward with the curriculum without taking time to really ask one of Stein's key questions: Efficient at what? What are we busied up with in schools? Is this the direction we want to go?

> How does impatience and product orientation affect learners and learning? What is the appropriate role of efficiency in (teacher) education?

The Challenge of Group Work

Despite the perceived value of group work and the pre-service teachers' strong desire to include it in their classrooms, some of the pre-service teachers had strongly disliked working with others in previous educational settings. Most expressed that doing good group work was very challenging due to its complex and changing nature. They spoke about division of labour and control of group direction, among other things, as being significant and complex factors in the success of group work. Nicole shared:

Part of my vision was having [my students] work in groups more often than individually, so they could learn from each other and teach each other. But I found that with certain classes, the dynamics and stuff, it just doesn't work ... They have a hard time giving each other tasks. They have a hard time working together. And I think if you built upon it, they would have an easier time. But there are still going to be those kids who just sit off to the side and don't contribute much, and then also those kids that want to contribute everything and don't let anyone else do it.

Despite these types of challenges, the pre-service teachers felt that group work could be successful if the teacher was very attentive to the process and to the students who were having trouble engaging due to feelings of uncertainty or discomfort. Garrett (PST) said that developing patterns of good group work was a gradual process over time:

It's sort of a natural progression. I mean, if you're not used to working in groups, then it is going to be hard. So I realized that they needed to be introduced to it almost in baby steps [with] a lot of guidance ... The social thing was big for me, so it was a real good experience having it actually become a struggle. I think if I had my own classroom, I would prepare my students for that a lot more.

The pre-service teachers also felt that some students needed to learn how to take a step back so that others could be more engaged in the work of a group. This might mean embracing patience and stepping back from the perils of expecting perfection.

The pre-service teachers went on to say that the group work they were used to doing in the teacher education program was typical of the type of group work that happened in schools. Those groups often were competitive and emphasized the work of individuals, which took away from the focus on a common goal and group cohesiveness. The following discussion from one of the focus groups makes this clear:

GARRETT: So often when we get in groups in our program, it's just [about focusing on] the most efficient way. We'll get down and we'll divide everything up – you do this, you do this. I'll do this *[laughter and agreement from others].*

NICOLE: And it's individual work, just put together.

GARRETT: So we never have to meet again.

ANIELLE: Because we don't have time.

GARRETT: But with my [cedar bark] group, we did everything together, and we took it task by task.

HEATHER: Yeah, we did too.

GARRETT: So it wasn't like it was divided up or anything.

MICHELE: So your identity was as a group, not as an individual there?

GARRETT: Yeah ... and when you're dividing it up like that, you're going to compare yourself to another person in the group. Because if you come back and meet, and you put down what you did, and [Heather] didn't do anything, and I did a lot of stuff *[laughter]*, then sure there's going to be comparisons there, right? But when we do it all together step-by-step then there's not so much of that comparing and all that.

The members of this focus group went on to discuss other issues, such as whether it was possible to have individual and team focus at the same time within a group, the lack of time available in classrooms for good group work, the role of external motivation in group work, and how a drive towards efficiency might be affecting group work processes.

The earth fibres course indicates that healthy group work is possible. It takes a certain kind of attention, patience, space, and time. It requires us to move away from our fixation with efficiency, and perhaps, to pay better attention to the learning spirit of the group.

> How do we create more experiences for pre-service teachers to engage in healthy group work? How might having such experiences transfer to their teaching practice?

The Challenge of Reflection

After returning from their final practicum experiences, the pre-service teachers considered the act of reflection. Courtney, Jade, and Kevin spoke about how reflection in teaching practice was different from reflection as an assignment:

COURTNEY: In a way, reflection over the past five years [in the program] has been skewed for me. [In practicum] I reflect every day, but it comes at its own time and in its own pace and its own way.

JADE: Definitely.

COURTNEY: But it's definitely important. But that's something I've learned through the program is that you cannot force your children to reflect.

KEVIN: [It's also about] learning *how* to reflect as well. Not simply writing a summary of what happened, but interpreting the results, or interpreting what happened and making sense of it. The strategies.

JADE: Yeah, I definitely found over a practicum your reflection is genuine and you honestly care, you honestly want to know or want to grow. But in the university you just …

COURTNEY: It's not a natural place to reflect.

JADE: No. I don't even think it's a process really, when you're forced to do it.

COURTNEY: It has to come from within, from your own desire to change or to question.

JADE: Which happens completely naturally when you're in a classroom setting.

The embedded and endogenous way of reflecting in practice was similar to the type of reflection that the pre-service teachers did within the course.

Since Dewey (1933) identified reflection as being essential to problem-solving skills, many educators have acknowledged the importance of the role of this type of thoughtfulness in teacher practice. Schön (1983, p. 3) recognized the tacit intuitive knowledge-in-action of the teacher, describing it as a process of going deeper into teaching in ways that may be less empirically controlled: "The practitioner must choose. Shall he [sic] remain on the high ground where he can solve relatively unimportant problems according to prevailing standards of rigor, or shall he descend to the swamp of important problems and nonrigorous inquiry?"

How do pre-service teachers keep their reflection in practice focused on transformative reflexivity rather than re-creating the monoculture of schools?

There is debate over the nature of reflection, as well as its effectiveness; therefore, clarity of both conceptualizations and intent in reflection are important (Grimmett, Erickson, Mackinnon, and Riecken, 1990; Hyatt and Beigy, 1999). Current definitions of reflection are strongly influenced by Euro-Western cultural beliefs. Using a positivist paradigm to study or frame reflection reduces it to a technical process rather than honouring the complex, lived experience that it is (Richardson, 1990). In addition, it makes it difficult to see the culture of positivism in which we are immersed. Developing cross-cultural inquiry enhances our understanding and use of reflective practice (Houston and Clift, 1990), thus enriching awareness of personal culture.

While teachers need to reflect on a technical level, they must also consider the contexts in which they teach (institutional, social, cultural, and so on), and any related moral and ethical issues (Zeichner, 1987). Teachers can use autobiographical processes as reflective tools to assist them in embracing the lived experience in educational practice (Grumet, 2006; Pinar and Grumet, 1976). This self-reflection can increase their pedagogical thoughtfulness as they develop a more mindful orientation to others (van Manen, 1991). There are rich possibilities for knowing based in personal constructions of experience for both the teacher and the learner. Knowledge gained in practice can be a useful source of understanding for teachers, and this practical knowledge can be explored and informed by a reflective practice (Clandinin and Connelly, 2000).

Referencing Shor (1993), Leonardo (2004, p. 13) suggests that educators interested in social well-being should "ask questions about common answers rather than ... answer questions" on issues of power and privilege. This notion is based on Freire's pedagogy of the question, giving learners a language with which to challenge social-cultural constructs, thus moving beyond a shallower and less intellectually challenging pedagogy of the answer (Bruss and Macedo, 1985). In addition, social critique theorists promote sustained dialogue with community members on issues of social justice that lead to action (Gomez, 1994; Goodlad, 2008).

Typically, white pre-service teachers feel unprepared to teach students of cultures other than their own (Birrell, 1995), despite having altruistic intentions (Marx, 2003). These intentions are often limited by unexamined habits of privilege that lead them "to think of their lives as morally neutral, normative and average, and also ideal, so that when we work to benefit others, this is seen as work that will allow 'them' to be more like 'us'" (McIntosh, 1990, p. 32). White educators feel a sense of unease about dealing with race, and somehow, must work humbly to transform their own privilege and that of dominant institutions (Howard, 2004). Strong reflexive practice can help educators to realize that they are viewing the world through their own cultural lens shaped by their own lifeworld beliefs (Irvine, 2003). The earth fibres course provided space and time within a non-judgmental environment for pre-service teachers to engage in reflexive work that illuminated their own cultural positioning.

Reflection and reflexivity can be contentious practices among pre-service teachers. As an instructor, I have experienced first-hand the reluctance of students who prefer not to reflect, especially when deeper processes of reflexivity regarding their own power and privilege are involved. Reasons for a lack of reflection among pre-service teachers include biographical, situational, and cultural factors that are complex and interconnected (Gore and Zeichner, 1991). Beginning teachers tend to be either *commonsense thinkers,* who often ask how, when, and to what standard, *or reflective thinkers,* who tend to ask the deeper question, why (Labosky, 1994).

In the context of the earth fibres course, the pre-service teachers appreciated the importance of reflective practice, and saw how it would be especially useful within the complexities of their multicultural practicum classrooms. Chelsea explained how her reflection happened in relationship with her students: "[I need to be] making sure I'm aware of if my students are learning and how much. And if they want to talk to me about something, then actually listening to them, not just sort of brushing them off – *actually* listening so I can improve myself." Chelsea's image of the learner and teacher placed them both in a relationship where, through discussion, one taught the other in a circular process similar to that encouraged by the wisdom keepers.

Reflexivity with peers was also seen as an important aspect of teaching, as Heather said:

I think it is really important to be intentional about your work and to be able to sit down with somebody and to have them challenge you and to be like, "Well, why do you think that?" And then you be like, "Well, I have no idea.

Somebody told it to me and I am regurgitating it," you know? Wait a minute, stop and go back and think about that. Like, where is that coming from? That's a really good process, if you have time for the process, and if you're going to give time for the process.

How do we build time into a teacher's busy day to be reflexive? How can professional development days become an avenue for this important work?

Heather's insistence on attending to where her beliefs are coming from brings her more fully into an awareness of herself as a cultural being; dominant culture is no longer invisible, but alive and worthy of critical attention.

The next chapter suggests ways that teacher education programs might change to better serve our needs in this regard.

11

Re-envisioning (Teacher) Education

The pre-service teachers left the earth fibres course acutely aware of two fundamentally different worldviews. They had experienced a particular version of indigenous pedagogy, a viable way of learning and teaching that resonated with them on deep and vibrant levels. They went into their practica inclined towards integrating new ideas and ways of being into their classrooms. The schools they entered were steeped in long-held traditions of mainstream educational culture, contexts in which they faced deeply ingrained habits of the industrial model and resistance towards the possibilities of new paradigms. Many of the pre-service teachers in the study felt hesitant to try out ideas from the earth fibres course in these settings. This hesitancy was due in part to the fact that they were under intense pressure to succeed in the practicum situation in order to get their teaching certificates. The mostly implicit rules of achievement required them to teach in the ways already established. Their task was also complicated by the prevalence of the positivist paradigm whose basic tenets are established in a particular ontological and epistemological view of education. Straddling both the indigenous and positivist worlds, how could they develop something workable, considering the deep tensions between the two paradigms?

Teacher education programs can be rich sites for the transformative work of embracing new paradigms, and teacher educators hold the responsibility of establishing appropriate spaces conducive to and supportive of this work. The context of teacher education is the focus of this chapter, yet I continue to use the terms (teacher) education and (teacher) educators to emphasize the intimate overlaps between what happens in university programs and what happens in the schools. Change will need to come from all areas, and may arise from unexpected places. As a teacher educator, I am located in the university setting, and the critical questions within text boxes in previous chapters describe some of the tensions that I notice as significant in this particular context. They are things that niggle in the back of my consciousness as not being right about what we do. Further discussion around these and related questions will help us in our efforts to indigenize educational settings.

The tensions I refer to are set against a larger cultural backdrop in which (teacher) education has become, in the words of Britzman (1990/2003, p. 1), one of the "great anxieties" of the century. Britzman argues that, as teachers, we each bring to our teaching a school biography based on our experiences as past students. This inherited familiarity with teaching is typically privileged over any theoretical knowledge we might encounter. In addition, "the practice of teaching, because it is concocted from relations with others and occurs in structures that are not of one's own making is, first and foremost, an uncertain experience that one must learn to interpret and make significant" (p. 3). The pre-service teachers in this study spoke of having surprisingly deep feelings of anxiety about the overall teacher education program. Many spoke of feeling enormous pressure and concern about being prepared enough, about having the right toolkit in order to do their job.

In *The Courage to Teach*, Palmer (1998) discusses the frustration and despair teachers experience in the relentless complexities of practice; in particular, he describes how teachers often struggle with issues of identity and integrity. Frustration and despair are fuelled by the fact that education is often driven by a culture of efficiency that compels us to move, to improve, and to outdo ourselves, at an incessant and exponentially faster and faster pace (Stein, 2002). When left unattended, these issues can get out of hand and affect us deeply, resulting in alarming statistics on new-teacher burnout and attrition, with reports of up to 50 percent of new teachers leaving the profession within the first three years of practice (Karsenti and Collin, 2013).

How do we turn these tensions into possibility? This chapter focuses on six actions I suggest for (teacher) educators as we re-envision what is possible in the field: finding collaborative purpose, developing relational accountability, walking alongside each other, enacting a pedagogy of spirit, being-becoming mindful inquirers, and walking our talk. These issues are described separately but in reality are deeply interconnected, reciprocal, and interactive.

Finding Collaborative Purpose

Living in North America, we are "marinated in euro-centric thought" (Battiste, 2010). Everything we do resides with the undercurrent or within the atmosphere of the prevailing positivist worldview. The earth fibres course provided a brief, unusual, and *consciously planned* opportunity to absorb an alternative existence of indigenous ways. At the same time, it was an invitation to the wisdom keepers and the pre-service teachers to braid their stories together and have conversations across cultures about learner-teacher well-being. As we talked together, we developed a sense of mutual agreement and support in terms of how we might create classrooms that promote optimum conditions for both indigenous and non-indigenous learners. This combined sense of purpose from our deepening relationships gave the pre-service teachers a sense of how social justice work is, at its heart, a deeply collaborative process (Bell, 1997; Grant and Agosto, 2008). Our thinking about how we view education and conceptualize schooling is enhanced when done in community and can be modelled in teacher education (Prawat, 1992). Unfortunately, in the context of their practica, the pre-service teachers had little or no opportunity, as Garrett (PST) said, to build community "together, step-by-step."

The course was an ambitious project that tried to balance the needs of many, including the individual course participants, the small groups, the large group, the university community, and members of local First Nations. You may recall Leanne's image in Chapter 5 of the learner surrounded by concentric circles of community influence (see page 121). There was a complicated web of interactions within the course, which sometimes created tensions. However, having an overarching common goal led to a sense of reciprocity within the learning community (Lave and Wenger, 1991/2003; Wenger, 1998).

There was a remarkable balance between nourishing the learning spirit as a personal individual process and keeping a relational tie between the individual and the communities involved. Zeichner (2006, p. 328) points out that while many teacher education programs use the term "social justice education," most of this work "seems to focus on the actions of individual teacher educators in their college and university classrooms and has not included the kind of proposals for structural changes in teaching as an occupation and teacher education." The earth fibres experience shifted organizational structures towards indigeneity.

Not only should educational purpose be collaborative, but it should also be made as clear as possible. Many of the problems in education are really better described as problems *of* education (Orr, 1994/2004). Leaders in the field have called for significant change that focuses on more than surface patterns of teacher practice, suggesting a re-imagining of the deep conceptual structures within teacher education (Cochran-Smith, 2000; Wideen and Grimmett, 1995). Educators are called upon to think carefully about the purpose of teacher education before addressing the role of teachers within the field (Cochran-Smith, Feiman-Nemser, McIntyre, and Demers, 2008). Clarity of intent leads to clarity of roles. From there, the types of dispositional change necessary to serve the diversity of students in our classrooms can be addressed.

Prominent values affecting the scope and structure of Western-influenced teacher education are described as being the overlapping areas of academic learning, preparation for a productive life, individual human development, and social justice (Hansen, 2008). This sentiment is strikingly different from the spirit inherent in Cajete's (2009) questions: How do we remedy the environmental crisis on the planet? How do we learn to live with each other? How do we nourish our souls? Cajete's queries shift the focus away from a narcissistic, knowledge-as-commodity attitude towards one that honours relational knowing and interdependency. His indigenous viewpoint can serve (teacher) education well as a paradigmatic compass that guides conversations about educational purpose and focus. The indigenous concepts of ecological connectivity, nourishing the learning spirit, and knowing through relationships can have a significant impact within a multicultural classroom of diverse learners. Indigenous knowledges have unique power and transformational possibilities that can "promote rethinking our purpose as educators" (Kincheloe and Steinberg, 2008, p. 147).

On a fundamental level, teacher educators need to be conscious of why we do what we do (Hansen, 2008). When teacher educators think about educational intent, suggests Hansen, they must distinguish between function (maintenance) and purpose (the possibility of transformation); finding intellectual direction is a recursive, dialogic process that includes both. In the many hours, days, months, and years that teachers spend in schools, they are setting the tone of their classrooms (van Manen, 1986) and the direction of the learning that takes place within them. How we care for the planet, and how we care for each other and ourselves will determine in large part the health and wellness of students, our families, our communities, and the Earth. Obviously, these things matter, yet too often teachers are educated to reproduce the hegemonic culture of schools thoughtlessly, without examining the very foundational tasks of clarifying values and purpose towards imagining new ways forward. Many (teacher) educators find themselves caught up in the function of teaching – planning lessons, managing behaviours, invigilating exams, marking papers, keeping records. The transformational possibilities of knowing a collective purpose and acting upon it are often neglected.

What is education for? As Orr (1994/2004) suggests, this is perhaps the most important question that educators should be discussing today. We are on a ship without a point of reference, using an outdated compass. We need to reorient ourselves in order to address the crosscultural issues in today's classrooms. Our explorations must be done both collaboratively and individually. When my own sense of purpose is clear, then I can articulate this sense more easily in conversations with others. Together we can better think our way forward.

As a teacher educator, I set my compass towards the new-old paradigm of Cajete's (2009) questions. I say "new" because these questions are a new way of framing Western education; I say "old" because these questions are based on ancient wisdom. His questions ask us to build on what is *sustainable* by listening to both ancestral knowledge and the needs of generations to come. Cajete's questions offer us a touchstone to re-envision educational purpose. What do we want our classrooms, and our world, to be? By clarifying our purpose, we can more easily answer: What's next? What actions ring true to our intent?

Developing Relational Accountability

Learning and teaching are highly complex activities; there are many layers of teaching practice, and many layers to the experiences of both learners and teachers (Aoki, 2005). For example, learning involves multiple and embodied practices of listening, speaking, seeing, and feeling, requiring teachers to think carefully about the varied and difficult paths that learning inevitably takes (Smits, Towers, Panayotidis, and Lund, 2008). Educational scholars suggest that teacher education should actively address the less tangible, even hidden, but very real layers of teaching such as balancing the competing demands of practice (Rust, 1994) and integrating practice and theory (Brouwer and Korthagen, 2005). In crosscultural settings, the nuances of educational complexity increase exponentially. Teacher education can be improved by specifically attending to how teacher dispositions shift towards crosscultural awareness, and our relationality within that context.

As discussed earlier, indigenous worldviews embrace the idea that complexity such as that found in educational settings is about relationships more than things. *How* we teach matters more than *what* we teach. We exist *only* in relationship and our actions *always* affect the complex web of existence in which we are embedded (S. Wilson, 2008). The curriculum-as-lived trumps the curriculum-as-planned every time (Aoki, 2005). Our relationality obliges us to become accountable, whether we are aware of it or not. This, it seems, is especially true when we hold the kind of privilege that most teachers do – we are mostly white, members of dominant society, *and* we are "in charge" of the multitude of learners entering our classrooms. Not only are we well positioned to take an active, guiding role in the transformation of schooling but we are also relationally accountable to take on this task.

Unfortunately, new teachers often struggle to survive in the profession or even leave teaching entirely unless they can do the work of clarifying and then upholding their beliefs (Cole and Knowles, 1993). Pre-service teachers need knowledge and skills, and they also need to understand what they believe in and care about within the classroom context. Paradoxically, they also need to be able to let go of or shift their beliefs as they increasingly come to know that their worldview is one of many interdependent realities. We need to carefully develop ways of knowing while not knowing (Kumashiro, 2008), a "view of teacher education that can tolerate existential and ontological difficulties, psychical complexities, and learning from history" (Britzman, 2000, p. 200). In short, relational accountability occurs when we *speak to be revealed, listen to be changed* (Altman, 2012).

The earth fibres course highlights that those around us may hold views on what education is and what it could become that differ fundamentally from our views on the same subject. Each participant's sense of purpose grew out of a particular cultural perspective. It becomes important, then, not just to gain understandings of culture and cultural ways but also to become adept at examining the *why* of culture – both one's own culture and the culture of others – honing our ability to converse with those from whom we differ. It is within this realm of the *why* that we begin to deal more fully with complex social justice issues of power and inequity, to appreciate our diversity and at the same time to begin to locate our relational accountability.

Social critique theorists suggest that relational thinking should be a key ingredient in pre-service education, particularly within crosscultural settings (Hollingsworth et al., 1993). Because many teacher education programs do not systematically consider and incorporate a focus on social justice issues, courses that give pre-service teachers deep critical and reflective skills often are disconnected and separate rather than embedded throughout the program. Such programs leave few opportunities for pre-service teachers to critique and understand the worldview they are being encouraged to teach. Effective teacher education programs can explore relationality more deeply by embedding social justice within subject matter. Thus, pre-service teachers become more familiar with the existing state of classroom and school communities, and are presented with "opportunities to consider what they could become" (Grossman, McDonald, Hammerness, and Ronfeldt, 2008, p. 246).

In order to make schools and schooling more equitable places, teacher educators need to be open to other epistemological and ontological positions. This goes beyond merely tolerating difference to having a willingness to be changed. Pre-service teachers need an educational container that can hold such complexity, a place where they can feel safe enough to know that they don't know, to explore what might be possible, and to envision the future through crosscultural conversations.

While there is much overlap between the two paradigms, the social critique tradition is being troubled by indigenous scholars concerned that indigenous perspectives are being excluded from the social justice movement at an epistemological level (Denzin, Lincoln, and Smith, 2008; Donald and den Heyer, 2009; Grande, 2000). Grande (2000) writes that "while critical pedagogy may have propelled mainstream educational theory and practice along the path of social justice ... it has muted and thus marginalized the distinctive concerns of American Indian intellectualism and education" (p. 467). This concern has not gone unnoticed. For example, the editors of the *Handbook of Critical and Indigenous Methodologies* propose that through dialogue between indigenous and critical scholars critical pedagogy that typically has focused on issues of social class might be re-imagined to include epistemological differences of race (Denzin, Lincoln, and Smith, 2008).

It is alarming, however, that despite these efforts not a single chapter in the current edition of the *Handbook of Research on Teacher Education* (Cochran-Smith et al., 2008) is focused on either the issues or the potential of indigenous pedagogy within the field. Nor is there included in the handbook any work authored from an indigenous perspective. This is significant in part because many indigenous scholars raise important questions regarding the basic theoretical frameworks commonly used in education. In particular, indigenous perspectives are important because they focus on relational accountability.

Walking Alongside

The importance of community-based experiences within teacher preparation for work in diverse classroom environments is beginning to be recognized (Sleeter, 2008). But finding the time, space, and funding for these types of community exchanges to occur is difficult, and teacher educators are often unprepared to support these experiences due to their own unconscious habits of mind (Chou and Sakash, 2008). What is clear is that there is a need to develop and implement many more opportunities where indigenous and non-indigenous people can *walk alongside* each other and learn together. The earth fibres experience gave the pre-service teachers a living, breathing example of a different learning community within a classroom. The act of walking alongside became an embodied understanding for the pre-service teachers as they *felt* the holistic rhythms of other ways of knowing. This knowledge became embedded in their ways of being-doing-knowing, and they went into their practica eager to construct alternative environments.

This collaborative work of walking alongside is a series of multi-layered actions over time and is profoundly relational. It is also akin to what curriculum theorist Chambers (2006) describes as the deep *act of visiting with,* rather than merely *touring past,* another culture. Walking alongside over a longer time period, rather than a brief sightseeing tour, required all participants to embrace a sense of knowing while not knowing, careful and generous listening, and emotionally engaged reflexive practice. Together, we stepped outside of our respective comfort zones and went out of our way to be mutually engaged.

This crosscultural learning experience was both genuine in its indigeneity and highly immersive in nature. The intimate time spent in direct relationship with the wisdom keepers offered participants concrete knowledge of indigenous ways, and gave them powerful insights into the *why* of a different culture. Working together on creating the mural, relaying stories, and sharing mundane life experiences helped the pre-service teachers to gain confidence and develop skills for interacting with indigenous people and for incorporating indigenous pedagogy into their teaching practice.

In my work with pre-service teachers, I have often heard concern expressed over what students perceive to be the "do as I say, not as I do" attitude of their instructors. For example, they might be told that as teachers they should include students in the creation of evaluation tools yet not be asked to do the same as learners in the course in which they are enrolled. In the earth fibres course, this was not the case. *We were expected to do as the wisdom keepers did.* This was at the heart of the experience of walking alongside. The participants weren't *told* about indigenous pedagogy; rather, they *experienced it directly* as the wisdom keepers did what they believed to be good pedagogical practice. This act of doing developed the participants' embodied understanding. The earth fibres course demonstrated the subtleties of the wisdom keepers' approach: the power of finding one's own learning direction through direct, embodied experience as opposed to the more distant, less efficient delivery modes such as lectures, readings, and so-called group projects.

The heavily experiential nature of the course helped participants to grasp more fully the unfamiliar and sometimes conceptually challenging notions of indigenous pedagogy. The wisdom keepers showed the pre-service teachers what they knew, and the pre-service teachers chose ways of proceeding that suited their own learning needs. The concreteness of the earth fibres experience gave the pre-service teachers an authentic understanding that could be brought into their own teaching practice. For example, as the wisdom keepers trusted the pre-service teachers to find their own learning styles, the pre-service teachers engaged in a process whereby they meta-cognitively observed the gentle offering style of the wisdom keepers and, at the same time, paid close attention to their personal feelings as the learners. This lived experience as learner-teacher was an important tool for the pre-service teachers to further develop their teaching disposition and style.

The pre-service teachers came into the course wanting to increase their cultural understanding of indigenous peoples and to have genuine learning experiences. They were also looking for alternative ways to create inclusive classrooms and to promote lifelong learning in their students. The course gave them a concrete example of ways in which classroom communities could be different. By observing congruence between the instructors' intent and their actions, the pre-service teachers saw the integrity of a pedagogical practice that resonated deeply with the beliefs of the wisdom keepers. This observation led to wonderings about the congruence of their own beliefs and practice as well as that of others. The pre-service teachers were able to deepen their awareness and understanding of other cultures as well as their own. Understanding the *why* of another culture increased their willingness to incorporate other cultural perspectives into their teaching practice. In many cases, this called for the pre-service teachers to make adjustments to their own fundamental beliefs about pedagogy.

The successful earth fibres experience raises the question: How do we create more dedicated time and space within teacher education programs for activities intended for and clearly conducive to walking alongside those who are members of another culture? Finding such time and space requires concerted resistance to dominant social, cultural, and institutional structures as well as to deeply embedded personal ways of being-knowing-doing. As discussed in an earlier chapter, this is a tender resistance that requires courage. Where do we, as people of privilege, teacher educators, educators in our schools, administrators, find the courage to carve out space where such learning can happen? How can we transform and transfer the teachings of the earth fibres course into our own contexts? I have three specific suggestions.

First, be wary of thinking prescriptively. Within the Earth fibres course, Lorna, Charlene, and the other wisdom keepers pointedly held at bay the aggressive assumptions, habits, and values of dominant positivist-oriented culture, so that indigenous ways could flourish. While the Earth fibres experience was highly successful in this regard, re-creating such experiences will look different in different settings. Developed organically within the context of a particular environment and set of relationships, the course can't be duplicated. What can be brought forward is the intent, the spirit-knowledge of the course, which focused on creating a space for indigenous experience to thrive in as natural a state as possible. Non-indigenous people were welcomed into that environment in an effort to create shifts in the dominant paradigm towards more inclusivity and acceptance of indigenous ways within educational contexts.

Second, pay attention to the type of community collaborations you enact. Walking alongside suggests the specific intent to make space for a certain kind of inclusiveness. For example, inviting indigenous stories into a classroom by having indigenous storytellers come and participate reflects a very different intent from that of a project to raise money for school supplies to be delivered to a local reserve. I do not suggest here that a project to raise money should be avoided. But (teacher) educators must consider carefully if the intent of such a project really is to walk alongside. These types of projects are too often limited to a surface level of interaction with indigenous people and bestow on the "givers" a false sense of their own contribution. Does an offering of material supplies change in a positive way the relationships between indigenous and non-indigenous people? Does it reinforce a deficit view, or does it encourage a collaborative purpose? How is relational accountability enacted?

Third, consider the power dynamics between students and instructors. Opportunities for walking alongside other cultures need to be designed carefully to take place in safe enough spaces, where personal dispositions of learning, teaching, and crosscultural understanding can be more fully explored. Beliefs are held at deep, and sometimes fragile, psychological levels and require care and support, as they are uncovered, examined, and transformed. This study indicates that keeping these types of course experiences *ungraded* is essential to learner well-being. Dispositional transformation is difficult or impossible to measure. Because each individual brings to the course unique beliefs, values, and attitudes, each journey of transformation is also unique. A complete/incomplete setting lends itself to having each learner be primarily responsible for measuring and defining his or her own growth and success. The gentle offering approach of the wisdom keepers serves as a model for trusting and supporting the learner in this regard. The earth fibres course became a safe enough space in which the learning spirit was nourished and instructors embraced an atypical trust in each learner, who was then able to find personal meaning in his or her own educational journey.

Enacting a Pedagogy of Spirit

Indigenous perspectives are often intimately engaged in attending to spirit and spiritual points of view. The very conceptualization of knowledge from an indigenous viewpoint is embedded in spirit (Aluli Meyer, 2008). Issues of spirituality can be problematic in educational contexts, as they often become conflated with issues of religion. It is important to make a clear distinction between the two, and for our purposes, focus on the former. My definition of spirit is rooted in the Latin *spiritus*, literally, "breath." Spirit is that which animates us and gives us life. It is mysterious, likely impossible to understand fully through intellectual effort alone.

Within the field of critical theory, spirituality (the act of attending to spirit) is discussed briefly by some theorists (Delpit, 1995/2006; Grande, 2004; hooks, 1994), but too often is presented as only a footnote. Yet awareness of spirituality is at the heart of knowledge construction and transformative practice (Riley-Taylor, 2002; Tisdell, 2003). Delpit (1995/2006), an African American critical theorist, proactively includes spirituality in her writing. While her concerns are centred in the United States, they have global implications:

Poor people and people of colour are clearly in trouble in this country. And this means that we as a country are in trouble. Our "trouble" cannot be resolved by the creation and administration of standardized tests. Our "trouble" cannot be resolved by "teacher-proof" curricula. The troubles of our country – indeed, the troubles of our world – can be addressed only if we help ourselves and our children touch the deep humanity of our collective spirit and regain the deep respect for the earth that spawned us. Perhaps we can learn from traditional African education, where the role of teachers is to appeal to the intellect, the humanity, and the spirituality of their students. (p. xviii)

This quote echoes Bartolomé's (1994) notion of enacting a *humanizing pedagogy*, in which the learner is an active knower within the educational process and the teacher is required to move beyond an over-concentration on methods.

Including spirituality in educational theory carries with it the assumption that knowledge is more than an intellectual understanding. The earth fibres course clearly showed how spirituality could become a more integral focus within highly intellectualized academic contexts. If we ignore spirit and spirituality in the classroom, we ignore certain types of knowledge. We can grow corn in (teacher) education only if we recognize knowledge as spirit and treat it with sacred respect within the mundane setting of the classroom.

As an educator, I try to be mindful of the wisdom of our ancestors and pay attention to the spiritual energy of what we think we know. All around me, within the context of higher education, the concept of spirituality is avoided, despite evidence that it may be useful in crosscultural understanding (Tisdell, 2003, 2007). We can negotiate the terrain of spirituality in part by attending to and including in our teacher education programs theoretical perspectives such as those found in the field of transformative (adult) learning. Here, spiritual and relational cosmology are acknowledged as being crucial to human growth and well-being (Kremer, 2003; O'Sullivan, 2001; Tisdell, 2003). Transformative learning theory posits that spirituality can be defined outside of the often divisive constructs of religion, and instead be understood in the context of the relationality that exists all around us.

Being-Becoming Mindful Inquirers

The interwoven acts of examining purpose, engaging in relational accountability, walking alongside, and embracing spirit renew ideas about what it means to be a teacher. Too often, the very structures of learning to teach are unsound in that one's readiness to teach is judged based on simplistic notions of whether one is prepared or ill-prepared (e.g., in gathering skills and knowledge) rather than on whether one has developed deep reflective skills (e.g., inspiriting dispositions) (Britzman, 1990/2003). Tender resistance requires reflexive attention to dispositional shifts; this resistance also requires a *mindful inquiry* orientation within (teacher) education.

Inquiry-based approaches, in which teachers take on some of the inquisitive tenets of a researcher persona, are often designed to engage pre-service teachers in meaningful ways to help them understand the practical complexities of learning (Ballenger, 2005; Grimmett, 1995). Further, an inquiry stance in crosscultural settings can take teachers beyond traditional pedagogical frameworks and encourage exploration and understanding of multiple epistemologies (Kincheloe and Steinberg, 2008). Within the earth fibres course, the authenticity of the experience engaged the pre-service teachers as learners but also as reflexive emerging teachers. The experience appeared to fuse their previously separate roles of learner-teacher-researcher, as they were being-becoming mindful inquirers.

There are many valuable approaches to teacher inquiry (e.g., see Cochran-Smith and Lytle, 2009; Fichtman Dana and Yendol-Hoppey, 2009; Meyer, 2008; Phillips and Carr, 2006; Tanaka, Stanger, and Tse, 2014). In the course, the informal inquiry approach of the pre-service teachers was affected by the cross-cultural nature of the situation. Their processes of reflection attended specifically to the socio-cultural context of education by examining the *why* of teaching beyond the *what* and the *how*. They began to ask: Why am I engaging in this particular pedagogical practice? Do my practices support my vision of a healthy society? How do I envision learning? This critical reflection has the dual purpose of encouraging a more profound understanding of power issues and eliciting a reexamination of some of the assumptions that underlie current curricula and educational structures (Brookfield, 1995).

In addition, and perhaps more importantly, the pre-service teachers' approach to being-becoming inquiring professionals was influenced by indigenous sensibilities. Hawaiian scholar Aluli Meyer (2008) sheds light on some of the subtleties of indigenous research approaches. She bases her approach on the belief that knowledge is spiritual, connects directly to physical place, engages all the senses, is based in relation with others, and is useful. She suggests that educational researchers have a responsibility to pay attention to underlying intention, as well as to how the energy or "frequency" of that intent might in turn affect the world around us.

> It's not about how well you can quote theory; it's whether those ideas affect how you act ... How will you feel encouraged to go forth into the world to alter its frequency? How will you bring robustness to this flat land knowing literacy keeps undimensioned? How will you actualize these principles of being to expand what knowledge is at its core? Make your work useful by your meaning and truth. I know it sounds somehow ethereal, but this is the point: Knowledge that does not heal, bring together, challenge, surprise, encourage, or expand our awareness is not part of the consciousness the world needs now. This is the function we as indigenous people posit. And ... *we are all indigenous.* (pp. 221–22)

Aluli Meyer calls on all educators to acknowledge and embrace both the specificity (knowledge rooted in place) and the universality (knowledge that is true beyond place) that are present in every learning situation. At the same time, she suggests an integrity that is non-hierarchical and non-judgmental. The subtlety of this leads us to the practice of mindfulness, a state of active, open awareness of what is.

Aluli Meyer's work introduces perspectives beyond positivist frameworks and requires a deep paradigmatic shift towards relational awareness. Shawn Wilson (2008, p. 92) describes the moral significance of this:

> With [relationality] as a foundation of our ontology, we must build the epistemological beliefs in egalitarianism and inclusiveness ... if reality is based upon relationships, then judgment of another's viewpoint is inconceivable. One person cannot possibly know all of the relationships that brought about another's ideas. Making judgment of others' worth or values is also impossible. Hierarchy in belief systems, social structure and thought are totally foreign to this way of viewing the world. Thus, egalitarianism and inclusiveness become not merely a norm, but the epistemologically inevitable.

Wilson (2010) frames the process of research as ceremony. Therefore, the researcher, rather than taking on the role of objective observer, becomes a ceremony leader, hence the title of his book, *Research Is Ceremony* (S. Wilson, 2010). In this role, researchers are in active relationship with the topic of interest, and they are profoundly accountable to all relationships inherent to the topic. Accordingly, the teaching that was modelled in the course began to replace the familiar prototypical "teacher as expert" approach, and participants began to embrace an archetypal understanding of teacher as relational knower or ceremony leader.

Within the complex and dynamic environments of multicultural classrooms there is an urgent need for an inquiry approach that is fluid and open to the possibilities of indigenous worldviews. My suggestion is to put into practice what I call *Transformative Inquiry* (TI), a mindful approach to inquiry that is highly informed by and embedded in an indigenist sensibility (Tanaka, 2015; Tanaka et al., 2012; Tanaka, Stanger, et al., 2014). While similar to other forms of teacher inquiry, the TI approach is intimately informed by the pedagogical style of the wisdom keepers within the earth fibres course, along with my other indigenous pedagogical encounters (Tanaka, 2013). TI also uses the ethos of Cajete's (2009) questions as a type of paradigmatic compass, echoing the intent found in the Earth fibres course towards learner well-being. His questions become touchstones that guide and remind the learner-teacher-researcher of what is genuine to developing wellness within educational practices.

Since 2010, the TI approach has been implemented within the teacher education program at the University of Victoria, and is currently the topic of a long-term study funded by the Social Sciences and Humanities Research Council of Canada. In a required course, pre-service teachers choose a topic that they are personally and professionally passionate to explore. They then investigate the topic reflexively and relationally within the larger educational, sociocultural, and environmental contexts. The overall sensibility of TI is that of mindful, reflexive engagement and relational accountability. Another key aspect acknowledges the inner and personal direction of the learning spirit (Battiste, 2009) of each learner. Learner autonomy is encouraged through a series of mentoring conversations with the course instructor and dialogic writing sessions geared towards the personal exploration of each inquiry topic (Tanaka, Tse et al., 2014).

The TI approach requires deep reflexivity on personal pedagogical location within existing educational paradigms and encourages accessing other ways of knowing such as poetry (Tanaka and Tse, 2015) and creative imagery (Stanger, Tanaka, Starr, and Tse, 2013). By acknowledging and understanding personal situatedness within various traditions, each pre-service teacher can begin to recognize and articulate his or her own values, beliefs, and attitudes, and how one's personal disposition might affect teaching practice. To this end, emotions (which are often inadequately understood, acknowledged, or discussed) are engaged with so that they become beneficial catalysts towards transformation (Tanaka, Tse, et al., 2014). Simultaneously, the TI approach recognizes and is sensitive to moving forward with the intent of good hands, the inclusion of spirit-knowledge, and a growing understanding of relationships and ways of being accountable within those relationships. In contrast, inquiry steeped in dichotomous traditions of positivism can be limited by an over-reliance on rational inquiry processes, judgment, and hierarchical orders, thus restraining awareness of the richness of what is, and the possibilities for what we might become.

Walking Our Talk

Education is teetering on the edge of a paradigm shift. While we still lean heavily towards positivism, there is a growing pull towards an as yet undefined, more inclusive way of being. Educators can take on the responsibility of leading the way in these changes; we can model a different way forward. Therefore, we must make pedagogical choices carefully in these precarious times. Teacher educators have always been uniquely positioned to make a difference in the lives of the many learners we touch, as our actions ripple out into our schools, our communities, and the world. We now have a heightened responsibility to pay careful attention to the pedagogical choices we make on all levels, from everyday learner-teacher interactions to curriculum and policy design. And, as the wisdom keepers taught, good hands are essential to this work. What if we were able in full consciousness to say to our students, *Do as I do*?

To walk alongside indigenous peoples genuinely, with the intent of moving towards and enacting an indigenous educational paradigm, means embracing uncertainty; this can be dangerous and vulnerable work. As (teacher) educators who hold relative positions of power, we can choose to engage across difference proactively through honest and sometimes difficult conversations. If this work is risky, then it is also work that requires a certain type of courage in order to stay true to our course, to walk our talk, to be vulnerable in ways that lead to positive change. We need to foster the courage to re-imagine education through finding collaborative purpose, developing relational accountability, walking alongside, enacting a pedagogy of spirit, and being-becoming mindful inquirers.

Here I think of Lorna, steadfastly holding back the positivist tide of the academy so that the seeds of the earth fibres course might take root and grow. She had the courage and conviction to walk her talk despite adversity, and those seeds continue to grow corn in many ways. At this writing, adapted versions of the course have been offered over a dozen more times (with various themes, such as Earth songs, story sticks, caring for artefacts, and so forth). XAXE SIÁM SILA is installed properly now in the learning commons, and there is an accompanying interactive display that describes her history and the course itself. Occasionally, the wisdom keepers hear from earth fibres participants, who remark upon how the course stays with them in their teaching practice. Recently, I had a chance encounter with Leanne (PST), who was teaching on a reserve in a northern Vancouver Island community. She told me that she frequently thinks back to the course as she continues her process of being-becoming an educator. The legacy of XAXE SIÁM SILA plays out in rich and unexpected ways. It's worthwhile to walk our talk.

12

Touchstones for Future Teaching

The true power in the wheel is in the centre.

– Lynne (WK)

Coming again full circle, we return to centre with a renewed sense of place. The woven strands of the story have been told and the wheel has been walked. As offerings, these stories present possibilities of awareness in terms of what it meant for the pre-service teachers to work with the earth fibres, to feel the smooth grain of cedar bark as it split, and to smell the rich aroma as the cedar was woven. Offered, too, are some of the accompanying stories that the wisdom keepers shared about gathering the materials, listening to plant knowledge, and watching their elders. These experiences of walking alongside have had a significant transformative effect on the participants – the pre-service teachers, the wisdom keepers, and myself – bringing us closer to what it means to attend to the wisdom of this place, SI,ĆENEN̲. Perhaps this process extends even to the earth fibres themselves, in that the often subtle experiences may play out through our own good hands in ways that aim to nourish and heal TEṈEW~Earth. We have come to a fresh place of knowing what might be true of learning and teaching. I invite you to consider how this effect might even ripple out to change you, the reader.

The course created *formative touchstones* (Strong-Wilson, 2008), places that offered a sense of what might be true in education. As educators, the participants could choose to act from the base created within their personal touchstones (Tanaka, 2011). As mentioned in the introduction, touchstone experiences anchor us to what we believe to be true; they help us locate ourselves in the complexity of busy schools, and then from there, to imagine what steps might be best as we proceed. Significant touchstones were formed in the course as we went below the surface of our cultural islands and considered the depths of intertwining cultural stories. It was an experience full of special encounters that required us to *visit* culture rather than *tour* it (Chambers, 2006). This type of visiting took time and awareness. Thus, the course became "a way of renewing and recreating people, places and beings, and their relationships to one another" (Chambers, 2006, p. 35).

The course provided a time and place to have authentic visiting with the wisdom keepers, and the participants picked up various touchstones as they walked alongside. These touchstones took many forms. Some were stories that the wisdom keepers shared, or stories that were created in the context of the course. Others were tangible things, such as the cattail mats that the preservice teachers wove or the beadwork in a medicine pouch. Some of these significant touchstones may have been presented to others through Giveaway. The mural was a touchstone for some, as were the appliquéd HÍSW̱E hands along the bottom edge that lift up the work of women from around Turtle Island–North America. Courtney (PST) speaks about rain, one of her significant touchstones:

> COURTNEY: Now, every time it rains, I think of [Charlene] ... I don't even know how she worded it, but the concept of rain being these cleansing tears from above. There are these little catchphrases that are now in my head that weren't [before]. There was no PowerPoint lecture or anything, but they stick with [me]. And I was thinking gosh, that's true teaching, when something that you say sticks with your student and they think of it when they're out and about on their own daily busy lives.
>
> MICHELE: So why did those things stick like that for you?
>
> COURTNEY: I don't know. I'd like to know. I think of a couple of reasons. Perhaps because they are true, but it's a truth that's kind of awakened in yourself, that I've never taken the time to think of. You know, gosh, rainfall, it's really cleansing. Or gosh, it's the changing of the seasons, let's take a moment to be aware of that for a second. And I know the seasons change so it's nothing new, but to be [truly] aware of it.

This significant type of "awakening" was noted by many of the pre-service teachers. The earth fibres course went beyond a surface intellectual understanding to strike a deep chord in their being. The depth of Courtney's experience created a salient touchstone, from which new possibilities around the meaning of rain could emerge. Visiting in this way, over time and in liminal spaces between cultural stories, required the pre-service teachers to shift their understanding of indigenous peoples and of themselves; the stories they lived by were changed. How that might affect their lives and the lives of future students is open to tremendous possibility.

Through actively engaging in the knowledge of SI,ĆENEN, the physical landscape became "wedded to the landscape of the mind, to the roving imagination, and where the latter may lead is anybody's guess" (Basso, 1996, p. 107). In the course, the pre-service teachers were in a sense exiled from familiar landscapes; different perspectives, different dispositions, and a different sense of identity as teachers began to emerge. The pre-service teachers moved beyond a tourist-like experience of indigenous culture to cultivate a deeper, more meaningful understanding of the *why* of a different worldview. They began to take on what Mi'kmaq elder Albert Marshal and Dr. Cheryl Bartlett at Cape Breton University call *two-eyed seeing,* the ability to use both indigenous and Euro-Western ways of thinking (Institute for Integrative Science and Health, 2006). Their educational horizon of understanding (Greene, 1978) had been altered, and they were able to bring forward new understandings of indigenous ways to encourage healthy learning communities in their classrooms.

In the process of writing this book, I have tried to remain true to the lived experience of the participants of the course by focusing on relationships and by trying to describe the "shape and feel of [a] way of life rather than focusing on isolated factors" (Norberg-Hodge, 1991, p. 113). I hope that I have been able, in some small way, to shed light on Charlene's underlying questions about how we can bring the strength of the old teachings into the modern-day education system. Building on the gentle offerings of the wisdom keepers, the pre-service teachers moved forward from their university experience with a stronger sense of the ancient wisdom of the past embedded in their beliefs. Here, I share select quotes from these young professionals. Their words, more than mine, show the impact of the course as a touchstone for future teaching.

> If I were to summarize the impact, it would be that because of our course together, I was able to experience, and therefore will incorporate, a foundation of community and relationships [in my own classrooms]. And I like the *authentic* word. You know, stressing authentic learning in my classroom ...

Because of the direct link to the class ... we were able to experience the effects of that ourselves. (Courtney)

I think that it is important to be able to feel the difference between regular courses and [the earth fibres] course. People are always saying you need to create a sense of community in your classroom, but what does that feel like? What does that look like? I think that was really huge for me to experience that and to be able to feel the difference between the community [in the earth fibres course] and a regular classroom. (Jade)

Very simply, a real, inevitable outcome was having a deeper understanding of Aboriginal ways of knowing as a non-Aboriginal person that I can now relate and bring into my classroom through a more authentic experience than what perhaps I experienced in my own K to twelve education. And that's a huge benefit, knowing that I'm supposed to be a teacher of this as well. So that's pretty big, actually, when I think about it. (Courtney)

I think they should make this course mandatory for education students ... simply for the indigenous knowledge and having that exposure because we're expected to teach about it but hardly anyone has experienced it. (Danielle)

[Practically speaking,] I'm going to be able to do certain crafts that would not have been easy to have done before, such as sewing. [But it also] provided me with deep insight into the learning experience. (Kevin)

I really think that for me, something that I took out the most [from the course] is ... to really just be intentional about everything you teach. If you don't know why you're teaching it, you shouldn't be teaching it ... You need to find a bigger picture and why is this going to be important? And why is this going to affect this eleven-year-old in thirty years? Or why is this going to touch them in their lives now? Or how is this going to carry out somewhere outside of this class? Because if the only time that they look at this one thing is twenty minutes in your class because it's in the Integrated Resource Package, it's not going to stick. (Heather)

It's kind of cliché but I think that if you have such a big group together and you have a huge vision like we did, and you really get everybody on board and they put their minds to it, I think we can accomplish so much. Of everything I got from this course, that's probably the biggest one. (Garrett)

I like what Garrett said about having a vision – having a common goal but something that you can visually see, like a project. I was in a leadership group and we built a playground for a campsite out of nothing, and we had to do it ourselves … And I think implementing something like that in your class throughout the year, some sort of big vision or big project for them to all work towards and be proud of, can have a huge impact on how the rest of the class goes. I think that can be a really neat way to build community. (Nicole)

The earth fibres course was an exceptional crosscultural learning community in which we walked our talk by putting into practice a pedagogy that resonated deeply with a relational indigenous ontology and epistemology. It was an authentic experience that gave the pre-service teachers a lived sense of indigenous ways of knowing and opportunities to experience the possibilities of self-direction within a community-oriented learning environment. Despite pressures such as time constraints and product orientation, all of the pre-service teachers spoke of their learning processes being nourished in various ways: emotionally, spiritually, intellectually, and physically. Through their relationships with the wisdom keepers, the pre-service teachers developed deeper understandings of indigenous cultures and indigenous pedagogy, and they became more confident in engaging with indigenous people; as Janet (WK) described earlier, the experience was filled with busy bee activities of cooperation.

As these young educators were immersed in a lived crosscultural experience, they found space to imagine new possibilities for the multicultural children of their future classrooms. The occasion to walk alongside indigenous community members, and to participate in rich dialogue, reflection, and reflexivity, took them beyond comfortable positivist sensibilities to places where they found important touchstones to inform their educational practice. As their individual learning spirits were cultivated, their actions rippled out to strengthen the community, both within the course and beyond. It is encouraging to see how the pre-service teachers have taken the experiences and embodied understanding of the course forward into their early teaching careers. I have confidence that these new teachers really can make a difference in the lives of the many children they will teach.

Ongoing Wonderings

I, too, am compelled to live my life differently now that I've heard the stories of the earth fibres course. As I complete this writing, I find that I have more questions than when I began. Some are questions I've held since my childhood, while

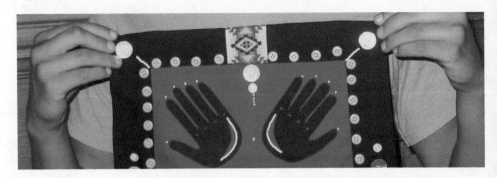

HÍSW̱KE Honouring hands on a Giveaway piece

others are new or transforming. My ways of listening for the answers have also changed. In fact, I don't really expect answers anymore, at least not tidy ones. As the poet Rilke (1986) suggests, I now strive for patience as I look for ways to be actively engaged within the possibilities of each question. For "the point is, to live everything. *Live* the questions now. Perhaps then, someday far in the future, you will gradually, without noticing it, live your way into the answer" (Rilke, 1986, p. 34).

The questions go on, but the point is that what I care about, and what I want pre-service teachers leaving teacher education programs to care about, are intimately related to questions inspired by Cajete (2009) and Orr (1994/2004). How will we sustainably care for the planet so that all sentient beings might prosper? How will we live with each other in ways that recognize and utilize the gifts of our diversity? How will we nurture our own souls so that we can heed the call of our learning spirits? And finally, what is the purpose of education, and can curricula be designed to address our deep and nuanced need? These questions must be held gently, with good hands. Often, they trouble and disturb my sense of complacency as I look for a path with heart and for learning-teaching-researching that *really* matters (Chambers, 2004).

On TEṈEW~Earth, there are red-black-white-yellow-brown peoples residing together, and our stories are inextricably linked. It is from a place of humble commonality that we must proceed as we explore our wonderings and watch them ripen and evolve. I believe that our way forward invites educators towards being-becoming indigenist (S. Wilson, 2007) – to connect deeply with and embody soul, place, and relational accountability. In fact, many scholars remind us that *we are all indigenous* (Aluli Meyer, 2008; Saul, 2008; S. Wilson, 2010). Such a positioning embraces both the specificity of indigenous wisdom derived from each unique place, and the universality of that wisdom across TEṈEW~Earth (Aluli Meyer, 2008). We are always both being and becoming. The question is: Upon what do we set our sights?

All my relations.

References

Alfred, T. (2005). *Wasáse: Indigenous pathways of action and freedom.* Peterborough, ON: Broadview Press.

Altman, K. (2012). All my relations: A 5Rhythms workshop. Offered at the White Eagle Hall in Victoria, BC, September 21–23.

Aluli Meyer, M. (2008). Indigenous and authentic: Hawaiian epistemology and the triangulation of meaning. In N.K. Denzin, Y.S. Lincoln, and L.T. Smith (Eds.), *Handbook of critical and Indigenous methodologies* (pp. 217–233). Thousand Oaks, CA: Sage. http://dx.doi.org/10.4135/9781483385686.n11

Alvord, L., and Van Pelt, E. (1999). *The scalpel and the silver bear.* New York: Bantam.

Aoki, T. (2005). Layered voices of teaching: The uncannily correct and the elusively true. In W.G. Pinar and R.L. Irwin (Eds.), *Curriculum in a new key: The collected works of Ted T. Aoki* (pp. 187–197). Mahwah, NJ: Lawrence Erlbaum.

Apple, M.W. (1995). *Education and power* (2nd ed.). New York: Routledge.

–. (2008). Is deliberative democracy enough in teacher education? In M. Cochran-Smith, S. Feiman-Nemser, D.J. McIntyre, and K.E. Demers (Eds.), *Handbook of research on teacher education: Enduring questions in changing contexts* (3rd ed., pp. 105–110). New York: Routledge.

Applebee, A. (1996). *Curriculum as conversation: Transforming traditions of teaching and learning.* Chicago: University of Chicago Press.

Archibald, J. (2008). *Indigenous storywork: Educating the heart, mind, body, and spirit.* Vancouver, BC: UBC Press.

Artz, S. (1994). *Feeling as a way of knowing.* Ottawa: Trifolium Books.

Ballenger, C. (2005). "I would sing every day": Skepticism and the imagination. In L. Pease-Alvarez and S.R. Schecter (Eds.), *Learning, teaching, and community: Contributions of situated and participatory approaches to educational innovation* (pp. 27–46). Mahwah, NJ: Lawrence Erlbaum.

Barab, S.A., and Roth, W.-M. (2006). Curriculum-based ecosystems: Supporting knowing from an ecological perspective. *Educational Researcher, 35*(5), 3–13. http://dx.doi.org/10.3102/0013189X035005003

Bartolomé, L. (1994). Beyond the methods fetish: Towards a humanizing pedagogy. *Harvard Educational Review, 64*(2), 173–194.

Basso, K.H. (1996). *Wisdom sits in places: Landscape and language among the Western Apache.* Albuquerque: University of New Mexico Press.

Battiste, M. (2007, April). *Nourishing the learning spirit.* Keynote address, AWASIS annual conference, Saskatoon, SK.

–. (2008). The struggle and renaissance of indigenous knowledge in Eurocentric education. In M. Villegas, S.R. Neugebauer, and K.R. Venegas (Eds.), *Indigenous knowledge and education: Sites of struggle, strength, and survivance* (pp. 85–91). Cambridge: Harvard Educational Review.

–. (2009). Nourishing the learning spirit: Living our way to new thinking. *Canadian Educational Association, 50*(1), 14–18.

–. (2010). Public lecture on the learning spirit. University of Victoria, BC. June 17.

Battiste, M., and Barman, J. (1995). *First Nations education in Canada: The circle unfolds.* Vancouver, BC: UBC Press.

Battiste, M., and Henderson, J.Y. (2000). *Protecting indigenous knowledge and heritage.* Saskatoon, SK: Purich Publishing.

Bell, L.A. (1997). Theoretical foundations for social justice education. In M. Adams, L.A. Bell, and P. Griffin (Eds.), *Teaching for diversity and social justice* (pp. 3–15). New York: Routledge.

Bentz, V., and Shapiro, J. (1998). *Mindful inquiry in social research.* Thousand Oaks, CA: Sage.

Birrell, J. (1995). "Learning how the game is played": An ethnically encapsulated beginning teacher's struggle to prepare black youth for a white world. *Teaching and Teacher Education, 11*(2), 137–147. http://dx.doi.org/10.1016/0742-051X(94)00017-Z

Bishop, R. (2008). Te Kotahitanga: Kaupapa Māori in mainstream classrooms. In N.K. Denzin, Y.S. Lincoln, and L.T. Smith (Eds.), *Handbook of critical and indigenous methodologies* (pp. 439–459). Thousand Oaks, CA: Sage. http://dx.doi.org/10.4135/9781483385686.n21

Boyd, R., and Myers, G. (1988). Transformative education. *International Journal of Lifelong Education, 7*(4), 261–284. http://dx.doi.org/10.1080/0260137880070403

Britzman, D. (1990/2003). *Practice makes practice: A critical study of learning to teach.* Albany: The State University of New York Press.

–. (2000). Teacher education in the confusion of our times. *Journal of Teacher Education, 51*(3), 200–205. http://dx.doi.org/10.1177/0022487100051003007

Britzman, D., Dippo, D., Searle, D., and Pitt, A. (1997). Toward an academic framework for thinking about teacher education. *Teaching Education, 9*(1), 15–26. http://dx.doi.org/10.1080/1047621970090103

Brookfield, S. (1995). *Becoming a critically reflective teacher.* San Francisco: Jossey-Bass.

Brouwer, N., and Korthagen, F. (2005). Can teacher education make a difference? *American Educational Research Journal, 42*(1), 153–224. http://dx.doi.org/10.3102/00028312042001153

Brown, F.L. (2004). *Making the classroom a healthy place: The development of affective competency in Aboriginal pedagogy.* Unpublished doctoral dissertation, University of British Columbia, Vancouver, British Columbia, Canada.

Brown, J.E. (1976). The roots of renewal. In W.H. Capps and E.F. Tonsing (Eds.), *Seeing with a Native eye: Essays on Native American religion* (pp. 79–85). New York: Harper and Row.

Bruss, N., and Macedo, D.P. (1985). Toward a pedagogy of the question: Conversations with Paulo Freire. *Journal of Education, 167*(2), 7–21.

Bullough, R.V., and Young, J. (2002). Learning to teach as an intern: The emotions and the self. *Teacher Development, 6*(3), 417–432.

Cajete, G. (1994). *Look to the mountain: An ecology of indigenous pedagogy*. Skyland, NC: Kivaki Press.

–. (2009, April). *Building healthy and sustainable indigenous communities through research*. Paper presented at the American Educational Research Association conference, San Diego, CA.

Canadian Council on Learning (2007). *Redefining how success is measured in First Nations, Inuit and Métis learning*. Ottawa: Canadian Council on Learning.

Capra, F. (1996). *The web of life*. New York: Random House.

Chamberlin, J.E. (2003). *If this is your land, where are your stories? Finding common ground*. Toronto: Knopf Canada.

Chambers, C. (2004). Research that matters: Finding a path with heart. *Journal of the Canadian Association for Curriculum Studies, 2*(1), 1–19.

–. (2006). "The land is the best teacher I ever had": Places as pedagogy for precarious times. *Journal of Curriculum Theorizing, 22*(2), 27–37.

Chávez, R.C., and O'Donnell, J. (Eds.) (1998). *Speaking the unpleasant: The politics of (non)engagement in the multicultural terrain*. Albany: State University of New York Press.

Chou, V., and Sakash, K. (2008). Troubling diversity. In M. Cochran-Smith, S. Feiman-Nemser, D.J. McIntyre, and K.E. Demers (Eds.), *Handbook of research on teacher education: Enduring questions in changing contexts* (3rd ed., pp. 686–692). New York: Routledge.

Clandinin, D.J., and Connelly, F.M. (2000). *Narrative inquiry: Experience and story in qualitative research*. San Francisco: Jossey-Bass.

Claxton, E., and Elliott, J. (1993). *The Saanich year*. Brentwood Bay, BC: Saanich Indian School Board.

Cochran-Smith, M. (2000). The future of teacher education: Framing the questions that matter. *Teaching Education, 11*(1), 13–24. http://dx.doi.org/10.1080/1047621005 0020327

–. (2005). The new teacher education: For better or worse? *Educational Researcher, 34*(7), 3–17. http://dx.doi.org/10.3102/0013189X034007003

Cochran-Smith, M., Feiman-Nemser, S., McIntyre, D.J., and Demers, K.E. (2008). *Handbook of research on teacher education: Enduring questions in changing contexts* (3rd ed.). New York: Routledge.

Cochran-Smith, M., and Lytle, S. (2009). *Inquiry as stance: Practitioner research in the next generation*. New York: Teachers College Press.

Cole, A.L., and Knowles, J.G. (1993). Shattered images: Understanding expectations and realities of field experiences. *Teaching and Teacher Education, 9*(5/6), 457–471. http://dx.doi.org/10.1016/0742-051X(93)90030-K

Cowley, P., and Easton, S. (2006). *Report card on Aboriginal education in British Columbia. Studies in educational policy*. Vancouver, BC: Fraser Institute.

Cranton, P. (1994). *Understanding and promoting transformative learning: A guide for educators of adults*. San Francisco: Jossey-Bass.

Csikszentmihalyi, M. (2007). *Flow: The psychology of optimal experience*. New York: Harper Perennial.

Davies, B., Browne, J., Gannon, S., Honan, E., Laws, C., Mueller-Rockstroh, B., and Petersen, E.B. (2004). The ambivalent practice of reflexivity. *Qualitative Inquiry, 10*(3), 360–389. http://dx.doi.org/10.1177/1077800403257638

Davis, W. (2009). *The wayfinders: Why ancient wisdom matters in the modern world*. Toronto: House of Anansi Press.

Delpit, L. (1988). The silenced dialogue: Power and pedagogy in educating other people's children. *Harvard Educational Review, 58*(3), 280–298.

–. (1995/2006). *Other people's children: Cultural conflict in the classroom*. New York: New Press.

Denzin, N.K., and Lincoln, Y.S. (1994). Introduction: Entering the field of qualitative research. In N.K. Denzin and Y.S. Lincoln (Eds.), *Handbook of qualitative research* (pp. 1–18). Thousand Oaks, CA: Sage.

Denzin, N.K., Lincoln, Y.S., and Smith, L.T. (Eds.). 2008. *Handbook of critical and indigenous methodologies*. Thousand Oaks, CA: Sage.

Dewey, J. (1933). *How we think*. Boston: D.C. Heath.

Donald, D., and den Heyer, K. (2009, May). *Curricular and pedagogical intents: Aboriginal perspectives, social studies, and teacher education*. Paper presented at the Canadian Society for Study of Education, Ottawa, ON.

Dressman, M. (1998). Confessions of a methods fetishist: Or, the cultural politics of reflective nonengagement. In R.C. Chávez and J. O'Donnell (Eds.), *Speaking the unpleasant: The politics of (non)engagement in the multicultural terrain* (pp. 108–126). Albany: State University of New York Press.

Ermine, W. (1995/1996). Aboriginal epistemology. In M. Battiste and J. Barman (Eds.), *First Nations education in Canada: The circle unfolds* (pp. 101–112). Vancouver, BC: UBC Press.

Esteve, J.M. (2000). Culture in the school: Assessment and the content of education. *European Journal of Teacher Education, 23*(1), 5–18. http://dx.doi.org/10.1080/713667265

Fichtman Dana, N., and Yendol-Hoppey, D. (2009). *Reflective educator's guide to classroom research: Learning to teach and teaching to learn through practitioner inquiry* (2nd ed.). Thousand Oaks, CA: Corwin Press.

Fisher, A. (2002). *Radical ecopsychology: Psychology in the service of life*. Albany: State University of New York Press.

Fixico, D. (2003). *The American Indian mind in a linear world: American Indian studies and traditional knowledge*. New York: Routledge.

Freire, P. (1970/2005). *Pedagogy of the oppressed*. New York: Continuum.

–. (1998). *Teachers as cultural workers: Letters to those who dare to teach*. Boulder, CO: Westview Press.

Futrell, M.H. (2008). Changing the paradigm: Preparing teacher educators and teachers for the twenty-first century. In M. Cochran-Smith, S. Feiman-Nemser, D.J. McIntyre, and K.E. Demers (Eds.), *Handbook of research on teacher education: Enduring questions in changing contexts* (3rd ed., pp. 534–539). New York: Routledge.

Gardner, H. (2006). *Multiple intelligences: New horizons*. New York: Basic Books.

Gay, G. (2000). *Culturally responsive teaching: Theory, research and practice*. New York: Teachers College Press.

Generett, G.G., and Hicks, M.A. (2004). Beyond reflective competency: Teaching for audacious hope-in-action. *Journal of Transformative Education, 2*(3), 187–203. http://dx.doi.org/10.1177/1541344604265169

Gillette, M.D., and Schultz, B.D. (2008). Do you see what I see? Teacher capacity as a vision for education in a democracy. In M. Cochran-Smith, S. Feiman-Nemser, D.J. McIntyre, and K.E. Demers (Eds.), *Handbook of research on teacher education: Enduring questions in changing contexts,* (3rd ed., pp. 231–237). New York: Routledge.

Giroux, H.A. (1992). *Border crossings: Cultural workers and the politics of education*. New York: Routledge.

Goleman, D. (1995). *Emotional intelligence: Why it can matter more than IQ*. New York: Bantam.

Gomez, M.L. (1994). Teacher education reform and prospective teachers' perspectives on teaching "other people's" children. *Teaching and Teacher Education, 10*(3), 319–334. http://dx.doi.org/10.1016/0742-051X(95)97312-A

Goodlad, J.I. (2008). Advancing the public purpose of schooling and teacher education. In M. Cochran-Smith, S. Feiman-Nemser, D.J. McIntyre, and K.E. Demers (Eds.), *Handbook of research on teacher education: Enduring questions in changing contexts* (3rd ed., pp. 111–116). New York: Routledge.

Goodlad, J.I., Mantle-Bromley, C., and Goodlad, S.J. (2004). *Education for everyone: Agenda for education in a democracy*. San Francisco: Jossey-Bass.

Gore, J.M. (1993). *The Struggle for pedagogies: Critical and feminist discourses as regimes of truth*. New York: Routledge.

Gore, J.M., and Zeichner, K.M. (1991). Action research and reflective teaching in pre-service teaching education: A case study from the United States. *Teaching and Teacher Education, 7*(2), 119–136. http://dx.doi.org/10.1016/0742-051X(91)90022-H

Grande, S.M. (2000). American Indian geographies of identity and power: At the crossroads of Indígena and Mestizaje. *Harvard Educational Review, 70*(4), 467–498.

–. (2004). *Red pedagogy: Native American social and political thought*. New York: Rowman and Littlefield.

Grant, C.A. (2008). Teacher capacities: Knowledge, beliefs, skills and commitments. In M. Cochran-Smith, S. Feiman-Nemser, D.J. McIntyre, and K.E. Demers (Eds.), *Handbook of research on teacher education: Enduring questions in changing contexts* (3rd ed., pp. 123–133). New York: Routledge.

Grant, C.A., and Agosto, V. (2008). Teacher capacity and social justice in teacher education. In M. Cochran-Smith, S. Feiman-Nemser, D.J. McIntyre, and K.E. Demers (Eds.), *Handbook of research on teacher education: Enduring questions in changing contexts* (3rd ed., pp. 175–200). New York: Routledge.

Grant, C.A., and Tate, W. (2001). Multicultural education through the lens of the multicultural education research literature. In J.A. Banks and C.A. McGee Banks (Eds.), *Handbook of research on multicultural education* (pp. 801–820). San Francisco: Jossey-Bass.

Grauerholz, L. (2001). Teaching holistically to achieve deep learning. *College Teaching, 49*(2), 44–50. http://dx.doi.org/10.1080/87567550109595845

Greene, M. (1978). *Landscapes of learning*. New York: Teachers College Press.

Grimmett, P.P. (1995). Reconceptualizing teacher education: Preparing teachers for revitalized schools. In M.F. Wideen and P.P. Grimmett (Eds.), *Changing times in teacher education: Restructuring or reconceptualization* (pp. 202–225). Bristol, PA: Falmer Press.

Grimmett, P.P., Erickson, G.L., Mackinnon, A.M., and Riecken, T.J. (1990). Reflective practice in teacher education. In R.T. Clift, W.R. Houston, and M.C. Pugach (Eds.), *Encouraging reflective practice in education: An analysis of issues and programs* (pp. 20–38). New York: Teachers College Press.

Grossman, P., McDonald, M., Hammerness, K., and Ronfeldt, M. (2008). Dismantling dichotomies in teacher education. In M. Cochran-Smith, S. Feiman-Nemser, D.J. McIntyre, and K.E. Demers (Eds.), *Handbook of research on teacher education: Enduring questions in changing contexts* (3rd ed., pp. 243–248). New York: Routledge.

Grumet, M.R. (2006). Where does the world go when schooling is about schooling? *Journal of Curriculum Theorizing, 22*(3), 47–54.

Hampton, E. (1995). Towards a redefinition of Indian education. In M. Battiste and J. Barman (Eds.), *First Nations education in Canada: The circle unfolds* (pp. 5–46). Vancouver, BC: UBC Press.

Hansen, D.T. (2008). Values and purpose in teacher education. In M. Cochran-Smith, S. Feiman-Nemser, D.J. McIntyre, and K.E. Demers (Eds.), *Handbook of research on teacher education: Enduring questions in changing contexts* (3rd ed., pp. 10–26). New York: Routledge.

Hargreaves, A. (1996). *Changing teachers, changing times: Teachers' work and culture in the postmodern age.* New York: Teachers College Press.

Hart, M. (2001). Transforming boundaries of power in the classroom: Learning from La Mestiza. In R. Cervero and A. Wilson (Eds.), *Power and practice: Adult education and the struggle for knowledge and power in society* (pp. 145–163). San Francisco: Jossey-Bass.

Hawken, P. (2007). *Blessed unrest: How the largest movement in the world came into being and why no one saw it coming.* Toronto: Penguin.

Hayes, D. (2003). Emotional preparation for teaching: A case study about trainee teachers in England. *Teacher Development, 7*(2), 153–171. http://dx.doi.org/10.1080/136645 30300200196

Hirsh, S. (2005). Professional development and closing the achievement gap. *Theory into Practice, 44*(1), 38–44. http://dx.doi.org/10.1207/s15430421tip4401_6

Hoffman-Kipp, P., Artiles, A.J., and López-Torres, L. (2003). Beyond reflection: Teacher learning as praxis. *Theory into Practice, 42*(3), 248–254. http://dx.doi.org/10.1207/ s15430421tip4203_12

Hollingsworth, S., Dybdahl, M., and Minarik, L.T. (1993). By chart and chance and passion: The importance of relational knowing in learning to teach. *Curriculum Inquiry, 23*(1), 5–35. http://dx.doi.org/10.2307/1180216

Hollins, E.R. and Guzman, M.T. (2005). Research on preparing teachers for diverse populations. In M. Cochran-Smith and K.M. Zeichner (Eds.), *Studying teacher education: The report of the AERA Panel on Research and Teacher Education* (pp. 477–548). New York: Routledge.

hooks, b. (1994). *Teaching to transgress.* New York: Routledge.

Houston, W.R., and Clift, R.T. (1990). The potential for research contributions to reflective practice. In R.T. Clift, W.R. Houston, and M.C. Pugach (Eds.), *Encouraging reflective practice in education: An analysis of issues and programs* (pp. 208–222). New York: Teachers College Press.

Howard, G. (2004). How we are white. *Teaching Tolerance, 26,* 50–52.

Howard, T.C., and Aleman, G.R. (2008). Teacher capacity for diverse learners. In M. Cochran-Smith, S. Feiman-Nemser, D.J. McIntyre, and K.E. Demers (Eds.), *Handbook of research on teacher education: Enduring questions in changing contexts* (3rd ed., pp.157–174). New York: Routledge.

Hutchins, R.M. (1936/1952). *The higher learning in America.* New Haven: Yale University Press.

Hutchison, D., and Bosacki, S. (2000). Over the edge: Can holistic education contribute to experiential education? *Journal of Experiential Education, 23*(3), 177–182. http://dx.doi.org/10.1177/105382590002300310

Hyatt, D.F., and Beigy, A. (1999). Making the most of the unknown language experience: Pathways for reflective teacher development. *Journal of Education for Teaching, 25*(1), 31–40. http://dx.doi.org/10.1080/02607479919655

Institute for Integrative Science and Health (2006). *Two-eyed seeing.* Spirit of the East Knowledge Sharing Series, Cape Breton University. Video retrieved October 1, 2008, from: http://marcatodigital.com/iish/index.php?section=10

Irvine, J.J. (2003). *Educating teachers for diversity: Seeing with a cultural eye.* New York: Teachers College Press.

Kanu, Y. (2003). Curriculum as cultural practice: Postcolonial education. *Journal of the Canadian Association for Curriculum Studies, 1*(1), 67–81.

–. (2005). Teachers' perceptions of the integration of Aboriginal culture into the high school curriculum. *Alberta Journal of Educational Research, 51*(1), 50–68.

–. (2006, April). *Decolonizing Indigenous education: Beyond culturalism: Towards post-cultural strategies.* Paper presented at the American Educational Research Association, San Francisco, CA.

Karsenti, T., and Collin, S. (2013). Why are new teachers leaving the profession? Results of a Canada-wide survey. *Education, 3*(3), 141–149.

Kennedy, M.M., Ahn, S., and Choi, J. (2008). The value added by teacher education. In M. Cochran-Smith, S. Feiman-Nemser, D.J. McIntyre, and K.E. Demers (Eds.), *Handbook of research on teacher education: Enduring questions in changing contexts* (3rd ed., pp. 1247–1272). New York: Routledge.

Kincheloe, J.L., and Steinberg, S.R. (2008). Indigenous knowledges in education: Complexities, dangers, and profound benefits. In N.K. Denzin, Y.S. Lincoln, and L.T. Smith (Eds.), *Handbook of critical and indigenous methodologies* (pp. 135–156). Thousand Oaks, CA: Sage. http://dx.doi.org/10.4135/9781483385686.n7

King, T. (2003). *The truth about stories: A native narrative.* Toronto: House of Anansi Press.

Kremer, J.W. (1997). Transforming learning transforming. *ReVision, 20*(1), 7–15.

–. (2003). Ethnoautobiography as practice of radical presence: Storying the self in participatory visions. *ReVision, 26*(2), 5–15.

Kumashiro, K.K. (2008). Partial movements toward teacher quality ... and their potential for advancing social justice. In M. Cochran-Smith, S. Feiman-Nemser, D.J. McIntyre, and K.E. Demers (Eds.), *Handbook of research on teacher education: Enduring questions in changing contexts* (3rd ed., 238–242). New York: Routledge.

Kuokkanen, R. (2007). *Reshaping the university: Responsibility, indigenous epistemes, and the logic of the gift.* Vancouver, BC: UBC Press.

Labosky, V.K. (1994). *Development of reflective practice: A study of pre-service teachers.* New York: Teachers College Press.

Ladson-Billings, G. (1995). Multicultural teacher education: Research, practice, and policy. In J.A. Banks and C.A. McGee Banks (Eds.), *Handbook of research in multicultural education* (pp. 747–759). New York: Macmillan.

–. (1999). Preparing teachers for diverse student populations: A critical race theory perspective. *Review of Research in Education, 24,* 211–247.

–. (2001). Multicultural teacher education: Research, practice, and policy. In J.A. Banks and C.A. McGee Banks (Eds.), *Handbook of research on multicultural education* (pp. 747–759). San Francisco: Jossey-Bass.

Lakoff, G., and Johnson, M. (1999). *Philosophy in the flesh: The embodied mind and its challenge to western thought.* New York: Basic Books.

Lane, P., Bopp, J., Bopp, M., Brown, L., and elders (1984). *The sacred tree.* Twin Lakes, WI: Lotus Press.

Lave, J., and Wenger, E. (1991/2003). *Situated learning: Legitimate peripheral participation.* New York: Cambridge University Press. http://dx.doi.org/10.1017/CBO9780511815355

Leonardo, Z. (2004). Critical social theory and transformative knowledge: The function of criticism in quality education. *Educational Researcher, 33*(6), 11–18. http://dx.doi.org/10.3102/0013189X033006011

Liston, D.P., and Zeichner, K.M. (1991). *Teacher education and the social conditions of schooling.* New York: Routledge.

Little Bear, L. (2009, May). *Indigenous philosophies of land and life.* Public lecture given at the Indigenous Governance Leadership Forum, University of Victoria, BC.

Lortie, D.C. (1975). *Schoolteacher: A sociological study.* Chicago: University of Chicago Press.

Lowenstein, K. (2009). The work of multicultural teacher education: Reconceptualizing white teacher candidates as learners. *Review of Educational Research, 79*(1), 163–196. http://dx.doi.org/10.3102/0034654308326161

Marx, S. (2003). Entanglements of altruism, whiteness, and deficit thinking. *Educators for Urban Minorities, 2*(2), 41–56.

McDiarmid, G.W., and Clevenger-Bright, M. (2008). Rethinking teacher capacity. In M. Cochran-Smith, S. Feiman-Nemser, D.J. McIntyre, and K.E. Demers (Eds.), *Handbook of research on teacher education: Enduring questions in changing contexts* (3rd ed., pp. 134–156). New York: Routledge.

McIntosh, P. (1990). White privilege: Unpacking the invisible knapsack. *Independent School,* Winter, 31–36.

Merryfield, M.M., and Wilson, A. (2005). *Social studies and the world: Teaching global perspectives.* Washington, DC: National Council for the Social Studies.

Meyer, K. (2008, June). *Teaching practices of living inquiry.* Paper presented at Canadian Society for the Study of Education, Vancouver, BC.

Mezirow, J. (1978). *Education for perspective transformation: Women's re-entry programs in community colleges.* New York: Teachers College Press.

–. (1997). Transformative learning: Theory to practice. *New Directions for Adult and Continuing Education, 74,* 5–12. http://dx.doi.org/10.1002/ace.7401

Miller, J. (2007). *The holistic curriculum* (2nd ed.). Toronto: University of Toronto Press.

Moll, L.C., and Arnot-Hopffer, E. (2005). Sociocultural competence in teacher education. *Journal of Teacher Education, 56*(3), 242–247. http://dx.doi.org/10.1177/0022487105275919

Momaday, L.S. (1976). Native American attitudes to the environment. In W.H. Capps and E.F. Tonsing (Eds.), *Seeing with a Native eye: Essays on Native American religion* (pp. 79–85). New York: Harper and Row.

Moodley, K.A. (2001). Multicultural education in Canada: Historical development and current status. In J.A. Banks and C.A. McGee Banks (Eds.), *Handbook of research on multicultural education* (pp. 801–820). San Francisco: Jossey-Bass.

Neumann, A. (2006). Professing passion: Emotion in the scholarship of professors at research universities. *American Educational Research Journal, 43*(3), 381–424. http://dx.doi.org/10.3102/00028312043003381

Nhất Hạnh, T. (1991). *Peace is every step: The path of mindfulness in everyday life.* New York: Bantam Books.

Noddings, N. (2003). *Happiness and education.* New York: Cambridge University Press. http://dx.doi.org/10.1017/CBO9780511499920

Norberg-Hodge, H. (1991). *Ancient futures: Learning from Ladakh.* Berkeley: University of California Press.

Oberg, A. (2004). Reflecting on reflecting. *Journal of the Canadian Association for Curriculum Studies, 2*(1), 239–244.

Okri, B. (1997). *A way of being free.* London: Phoenix House.

Oosterheert, I.E., and Vermunt, J.D. (2003). Knowledge construction in learning to teach: The role of dynamic sources. *Teachers and Teaching: Theory and Practice, 9*(2), 157–173. http://dx.doi.org/10.1080/13540600309376

Orr, D. (1994/2004). *Earth in mind: On education, environment, and the human prospect.* Washington, DC: Island Press.

–. (2005). Foreword. In M.K. Stone and Z. Barlow (Eds.), *Ecological literacy: Educating our children for a sustainable world* (pp. ix-xi). San Francisco: Sierra Club Books.

O'Sullivan, E. (2001). Beyond globalization: Visioning transformative education within a politics of hope. *Review of Education, Pedagogy and Cultural Studies, 23*(3), 317–333. http://dx.doi.org/10.1080/1071441010230305

–. (2003). Bringing a perspective of transformative learning to globalized consumption. *International Journal of Consumer Studies, 27*(4), 326–330. http://dx.doi.org/10.1046/j.1470-6431.2003.00327.x

O'Sullivan, E.V., Morrell, A., and O'Connor, M. (Eds.). (2002). *Expanding the boundaries of transformative learning.* New York: Palgrave.

Palmer, P. (1998). *The courage to teach: Exploring the inner landscape of a teacher's life.* San Francisco: Jossey-Bass.

Phillips, D., and Carr, K. (2006). *Becoming a teacher through action research: Process, context and self-study.* New York: Taylor and Francis Group.

Piaget, J. (1960). *The psychology of the child.* New York: Basic Books.

Pinar, W.F. (2004). *What is curriculum theory?* Mahwah, NJ: Lawrence Erlbaum.

Pinar, W.F., and Grumet, M.R. (1976). *Toward a poor curriculum.* Dubuque, IA: Kendall/Hunt.

Polkinghorne, D. (1988). *Narrative knowing and the human sciences.* Albany, NY: State University of New York Press.

Prawat, R.S. (1992). Teachers' beliefs about teaching and learning: A constructivist perspective. *American Journal of Education, 100*(3), 354–395. http://dx.doi.org/10.1086/444021

Preece, A. (2004). Gândirea critică în sala de clasă: niciodată nu e prea devreme pentru a începe [Critical thinking in the classroom: Never too soon to start]. *Şcoala Reflexivă, 1*(2), 2–9.

Richardson, V. (1990). The evolution of reflective teaching and teacher education. In R.T. Clift, W.R. Houston, and M.C. Pugach (Eds.), *Encouraging reflective practice in education: An analysis of issues and programs* (pp. 3–19). New York: Teachers College Press.

–. (1996). The role of attitudes and beliefs in learning to teach. In J. Sikula, T. Bettery, and E. Guyton (Eds.), *Handbook of research on teacher education* (2nd ed., pp. 102–119). New York: Macmillan.

Riley-Taylor, E. (2002). *Ecology, spirituality and education: Curriculum for relational knowing*. New York: Peter Lang.

Rilke, R.M. (1986). *Letters to a young poet* (S. Mitchell, Trans.). New York: Vintage.

Robertson, E. (2008). Teacher education in a democratic society: Learning and teaching the practices of democratic participation. In M. Cochran-Smith, S. Feiman-Nemser, D.J. McIntyre, and K.E. Demers (Eds.), *Handbook of research on teacher education: Enduring questions in changing contexts* (3rd ed., pp. 27–44). New York: Routledge.

Ross, R. (1996/2006). *Returning to the teachings: Exploring Aboriginal justice*. Toronto: Penguin Canada.

Rust, F.O. (1994). The first year of teaching: It's not what they expected. *Teaching and Teacher Education, 10*(2), 205–217. http://dx.doi.org/10.1016/0742-051X(94)90013-2

Sanford, K., Williams, L., Hopper, T., and McGregor, C. (2012). Indigenous principles decolonizing teacher education: What we have learned. *in education, 18*(2), unpaginated. http://ineducation.ca/index.php/ineducation/article/view/61/547

Saul, J.R. (2008). *A fair country: Telling truths about Canada*. Toronto: Viking Canada.

Schaefer, C. (2006). *Grandmothers counsel the world: Women elders offer their vision for our planet*. Boston: Trumpeter Books.

Schmidt, P.R. (1999). Know thyself and understand others. *Language Arts, 76*(4), 332–340.

Schön, D. (1983). *The reflective practitioner*. New York: Basic Books.

Schultz, K. (2003). *Listening: A framework for teaching across difference*. New York: Teachers College Press.

Sharp, K.M. (2003). Teacher reflection: A perspective from the trenches. *Theory into Practice, 42*(3), 243–247. http://dx.doi.org/10.1207/s15430421tip4203_11

Shepard, L. (1990). Inflated test score gains: Is the problem old norms or teaching to the test? *Educational Measurement: Issues and Practice, 9*(3), 15–22. http://dx.doi.org/10.1111/j.1745-3992.1990.tb00374.x

Shor, I. (1986). Equality is excellence: Transforming teacher education and the learning process. *Harvard Educational Review, 56*(4), 406–426.

–. (1993). Education is politics: Paulo Freire's critical pedagogy. In P. McLaren and P. Leonard (Eds.), *Paulo Freire, a critical encounter* (pp. 25–35). New York: Routledge. http://dx.doi.org/10.4324/9780203420263_chapter_2

Shugurensky, D. (2002). Transformative learning and transformative politics: The pedagogical dimension of participatory democracy and social action. In E.V. O'Sullivan, A. Morrell, and M. O'Connor (Eds.), *Expanding the boundaries of transformative learning* (pp. 59–76). New York: Palgrave.

Sleeter, C.E. (2008). Preparing white teachers for diverse students. In M. Cochran-Smith, S. Feiman-Nemser, D.J. McIntyre, and K.E. Demers (Eds.), *Handbook of research on teacher education: Enduring questions in changing contexts* (3rd ed., pp. 559–582). New York: Routledge.

Smith, L.T. (1999). *Decolonizing methodologies: Research and indigenous peoples*. London: Zed Books.

Smits, H., Towers, J., Panayotidis, L., and Lund, D. (2008). Provoking and being provoked by embodied qualities of learning: Listening, speaking, seeing, and feeling (through) inquiry in teacher education. *Journal of the Canadian Association for Curriculum Studies, 6*(2), 43–81.

Snipp, C.M. (2001). *American Indian studies. Handbook of research on multicultural education.* San Francisco: Jossey-Bass.

Spradley, J. (1980). *Participant observer.* New York: Holt, Rinehart and Winston.

Stanger, N.R.G., Tanaka, M., Starr, L., and Tse, V. (2013). Winter counts as transformative inquiry: The role of creative imagery as an interpretation of adaptive change. *Complicity, 10*(1/2), 87–110.

Statistics Canada (2005a). *Aboriginal peoples living off-reserve in Western Canada: Estimates from the labour force survey.* (Cat. No. 71–587-XIE). Ottawa: Ministry of Industry.

–. (2005b). *Projections of the Aboriginal population, Canada, provinces and territories: 2001 to 2017.* (Cat. No. 91–547-XIE). Ottawa: Ministry of Industry.

Stein, J.G. (2002). *The cult of efficiency.* Toronto: House of Anansi Press.

Stone, M.K., and Barlow, Z. (Eds.). (2005). *Ecological literacy: Educating our children for a sustainable world.* San Francisco: Sierra Club Books.

Strong-Wilson, T. (2008). *Bringing memory forward: Storied remembrance in social justice education with teachers.* New York: Peter Lang.

Tafoya, T. (1995). Finding harmony: Balancing traditional values with western science in therapy. *Canadian Journal of Native Education, 21*(supplement), 7–27.

Tanaka, M.T. (2009). *Transforming perspectives: The immersion of student teachers in indigenous ways of knowing.* Unpublished doctoral dissertation, University of Victoria, BC. Available at: https://dspace.library.uvic.ca//handle/1828/1664

–. (2011) Formative touchstones: Finding place as a teacher through an indigenous learning experience. In C. Mitchell, T. Strong-Wilson, K. Pithouse, and S. Allnutt (Eds.), *Memory and pedagogy* (pp. 60–77). New York: Routledge.

–. (2013). Learning to dwell aright in the tensionality of a sweat lodge. In W. Hurren and E. Hasebe-Ludt (Eds.), *Contemplating curriculum: Genealogies/times/places* (pp.174–186). New York, NY: Routledge.

–. (2015). Transformative inquiry in teacher education: Evoking the soul of what matters. *Teacher Development, 19*(2), 133–150. http://dx.doi.org/10.1080/13664530.2014.992459

Tanaka, M.T., Nicholson, D., and Farish, M. (2012). Committed to transformative inquiry: Three teacher educators' entry points into the mentoring role. *Journal of Transformative Education, 10*(4), 257–274. http://dx.doi.org/10.1177/1541344612472396

Tanaka, M.T., Stanger, N., and Tse, V. (2014). *Transformative inquiry* (iBook, v. 4.0). Available at: http://transformativeinquiry.ca/downloads/

Tanaka, M.T., and Tse, V.V. (2015). Touching the inexplicable: Poetry as transformative inquiry. *Journal of Curriculum Theorizing, 30*(3), 45–62.

Tanaka, M.T., Tse, V., Farish, M., Doll, J., Nicholson, D. and Archer, E. (2014). Carried along in the tide of another's knowing: The vulnerability of mentor~mentee relationships in Transformative Inquiry. *Journal of Transformative Education, 12*(3), 206–225. DOI: 10.1177/1541344614545129

Tanaka, M., Tse, V., Stanger, N., Piché, I., Starr, L., Farish, M. Abra, M. (2014). The edge of counselling: Mindful negotiation of emotions towards transforming learning~teaching. In L. Thomas (Ed.), *Becoming teacher: Sites for development of Canadian Teacher Education* (pp. 467–502). https://sites.google.com/site/cssecate/fall-working-conference

Tanaka, M., Williams, L., Benoit, Y.J., Duggan, R.K., Moir, L., and Scarrow, J.C. (2007). Transforming pedagogies: Pre-service reflections on learning and teaching in an indigenous world. *Teacher Development, 11*(1), 99–109. http://dx.doi.org/10.1080/13664530701194728

Thomas, S.P, and Pollio, H.R. (2002). *Listening to patients: A phenomenological approach to nursing research and practice.* New York: Springer Publishing.

Tisdell, E.J. (2001). The politics of positionality: Teaching for social change in higher education. In R. Cervero and A. Wilson (Eds.), *Power and practice: Adult education and the struggle for knowledge and power in society* (pp. 145–163). San Francisco: Jossey-Bass.

–. (2003). *Exploring spirituality and culture in adult and higher education.* San Francisco: Jossey-Bass.

–. (2007). In the new millennium: The role of spirituality and the cultural imagination in dealing with diversity and equity in higher education. *Teachers College Record, 109*(3), 531–560.

Traudt, K. (2002). Survey says ... : Can a white teacher effectively teach students of color? In L. Darling-Hammond, J. French, and S.P. Garcia-Lopez (Eds.), *Learning to teach for social justice* (pp. 43–51). New York: Teachers College Press.

Valli, L., and Buese, D. (2007). The changing role of teachers in an era of accountability. *American Educational Research Journal, 44*(3), 519–558. http://dx.doi.org/10.3102/0002831207306859

van Manen, M. (1977). Linking ways of knowing with ways of being practical. *Curriculum Inquiry, 6*(3), 205–228. http://dx.doi.org/10.2307/1179579

–. (1986). *The tone of teaching.* Richmond Hill, ON: Scholastic.

–. (1990/1997). *Researching lived experience: Human science for an action sensitive pedagogy.* London, ON: Althouse Press.

–. (1991). *The tact of teaching.* London, ON: Althouse Press.

Vella, J. (2002). *Learning to listen, learning to teach: The power of dialogue in educating adults.* San Francisco: Jossey-Bass.

Villegas, A.M. (2008). Does difference make a difference? In M. Cochran-Smith, S. Feiman-Nemser, D.J. McIntyre, and K.E. Demers (Eds.), *Handbook of research on teacher education: Enduring questions in changing contexts* (3rd ed., pp. 547–550). New York: Routledge.

Villegas, A.M., and Lucas, T. (2002). Preparing culturally responsive teachers: Rethinking the curriculum. *Journal of Teacher Education, 53*(1), 20–32. http://dx.doi.org/10.1177/0022487102053001003

Weenie, A. (1998). Aboriginal pedagogy: The sacred circle concept. In L. Stiffarm (Ed.), *As we see ... Aboriginal pedagogy* (pp. 59–66). Saskatoon, SK: University Extension Press.

Wenger, E. (1998). *Communities of practice: Learning, meaning, and identity.* New York: Cambridge University Press. http://dx.doi.org/10.1017/CBO9780511803932

Wideen, M.F., and Grimmett, P.P. (Eds.). (1995). *Changing times in teacher education: Restructuring or reconceptualizing.* Bristol, PA: Falmer Press.

Wideen, M.F., Mayer-Smith, J., and Moon, B. (1998). A critical analysis of the research on learning to teach: Making the case for an ecological perspective on inquiry. *Review of Educational Research, 68*(2), 130–178. http://dx.doi.org/10.3102/00346543068002130

Williams, L. (2006). *Course description for EDCI 499 Fall 2006, Earth Fibres, Weaving Stories: Learning and teaching in an indigenous world.* University of Victoria.

Williams, L., and Tanaka, M. (2007) Schalay'nung Sxwey'ga: Emerging cross cultural peda-gogy in the academy. *Educational Insights, 11*(3), 1–21. http://einsights.ogpr.educ.ubc. ca/v11n03/articles/williams/williams.html

Williams, L., Tanaka, M., Leik, V., and Riecken, T. (2014). Walking side by side: Living indigenous ways in the academy. In C. Etmanski, B. Hall, and T. Dawson (Eds.), *Learning and teaching community based research: Linking pedagogy to practice* (pp. 229–252). Toronto: University of Toronto Press.

Wilson, S. (2007). Guest editorial: What is an indigenist research paradigm? *Canadian Journal of Native Education, 30*(2), 193–195, 322.

–. (2008). *Research is ceremony*. Halifax: Fernwood.

–. (2010, April). Public lecture on indigenous research. University of Victoria, BC.

Wilson, T. (2002). Excavation and relocation: Landscapes of learning in a teacher's auto-biography. *Journal of Curriculum Theorizing, 18*(3), 75–88.

Zeichner, K. (1987). Preparing reflective teachers: An overview of instructional strategies which have been employed in pre-service teacher education. *International Journal of Educational Research, 11*(5), 565–575. http://dx.doi.org/10.1016/0883-0355(87) 90016-4

–. (2006). Reflections of a university-based teacher educator on the future of college- and university-based teacher education. *Journal of Teacher Education, 57*(3), 326–340. http:// dx.doi.org/10.1177/0022487105285893

Index

Note: (i) refer to illustrations; PST stands for "pre-service teachers"; WK, for "wisdom keepers"; TI, for "Transformative Inquiry."

Cree. *See* Memnook, Carolyn (Hesqiaht Saddle Lake/Cree); Memnook, Fran (Hesqiaht Saddle Lake/Cree)

critical questions: about, 210–11; Cajete's questions, 11–12, 129, 151–53, 192–93; clarifying purpose, 192–93; Does it grow corn?, 159–61, 200; Orr's questions, 12, 193, 210; Transformative Inquiry (TI), 202–3; transformative learning, 172, 200. *See also* Cajete, Gregory, critical questions

crosscultural understanding, 6, 46–47, 58, 115–17, 149, 165, 196, 205–11

cultural appropriation, 165

Danielle (PST), 53, 92, 105, 110, 122, 123(i), 208

deer, 34–35

Della. *See* Sylvester, Della Rice (Cowichan)

Delpit, L., 169, 199

Dewey, John, 185

dispositional change in PSTs. *See* preservice teachers, dispositional changes

Dressman, M., 10

Earth. *See* environmental sustainability; TEN̲EW̲~Earth

earth fibres: classroom materials, 17, 40–41; creative process, 50, 60, 93, 103–4, 145, 158, 161; eco-social-spiritual awareness, 159–60; stories of place, 17; woven braid metaphor, 15–17, 20. *See also* buckskin blankets; button blankets; cattails; cedar bark

earth fibres course: about, 3–8; adapted versions of, 204; course description, 3–4; creation of mural, 7, 26(i), 57; creative ownership, 108, 110; group work, 83–85, 94–95, 184; intent of course, 3–4, 53–54, 57–58; location and time, 7; materials and supplies, 5, 17, 40–41; meanings of the crafts, 64; medicine wheel framework, 15, 18(i), 18–20, 21(i), 70–71, 91–92, 114; opening circles, 22, 65–69, 66(i), 133; opening prayers, 68–69, 144; product vs process, 84–85, 132, 145, 158; as

resistance, 162; spirituality, 60; stories, 140, 148–50; terminology, 8–9; textile skills, 57, 60; touchstones for teaching, 7, 10–11, 202, 205–11; university environment, 93–94, 111–12, 131–32, 144–46, 152, 158, 200; woven braid metaphor, 15–17, 20. *See also* Honoured Grandmother mural; research project

earth fibres course and PSTs: assessment, ungraded, 88, 146, 180–81, 198–99; choosing to participate, 140–41; class size, 4; cultural translation and sense of unknowing, 63–64, 141–42, 145–46; dispositional change in PSTs, 196; equal partnership with WKs, 74–76; expectations of PSTs, 55–56; indigenous languages, 64–65; journal writing, 101–2; lack of note-taking, 62–63, 73–74, 88, 125, 141; listening and observing, 62–63, 164; motivation of PSTs, 17, 22, 45, 55, 61–62, 76, 88, 99–100, 140–41; political correctness, 55, 163; pseudonyms for PSTs, 4; putting aside the familiar, 141–42; reasons to not take the course, 55; sense of community, 51–52, 56; walking alongside, 195–99. *See also* pre-service teachers (PST)

education, terminology, 9

education of teachers. *See* pre-service teachers (PST); teacher education

efficiency goals, 104–5, 181–83, 190

Elder–Grandma Moon (story), 36–37

elders, 154. *See also* wisdom keepers (WK)

emotions: counselling skills, 46, 148; discomfort of, 7, 46, 145–46, 148; emotional sharing, 142–44, 146–47, 149, 164, 170–71; holistic learning, 59, 80–82, 119–20, 133–36, 153–55; reflectivity, 7, 9–11, 172–73; role in learning, 11; safe enough space, 71, 86–90, 142–44, 169, 172; social justice work, 172–73; Transformative Inquiry (TI), 202–3; transformative learning, 169–72, 200. *See also* reflection; spirituality

English language, 131, 157. *See also* worldview, Euro-Western environmental sustainability: about, 24, 151–53; academic scholarship on, 12; connection vs disconnection from TENEW~Earth, 11, 24, 151–52, 206–7; consumerism, 43, 47–48; Does it grow corn?, 159–61, 200; earth fibres course goals, 54; ecological balance, 154–55; How will we deal with the environmental crisis? (Cajete), 12, 23, 24, 151–53; indigenous worldview, 152–56; interconnected relations, 145, 156–59, 210–11; nature walks, 4, 42–46, 68, 75, 151–54; planetary changes, 54; practicum experiences, 151–52; tender resistance, 24, 164–65. *See also* place; TENEW~Earth

Ermine, W., 155

Euro-Western pedagogy. *See* pedagogy, Euro-Western

Euro-Western worldview. *See* worldview, Euro-Western

evaluation. *See* assessment and evaluation

fibres. *See* earth fibres

First Nations indigenous pedagogy. *See* earth fibres course; pedagogy, indigenous; wisdom keepers (WK)

fish: connection to place, 42; salmon in moon stories, 31–37

focus groups, post-practicum. *See* research project

food making and sharing, 48–49, 65–66

Fran. *See* Memnook, Fran (Hesqiaht Saddle Lake/Cree)

Freire, Paulo: banking model of education, 175; conscientization, 170; death of the professor, 23, 138; dispositional qualities and social justice, 166; pedagogy of the question, 186

frogs, xv, 27, 30–31

Gardner, Howard, 133–34

Garrett (PST), 40, 43, 52, 56, 66–67, 75, 81, 88–90, 100, 109, 112, 121–22, 138, 183–84, 191, 208

Gay. *See* Williams, Gay (Lil'wat)

gender balance, 28, 31, 83, 132

gentle offerings, 22, 76–78, 122, 129, 130, 197, 198–99. *See also* learner-teacher relationships

George, Charlene, kQwa'ste'not (T'Sou-ke), lead instructor: cattail mats activity, 39–40, 40(i); cedar bark group, 83–84; course design by, 4–5, 54, 65; cultural translation, 63–64; cyclical activities, 41–42; gentle offerings, 76, 77, 129, 130; good hands, 8, 92; holistic learning, 80–82; learner-teacher relationships, 71, 77; marbles and learners metaphor, 87; moon stories, 5, 27–29; perfectionism, 97; personal positioning, 44–45; rain as cleansing tears, 206; reflexivity, 99, 102; safe places, 87–88; time to peel cedar bark, 41–42; university environment, 93–94, 113, 152, 158; unveiling ceremony, 113, 158; work sessions at her home, 112–13

Gina. *See* Robertson, Gina (Laichwiltach/Kwakuitl)

Giveaway: about, 37, 94–99, 157–58; first pieces, 96–97; indigenous worldview, 157–58; modelling of, 95–96; moon stories, 36; pieces created for, 98(i), 210(i); reciprocity, 95–96, 132, 191; unveiling ceremony, 96–98

goals of teaching. *See* why we teach

good hands: about, 8, 22–23, 91–94, 136; first pieces, 96–97; generosity, 96; Giveaway, 94–99, 98(i), 210(i); handwork and knowing, 81–82, 91–92; image of offering of thanks \0/, 28–29, 38, 206, 210(i); learning rhythms, 94; medicine wheel framework, 17–20, 18(i), 21(i), 22–23, 91–92; mistakes, 97; mural feature, 26(i), 28, 37; patience, 104–5, 109–10; perfectionism, 96–97, 105–6, 124, 142; reflection, 99, 103–4; spirituality, 160; Transformative Inquiry (TI), 202–3

Grande, S.M., 195

Grandmother mural. *See* Honoured Grandmother mural

gratitude, 28, 38, 67

group work: in earth fibres course, 4, 83–85, 94–95, 132; individual vs group identity, 94–95, 106–7, 184; patience, 184–85; in practicum placements, 183–85; stories, 140

groups, circle. See circles, opening

Grumet, M.R., 176

hands, good. See good hands; HÍSW̱ḴE (thanks for gifts) hands

Heather (PST), 52, 86, 108, 116, 119, 120(i), 123–24, 126, 187–88, 208

Hemry, James (Métis), 50, 93, 95

Hemry, Lynne (Métis), 4, 18–20, 71, 77, 86, 96, 159, 205

Hesqiaht Saddle Lake/Cree. See Memnook, Carolyn (Hesqiaht Saddle Lake/Cree); Memnook, Fran (Hesqiaht Saddle Lake/Cree)

HÍSW̱ḴE (thanks for gifts) hands: image of offering of thanks \0/, 28–29, 38, 206, 210(i)

holistic learning (physical, emotional, spiritual, mental), 59, 80–82, 119–20, 133–36, 153–55

Honoured Grandmother mural: about, 4, 26(i), 27–29; ceremonial shawl, 4, 60, 83–84, 84(i); creation of, 7, 28, 57, 84–85; display at U of Victoria, 28, 57, 204; features in, 26(i), 27–28, 110, 206; gender balance, 28, 31, 83, 132; honouring of women, 27–28, 57, 110–11; installation ceremony, 113, 158; moon stories, 4, 27–29, 37, 158–59; theé lellum (honoured home), 4, 5; unveiling ceremony, 96–98, 98(i), 106–13, 107(i), 158–59. See also Moons of XAXE SIÁM SILA

how and why we teach. See teacher education; why we teach

Hummingbird, mural feature, 28

Hutchins, R.M., 175–77

indigenous, terminology, 8

indigenous education course. See earth fibres course; pre-service teachers (PST); wisdom keepers (WK)

indigenous pedagogy. See pedagogy, indigenous

indigenous worldview. See worldview, indigenous

inquiry approach, 9, 200–203

instructors, Aboriginal. See George, Charlene, kQwa'ste'not (T'Sou-ke), lead instructor; wisdom keepers (WK)

intent in teaching. See why we teach

introductions, personal, 4–5, 52–53

Jade (PST), 45–46, 97, 99, 106–7, 110–12, 118–19, 124–25, 127(i), 128, 136, 185, 208

James. See Hemry, James (Métis)

Janet. See Rogers, Janet (Mohawk/Tuscarora)

Jayne (PST), 61, 126, 137

journal writing, 101–2

Kanu, Y., 166–67

Kevin (PST), 41, 52–53, 56, 68–69, 81–82, 98–99, 115, 160, 185, 208

King, Thomas, 13, 130

kQwa'ste'not. See George, Charlene, kQwa'ste'not (T'Sou-ke), lead instructor

Kumashiro, K.K., 169

Kwakuitl. See Robertson, Gina (Laichwiltach/Kwakuitl)

Laichwiltach/Kwakuitl. See Robertson, Gina (Laichwiltach/Kwakuitl)

Lane, P., 19

languages, 8–9, 64–65, 131, 135–36, 157. See also SENĆOŦEN (language of W̱SÁNEĆ peoples)

Leanne (PST), 46, 54, 56, 62, 78, 86, 91, 92, 95, 103–4, 108–9, 112–13, 116, 121–22, 132, 136, 177, 182, 191, 204

learner-teacher relationships: about, 9, 70–71, 90; basic skills, 78; boundaries, 122; defined, 9; encouragement, 72; equal partners, 74–76, 115, 122–25; expertise and skills, 74–76, 78; faith in the learner, 78–80; focus group notebook images, 115, 120(i)–121(i),

nature walks: connection to place, 42–44, 45–46, 68, 151–52; equality of PSTs and WKs, 75; leadership, 4; nature in indigenous worldview, 153–54. *See also* environmental sustainability; place

Nicole (PST), 42, 45, 55, 73–75, 86, 88, 99–100, 115–17, 123, 124(i), 126, 134–35, 136, 144, 178–80, 183, 209

non-indigenous people. *See* pedagogy, Euro-Western; worldview, Euro-Western

O'Connor, M., 171–72

Okri, Ben, 14

Old Man welcoming totem pole, xiv, 28, 83, 132, 142

opening circle. *See* circles, opening

Orr, David, 12, 193, 210

O'Sullivan, E.V., 171–72

Palmer, Parker, 9, 190

participants, terminology, 8. *See also* pre-service teachers (PST); wisdom keepers (WK)

patience, 38, 104–5, 109–10, 118, 181–83, 210

pedagogy, Euro-Western: academic emphasis, 80; assessment, 88, 180–81; banking model of education, 175–76; dichotomous thinking, 157; disconnection from environment, 151–52; efficiency goals, 104–5, 181–83, 190; inclusion in education, 155; industrial model, 23–24; language and way of knowing, 131; learner-teacher relationships, 71–72; learning styles, 54, 197; notetaking, 62–63, 73–74, 141; positivism, 24, 155, 175–79, 181, 186, 189; subjective vs objective truth, 176; teacher perfection, 124, 144; transmissive teaching, 45, 131, 176, 181; tree metaphor, 134. *See also* worldview, Euro-Western

pedagogy, indigenous: about, 155; academic scholarship on, 12, 195, 201–3; creative process, 50, 60, 93, 145, 158; earth fibres course, 3–4, 15–20; experiential learning, 196–97; handwork and knowing, 81–82, 91–92; holistic learning, 59, 80–82, 119–20, 133–36, 153–55; inclusion in education, 155; indigenous worldview, 153–56; interconnected relations, 48–49, 176, 193–95; internal motivation, 49–50, 99–100, 131–32, 145; language and way of knowing, 131; listening and observing, 54, 62–63, 164; local cultural knowledge, 135, 149; marginalization of, 54; patience, 38, 104–5, 109–10, 118, 181–83, 210; spirituality, 59–60, 199–200; teacher concept as problematic, 50; tender resistance, 24, 164–65; Transformative Inquiry (TI), 202–3; tree metaphor, 134; unity in diversity, 156; ways of knowing, 152–56; woven braid metaphor, 15–17, 20. *See also* medicine wheel framework; wisdom keepers (WK); worldview, indigenous

perfectionism, 62–63, 96–97, 105–6, 124, 142

personal introductions. *See* introductions, personal

pipe ceremony, 96

place: about, 17, 21–22, 58; cattail mats activity, 39–40, 40(i), 133; connection vs disconnection from, 40–44, 47, 151–52; cultural beliefs and social position, 167–69; earth fibres and connection to place, 4–5, 17, 40–41; environmental changes, 41; indigenous worldview, 153–54, 207; institutionalized settings, 42–43, 93–94; medicine wheel framework, 17–20, 18(i), 21(i), 21–22; personal positioning, 12, 44–45; spirituality and place, 59–60; unconscious learning, 48–49. *See also* community; environmental sustainability; SI,ĆENEN (land where course took place); TENEW~Earth

placement of PSTs in schools. *See* pre-service teachers, practicum experiences

political correctness, 55, 163

positivism: academic scholarship on education and, 176; banking model of education, 175–76; fragmentation of existence, 155, 177; paradigm shift away from, 203–4; practicum as positivism soup, 24, 175–79, 181, 186, 189; reflectivity as technical process, 186; subjective vs objective truth, 176; transmissive teaching approaches, 45, 131, 176, 181; worldview, Euro-Western, 24, 153, 155, 167–68, 175–79. *See also* pedagogy, Euro-Western; worldview, Euro-Western

potlatch, 95. *See also* Giveaway

power relations, 5, 169, 198, 204

practicum. *See* pre-service teachers, practicum experiences

pre-service teachers (PST): (teacher) educator, terminology, 9; about, 17; assessment in courses, 88, 101–2, 146, 180–81, 198–99; constructivist learning, 45, 178–79; creative ownership, 108, 110; cultural beliefs and social position, 5, 44–45, 60–61, 167–69, 187–88, 194; discomfort of, 145–46, 148, 163, 169, 171, 190; identity and integrity issues, 190; images of learner and teacher roles, 47; learner-teachers, 9, 99–101, 137–38; perfectionism, 62–63, 96–97, 105–6, 124, 142; political correctness, 55, 163; PSTs' knowledge of difference, 46–47, 115–16, 163; social justice advocacy, 179; woven braid metaphor, 15–17, 20. *See also* earth fibres course and PSTs; teacher education

pre-service teachers, dispositional changes: about, 6–7, 128, 165–67; awkwardness, 172–73; change towards cultural inclusion, 7, 116–18; crosscultural understanding, 6, 115–18, 149, 196, 205–11; cultural appropriation, 165; defined, 6, 165–66; factors in, 165–67; focus groups, post-practicum, 114–15, 117, 174–75, 184–85; image data from interviews, 114–15; images of roles, initial, 47; learning spirit, 22, 88–89, 130–33, 155–56, 160, 179–80, 199; transformative communities, 169–72. *See also* reflection; social justice and resistance

pre-service teachers, practicum experiences: about, 24, 174–75, 189; assessment of PSTs, 189, 198–99; assessment of students, 180–81, 198; autonomy and ownership, 137–38, 177–79; efficiency, 181–83, 190; environmental sustainability, 151–52; external motivation for learning, 179–80; focus groups, post-practicum, 114–15, 117, 174–75, 184–85; group work by students, 183–85; opening circles, 146–48; planning for indigenous pedagogy, 56–57; positivism, 24, 153, 155, 175–79, 189; reflection, 185–88; safe enough space, 146–48

print buckskin, 4, 15(i), 17

PST. *See* pre-service teachers (PST)

purpose of teaching. *See* why we teach

Put Away Your Paddles Moon (story), 36

questions, critical. *See* critical questions

race and ethnicity: collective spirit, 199, 210–11; critical pedagogy, 195; dichotomous thinking, 157; institutional racism, 163; of PSTs, 5, 169, 187–88, 194; PSTs' knowledge of difference, 163

rain: as cleansing tears, 206–7; moon stories, 33, 34

reflection: about, 9–11, 99–106, 185–88; autobiographical processes, 186; during ceremonies, 113; conversations and dialogues, 102, 140, 144; cultural beliefs and social position, 167–69; defined, 186; good hands, 99, 103–4; inquiry approach, 200–3; island and iceberg metaphors, 167; journal writing, 101–2; knowing while not knowing, 169; learning processes, 117–18; medicine wheel framework, 20, 21(i); mindful reflexivity, 9–11, 99–106, 145–46, 168–69, 172–73; opening to reflexivity, 102–4, 194; patience, 38,

104–5, 109–10, 118, 181–83, 210; PSTs' lack of reflection, 187; PSTs' social positions and beliefs, 44–45, 187–88; reflection vs reflexivity, 10, 168–69; safe enough space, 146; social critique theory, 167–68, 194–95; stories we live by, 169–70; teacher as learner, learner as teacher, 99–101; Transformative Inquiry (TI), 202–3; transformative learning, 169–72, 200; on the why of culture, 194, 196. *See also* emotions; touchstones for teaching

religion vs spirituality, 199–200. *See also* spirituality

research project: about, 7–8, 12–13, 15–20; author, 4–5, 9–11, 16, 17, 171, 209–11; data analysis, 18–19; dispositional changes, 13; focus groups, 19, 114–15, 117, 174–75, 184–85; focus groups, notebooks, 114–15, 120(i), 120–21, 121(i), 123(i), 124(i), 127(i); interviews, 14, 19, 44, 47, 60–61, 102, 114–15, 140, 144, 160–61; medicine wheel framework, 17–20, 18(i), 21(i); narrative inquiry, 12–13, 14; overview of chapters on, 21–25; participant observer approach, 7, 140; phenomenological approach, 12–13; pre-service teachers, 16–17; spirituality, 60–61; terminology, 8–9; themes in data, 17–20; wisdom keepers, 16–17; woven braid metaphor, 15–17, 20. *See also* earth fibres course

resistance. *See* social justice and resistance

Richardson, V., 168

Rilke, R.M., 210

Robertson, Gina, (Laichwiltach/Kwakuitl), 4, 48–49, 55–56, 58, 64, 76, 85

Rogers, Janet (Mohawk/Tuscarora), 4, 50, 57, 60, 71, 95, 116, 132

ropes, cedar, 84

roses, cedar, 88–90, 89(i)

Ross, Rupert, 131

safety and well-being, 71, 86–90, 142–46, 162, 169, 172

Salish. *See* Coast Salish

salmon, moon stories, 31–37

Sam, May (Tsartlip), 4, 48, 72(i), 79–80, 92, 180

Sara (PST), 17, 44, 53–54, 62–63, 73, 92, 97, 101–2, 104, 105–6, 117–19, 125, 181–82

Schön, D., 185–86

SENĆOŦEN (language of W̱SÁNEĆ peoples): alphabet and orthography, 8–9; English translations, 38; language calendar, 29; pronunciation and glossary, xiii–xv; use of gesture of thanks \0/, 38; use of tilde (~), 38

Shapiro, J., 11

shawl, ceremonial cedar, 4, 60, 83–84, 84(i)

sheep's wool, 4

shells, 17

shift in teacher dispositions. *See* pre-service teachers, dispositional changes

SI,ĆENEN̲ (land where course took place), 3, 4, 5, 159, 161, 207. *See also* University of Victoria

Sleeter, C.E., 163

small groups. *See* group work

social justice and resistance: about, 24, 162–63; avoidance of thinking prescriptively, 198; collaboration, 191, 198; course as resistance, 162–63; cultural appropriation, 165; as dangerous work, 172–73; dispositional characteristics, 166; earth fibres course as, 24; multicultural education, 162–63; PSTs' knowledge of difference, 163; reflexivity, 168–69, 172–73; social critique theory, 167–68, 186, 194–95; social justice, 162–64, 179; tender resistance, 24, 164–65; transformative learning, 169–72, 200; willingness to engage, 166

Sockeye Moon (story), 32

souls. *See* spirituality

spindle whorl, mural feature, 28

Spiritual Birth Moon (story), 30

spirituality: about, 22, 59, 155–57, 160–61, 199–200; animate energy, 160; being-knowing-doing, 9, 59–60, 165;

of non-indigenous person, 11–12; indigenous knowledge interwoven with, 153; reflection, 186; social critique theory, 167–68, 194–95; subjective vs objective truth, 176; time systems, 29. *See also* pedagogy, Euro-Western; positivism

worldview, indigenous: about, 115, 152–56; basic elements in, 153; both worldviews (two-eyed seeing), 207–9; circular cosmology, 115, 153, 157–58; constant flux, 131–32, 156–57; diversity vs commonalities, 153–54; holistic learning, 59, 80–82, 119–20, 133–36, 153–55; "indigenist" worldview of non-indigenous person, 11–12; interconnected relations, 153, 156–59, 171, 193–95; languages, 64–65, 131; models of epistemology, 153; non-hierarchical web of being, 157–58; oral tradition, 153; PST awareness of, 115–16; spirituality, 153, 160–61; time systems, 29, 153; transformative learning, 169–72, 200; ways of knowing, 152–56. *See also* Giveaway; Honoured Grandmother mural; medicine wheel framework; pedagogy, indigenous

woven braid metaphor, 15–17, 20. *See also* pedagogy, indigenous

woven sashes, 4

W̱SÁNEĆ (east side of island). *See* SENĆOŦEN (language of W̱SÁNEĆ peoples); SI,ĆENEN (land where course took place)

XAXE SIÁM SILA, xv, 4, 158–59. *See also* Honoured Grandmother mural; Moons of XAXE SIÁM SILA

XEMŦOLTW̱, Nick Claxton, 9